Ha
Jan
Love,
Ron + Mary

The PERFECT GAME

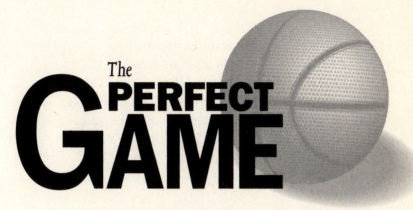

The PERFECT GAME

How Villanova's Shocking 1985 Upset of Mighty Georgetown
Changed the Landscape of College Hoops Forever

FRANK FITZPATRICK

Thomas Dunne Books ⋒ New York
St. Martin's Press

THOMAS DUNNE BOOKS.

An imprint of St. Martin's Press.

www.thomasdunnebooks.com

www.stmartins.com

Design by Omar Chapa

Library of Congress Cataloging-in-Publication Data

Fitzpatrick, Frank.

   The perfect game : how Villanova's shocking 1985 upset of mighty Georgetown changed the landscape of college hoops forever / Frank Fitzpatrick.

   pages cm.

ISBN 978-1-250-00953-1 (hardcover)

ISBN 978-1-250-02260-8 (e-book)

  1. Villanova University—Basketball.   2. Georgetown University—
Basketball.   3. NCAA Basketball Tournament—History.   4. Basketball—
United States—History.   I. Title.

  GV885.43.V55F58 2013

  796.323'63—dc23

2012037820

First Edition: January 2013

10 9 8 7 6 5 4 3 2 1

For Jim Diehl and his '54 Ford. Or was it a '53?

ACKNOWLEDGMENTS

Though I was never able to find it, I'm sure it's out there somewhere.

The eerily prescient tape that Alby Oxenreiter made in 1980—envisioning a 1985 NCAA title game between Villanova and Georgetown—was probably buried in a dusty attic or beneath mountains of boxes in a storage stall. Though Oxenreiter saved most of the recruiting recordings that, as a Villanova student broadcaster, he did for Rollie Massimino, the most historically interesting managed to slip away.

While Oxenreiter provided the gist of the long-lost tape, the authentic version would have been a welcome and fascinating find.

That's the trouble with recounting history: its edges gradually fray and disappear.

Tapes disappear. Newspaper libraries are dismantled. Memories wane. Principle figures die.

Fortunately, there's always plenty to peruse.

My thanks, initially, to all the sportswriters whose live first-hand accounts of that memorable 1985 game in Lexington,

Kentucky—as well as of the myriad events that surrounded and influenced it—provided unequaled insights.

This book wouldn't have been possible had not some diligent newspaper librarians—a profession now nearly as obsolete as newspapers themselves—preserved those dispatches, either on microfilm or in now-musty manila envelopes.

I also should thank the helpful special-collection staffs at both Villanova's and Georgetown's campus libraries who assisted me in unearthing various stories, statistics, and documents.

Unlike the book I did on the 1966 NCAA title game (*And the Walls Came Tumbling Down*), there also was a great deal of existing film and videotape relating to this game. Most helpful were the CBS broadcast from April 1, 1985, and the HBO documentary on the game ("The Perfect Upset") done twenty years later.

Villanova's players, especially Harold Jensen, Chuck Everson, Ed Pinckney, and Steve Pinone, provided help in a variety of ways, sharing their memories, their opinions and, in Everson's case, their photographs.

On the other hand, all these years later, the upset loss still stings Georgetown's players and coach John Thompson. Few wanted to talk of it with me, which made the one Hoya who was willing to do so in depth, assistant coach Craig Esherick, an even more valuable resource.

Also essential to this project were my editor at St. Martin's Press, Peter Wolverton; his saintly assistant, Anne Bensson; my agent, Frank Scatoni; and, of course, my understanding wife, Charlotte.

Everthing that grows
holds in perfection but a little moment.

-William Shakespeare
Sonnet 15

The PERFECT GAME

INTRODUCTION

How else can I explain those rainbows
When there is no rain? It's magic.

—Sammy Cahn, "It's Magic"

Alby Oxenreiter was a prophet.

Dwayne McClain finally understood that as he hugged a basketball to his chest and sprawled across Rupp Arena's polished, hard maple floor late on the night of April 1, 1985. At that moment, his underdog Villanova team led mighty Georgetown by two points and, though for him it seemed an interminable span, less than two seconds remained until the Wildcats would become college basketball's most unlikely champions ever.

McClain was in the spotlight, which is where'd he'd been for much of that NCAA championship game. He'd played as if possessed, doing whatever was needed, whatever he wanted, scoring a game-high 17 points, rebounding, defending, even spitting—literally spitting—at Georgetown. When the horn sounded, he would be holding the ball. He would be a hero, a champion, a 6-foot-6 slice of history.

Suddenly, as if he were being granted an opportunity to absorb the historic moment, to preserve the scene forever like some snow-globe village beneath glass, the chaos around him froze. The din of 23,214 voices throbbed in McClain's head as Georgetown's Horace Broadnax hovered helplessly above him. Villanova fans already were thrusting arms and fingers into the air. His 5-foot-8 coach, Rollie Massimino, had begun moving toward his Georgetown counterpart and physical opposite, 6-foot-10 John Thompson, for a postgame handshake, the contrast of tiny mortal and giant a perfect symbol for the remarkable game that was now nearly complete. On two sides of the gleaming court, rows of sportswriters were bent over their keyboards, trying desperately to translate their astonishment into words. Behind them, in seats occupied by coaches and NCAA administrators, heads were raised toward the scoreboard in search of the final confirmation for this basketball miracle. And above it all, the lights in the Kentucky arena's girded ceiling glowed like a welcoming heaven.

It was a once-in-a-lifetime moment.

Or rather it should have been.

Instead, in that instant, McClain remembered he'd experienced it all before, nearly five years earlier. In the fall of 1980, he was a Massachusetts high school senior on a recruiting visit to Villanova. As he sat that day in a cramped office in the university's tiny field house, he listened to a tape recording by Alby Oxenreiter, the student play-by-play announcer on the Wildcats' radio station. The second most recruited player in New England—only a gifted 7-foot Cambridge center named Patrick Ewing drew more interest—McClain had yet to choose a college. Privately, he was leaning toward Villanova, in part because the two friends he'd made at a Pennsylvania basketball camp that summer, Ed Pinckney and Gary McLain, were talking about doing the same. They sensed things were changing fast at Villanova. That same year the Wildcats had become members of what would soon be the hottest basketball conference on the planet, the Big East. Comprised of schools from populous East Coast cities, the year-old league was well on its way to becoming a sporting phenomenon.

A small Catholic college on Philadelphia's tony Main Line, Villanova already had a noteworthy hoops tradition. In 1939, the Wildcats had played Brown in the first NCAA tournament game ever played. Paul Arizin, named one of the NBA's fifty greatest players on the league's fiftieth anniversary in 1996, had starred at Villanova after World War II. And in 1971, just nine years before McClain's visit, Villanova had reached the NCAA title game, only to be beaten there by one of John Wooden's UCLA juggernauts.

Massimino, the wily son of an immigrant shoemaker, had succeeded Jack Kraft in 1973 as the Wildcats coach. He saw the Big East as an opportunity, a way to pry Villanova away from its Philadelphia roots and transform it into a national program. To accomplish that, he understood, he would need to intensify his recruiting efforts. He might not be able to go nationwide yet, but any hotshot senior on the East Coast certainly was going to hear from him. And so Massimino contacted Oxenreiter, an energetic Central Pennsylvanian who called Villanova's games on student-run WKVU. The coach asked the communications major to create make-believe broadcasts in which the players he was recruiting would star in imaginary Villanova victories of the future. Massimino told Oxenreiter that his assistants would provide him with biographical material on the recruits. He could invent the rest. Eager to impress, the youthful broadcaster closeted himself in a campus audio booth. With a reel-to-reel tape player, a rudimentary splicer, and a young man's imagination, Oxenreiter began to mix reality and fantasy. The improvised play-by-play descriptions he created were surprisingly impassioned, the starring roles he devised for the recruits always dramatic. He layered on crowd noise, stirring music, interviews with coaches, even commercials.

Massimino was impressed by the tapes and requested several for 1980's hot recruiting season. One would be for Ewing, far and away the nation's greatest prize. The Jamaican-born center reportedly had narrowed his choice down to six schools, and Villanova was one of them. By the time Ewing visited there, however, it was clear he had already made up his mind. He listened politely to Oxenreiter's recording, but it didn't sway him. He was bound for Georgetown in Washington, D.C., to play for Thompson.

Oxenreiter then set out to produce a tape for McClain. The versatile and athletic swingman would, of course, be its hero. But what about the other details of this concoction? Oxenreiter decided the imaginary game would take place in 1985 since that would be the player's senior season. And it wouldn't be just any game. For ultimate effect, he made it the NCAA Championship, an event whose popularity had exploded the previous winter when Magic Johnson's Michigan State team defeated Larry Bird's Indiana State in what would be the most viewed college basketball telecast ever.

Choosing an arena was easy. Just a few months earlier, in July, the NCAA had announced that the venue for 1985's Final Four would be Rupp Arena, in Lexington, the University of Kentucky's home since 1976. Now Oxenreiter needed a championship-game opponent for McClain and the Wildcats. He'd used North Carolina on another recording. The era of UCLA dominance seemed over at last. He briefly considered Kentucky until he realized that both schools had Wildcats for mascots. Too confusing.

Then Oxenreiter remembered Ewing also would be a senior in 1985. Surely any team aspiring to a national title, real or imagined, would have to contend with him and his team. And it looked increasingly like Georgetown was going to be his team. Besides, Ewing and McClain knew each other. Surely, the Worcester schoolboy, who never was able to do so in their high school meetings, would relish beating the 7-footer in their final collegiate game. Then, just for good measure, he decided McClain would be the game's high scorer and have the ball in his hands when it concluded.

With those additions, the milieu for Oxenreiter's six-minute production was complete. It all sounded so implausible at the time: Villanova versus Georgetown. The 1985 NCAA Championship. Rupp Arena. The closing seconds. High scorer McClain with the ball and . . .

. . . and now a half-decade later, the player thought, as if it had been fated by some sorcerer's spell, the fantasy on the tape had come to life.

* * *

A day before that title game, a headline that topped a Lexington newspaper's interview with coach-broadcaster Al McGuire seemed to sense what was coming: "It Will Take Divine Intervention to Stop Georgetown." As far as Villanova's players and coaches are concerned, that's exactly what happened. They believed, then and now, that powers beyond their own were at work that night in Kentucky.

"There was," forward Harold Pressley said, "some extra karma going on." As evidence, they point to the eerily prescient recording Oxenreiter made for McClain in 1980, their unprecedented shooting touch that night, the death just hours before of a longtime Villanova basketball coach, and the way their diminutive, dying trainer willed them to victory. "Perfect" was the adjective instantly ascribed to Villanova's 66–64 victory. Many have since labeled it one of sports' all-time greatest upsets. While there is much truth in both themes, neither is entirely precise.

After all, the Wildcats were hardly perfect. They turned the ball over seventeen times and missed a couple of free throws in the final minute. And, although it often gets overlooked, while Villanova was indeed a sizable underdog and a No. 8 seed going against the tourney's top-seeded team, it had nearly beaten the Hoyas a few months earlier, losing in overtime by a single basket. No, as impressive as it was, the Wildcats' upset wasn't quite flawless or unprecedented. It was magical. For forty minutes the Wildcats played as if an unseen hand, a basketball Geppetto, were manipulating them to their unexpected destiny.

"I don't know what else is out there, but I definitely believe there are other forces at work," said Villanova's Harold Jensen. "And there's no question we had a little help that night. A little stardust fell on us."

As the years pass and the events grow more distant and gilded in legend, it seems any retelling of Villanova's upset of Georgetown ought to begin with the words, "Once upon a time . . ." Like the best fairy tales, Villanova's vanquishing of Thompson's fire-breathing Hoyas combined reality with implausibility, earnest heroes with compelling villains, and a familiar simplicity with a darker, more complex subtext. It took place in the mythical basketball realm of Kentucky, in a palace named for the evil King Adolph. It was played in the fading mists of an innocent era, one still without shot clocks, three-point baskets, and baggy shorts. There would be a misunderstood giant, a hovering angel, and even, sitting mutely at the end of Villanova's bench that night, a leprechaun.

Watch the game now, all these years later, and once you get past the players' laughably brief shorts, the cheerleaders' swollen hair, and the lack of twenty-first-century clutter on the fuzzy CBS image, it's impossible to miss its magic. Some recognized that immediately. Among the 370 credentialed sportswriters who witnessed the game in person were those whose next-day accounts called the performance "miraculous," "divine," "fantastic," "paranormal," and "magical." The fact that Villanova won was less astonishing than the *way* it won. No one had ever seen anything quite like it.

A team just didn't shoot 90 percent in the second half of a championship game—or any game, for that matter—especially not when in an earlier loss to Georgetown that same team had missed 26 of 32 shots after halftime. A team just didn't shoot 78.6 percent for a game, especially not when the rest of Georgetown's opponents that season shot a combined 39 percent. A team just didn't maintain its poise and precision when faced with the kind of relentless physical and psychological pressure Villanova encountered that night. Against the defending NCAA champions, in a game whose intensity meter was turned past its maximum setting, with thirty-one million people watching, when every shot, every pass, every moment became a drama in itself, Villanova never retreated.

When the Wildcats had gathered in a Ramada Inn ballroom that Monday afternoon for their game-day Mass, their chaplain, the Rev. Bernard Lazor, hinted at miracles to come. The team had learned that morning that Al Severance, Villanova's basketball coach from 1936 to 1961, had been found dead in that same hotel. A Philadelphia sportswriter who had been sharing a Ramada room with the seventy-nine-year-old ex-coach had returned from breakfast to find him lifeless on the floor, the victim of a heart attack. Severance had been a familiar presence for the players, even accompanying the Wildcats to Vermont for their season opener in November. Now, Lazor said, just hours before the long season that followed was about to end, he'd ascended into heaven.

"You should know," the priest told the players, "that you'll have a guardian angel watching over you tonight. Al Severance will be up on the baskets, swatting Georgetown shots away, guiding yours in."

Not far away, Jake Nevin sat in his wheelchair and listened. Nevin had known Severance better than anyone in the room. He'd been the trainer for all his teams, continuing in the job right through the Kraft and Massimino eras. Less than five feet tall, superstitious, fiercely Irish, and wise-cracking, Nevin had been diagnosed with Lou Gehrig's disease exactly a year ago. "How can that be?" he asked the doctor. "I never even played baseball."

When Villanova's players needed reassurance, a laugh, or a shoulder to cry on, they went to Nevin. When they were called in to games at crucial moments, they invariably stopped first at his wheelchair to tap into his magic. The more Nevin's tiny body withered, the greater his powers seemed. "I never met a more magical guy in my whole life than Jake," said Chuck Everson, a backup center on the '85 team. "If he said something was going to happen, it happened. And he had been telling us for weeks that we were going to win the national championship."

Few had expected him to survive the season, but he'd hung on gamely—for just this day, he told the players. Nevin could no longer tape ankles, but he remained the Wildcats' oracle, their talisman, the reason that they, like him, were still alive on April 1. "Win it for Jake!" had been their motivational mantra.

When the Mass and the subsequent team meeting ended, Massimino urged his players to return to their rooms and reflect on Severance's death, Nevin's illness, and their own date with history. "When you get there," he said, "close your eyes and picture yourself playing this game to win. Don't play this game not to lose. Play it to win. Believe you can win." By that point, if he had told them to click their heels together three times and chant, "There's no place like home," they'd have done it. They believed.

So did Villanova's coach. Defying logic and conventional wisdom, Massimino had been possessed by an air of unusual confidence that week. "I remember seeing Rollie at one of those banquets on the night before the championship game where everyone, even the two [title-game] coaches, had to go," recalled Craig Esherick, Georgetown's top assistant. "They asked him to say a few words. I listened to him talk, and I'm thinking, 'Wow, this guy is really confident. This guy is not afraid at all about playing us tomorrow.' You could hear that when he spoke. And you could see that when he walked out of the place."

Jensen, an erratic, talented, emotionally fragile sophomore guard from Connecticut, said the news of Severance's passing and the coach's inspiring message produced a strange calm on what otherwise was a long and tension-filled day. It felt, he and others would later say, as if an unseen spirit suddenly had possessed them all and was assuring their victory. "I could feel a real quiet confidence in the room," Jensen said. "It wasn't like we thought we were going to roll over Georgetown. But we knew them, and we knew we could play with them, and we knew we could beat them and be NCAA champions."

Just like Jake had been whispering to them for weeks.

That night, with just ten seconds remaining in the game and Villanova's victory virtually assured, Jensen approached Nevin's wheelchair. "This one," Jensen told him as he gently kissed the old man's head, "is for you."

* * *

Ed Pinckney, the Villanova center who outplayed Ewing that night in Lexington, was a Boston Celtic in 2004 when he watched the Red Sox make a historic comeback from a 3-0 hole in their American League Championship Series with the New York Yankees. When it became apparent that the Sox were going to accomplish something unprecedented, Fox broadcaster Joe Buck sought an appropriate sports analogy. That he came up with Villanova's upset of Georgetown didn't surprise Pinckney.

"I played with Larry Bird and Kevin McHale, with Alonzo Mourning and Tim Hardaway," Pinckney said, "and even those guys would look at me and say, '1985.' You knew it was going to be remembered forever."

The list of NCAA title-game Cinderellas is a short one: North Carolina besting Wilt Chamberlain's Kansas in triple overtime in 1957; Texas Western's culturally significant triumph over Adolph Rupp's all-white Kentucky team in 1966; Jim Valvano's North Carolina State defeating Houston's Phi Slamma Jamma in 1983. And yet, despite the fact that those Wildcats usually played tough and close-fought games with those Hoyas, Villanova's upset continues to be viewed as the most surprising of all, because of the almost absolute certainty among everyone outside the Wildcats family—from fans, to sportswriters, to oddsmakers—that Georgetown, the defending champions, winners of thirty-five games, seventeen straight, couldn't lose.

"[No one] knows how the Hoyas will do it," the *Miami Herald*'s Edwin Pope wrote the morning of the game, echoing in his column what was in virtually everyone's head, "only that they will." A *Boston Herald* columnist wrote, only half in jest, that "in the spirit of humanitarianism I must demand that tonight's game be canceled. Just hold the [Georgetown] coronation as planned, send the Villanova kids out for a hot meal, and God bless."

Like the best myths and fairy tales, the more fearsome the giant, the more heroic its slayer. The Hoyas dominated most opponents psychologically, physically, thoroughly. "They didn't just want to beat you," Pinckney said. "They wanted to destroy you."

There were plenty of rational reasons to think the Wildcats had no chance that night. Villanova had ten losses that season, including six in its last eleven regular-season games. In the nine-team Big East, the Wildcats' 9-7 record was barely good enough to get them into the upper half of the standings. They'd lost twice to Georgetown, three times to St. John's, and ended the regular season by getting blown out at Pitt, a loss so disconcerting that Massimino benched his starters for its final seventeen minutes. "It's all over," Pinckney had said after that dispiriting Pitt loss. "We're not making the tournament now."

A year earlier, he might have been correct. There were just fifty-three teams in the 1984 NCAA field. But the burgeoning popularity of March Madness—a marketing phrase that became reality when that Bird-Magic duel raised the stakes, ratings, and interest to unprecedented levels—had caused the NCAA to expand to sixty-four teams for 1985. The Wildcats backed in, drew a No. 8 seed, then discovered that they would open the tournament against Dayton, on Dayton's home court.

"We didn't think Villanova was going to get in," said Mike Tranghese, the future Big East commissioner who then was a league administrator. "Then the pairings came out and they get Dayton at Dayton. You figured they were going out right there."

Because of the seeding disparity, Villanova's road to Lexington was far more perilous than Georgetown's. The Hoyas, seeded No. 1 overall, had to defeat Lehigh, Temple, Loyola of Chicago, and Georgia Tech to get to the Final Four. Villanova, meanwhile, seemed to have been matched with the college basketball Hall of Fame. Not only would the Wildcats play Dayton on its home floor, they then had to go against Maryland, Michigan, and, in the Southeast Regional Final, North Carolina.

It almost ended for them in Dayton and then again in Birmingham, Alabama. In the first half of that regional final against Dean Smith's Tar Heels, the Wildcats looked suddenly unsure of themselves. As they ran to the locker room down five at halftime, they suspected Daddy Mass was going to tear into them the way he attacked a bowl of pasta, which they'd all seen him do often at the home-cooked Italian dinners they'd shared at the coach's house. But what came out of Massimino's mouth instead that day was something no one expected, something no one has forgotten. After assuring them they could play better, he concluded in a frenzy. "I don't really want to go to the Final Four," he screamed. "You know what I want? I want a big dish of linguini with clam sauce!

And lots of cheese!" Having turned his players' anxiety to laughter, he finished, "Just relax. And let's go out and play."

They did, outscoring Carolina 39-22 in the second half to win 56-44, and earning of spot in the Final Four.

A breathtaking thirty-one million viewers watched the Villanova-Georgetown game on CBS, the 23.3 rating still the second highest ever for a basketball game, college or pro. The enormous audience was both astounding and, on the surface anyway, perplexing. By any conventional measurement, the game's appeal ought to have been limited. After all, Villanova-Georgetown wasn't an intriguing intraconference game. Both teams came from the same league. There was no great mystery about how they might match up. It was their third meeting in less than three months. These weren't two large state schools with enormous alumni bases and built-in audiences scattered across the nation. Both were small Catholic colleges from a tiny sliver of the East Coast, their campuses a mere 125 miles apart. There was no crossover appeal for football fans. Villanova had dropped the sport and Georgetown played it at the club level. There was no potential for one of those high-speed, high-flying, high-scoring games fans liked so well. Georgetown limited opponents to 58 points a game that year, Villanova 63.

As for individual appeal, sure, Georgetown's Ewing was the nation's best player. But this was his and his team's third title-game appearance in four years. And few fans anywhere could name a single Villanova player. The coaches? Massimino was a virtual unknown and Thompson, for a large chunk of America, a turnoff.

None of the aspects that in retrospect make Villanova-Georgetown so compelling could have been foreseen. Who, after all, knew the Wildcats would shoot the lights out? Who knew the Wildcats' mercurial point guard, Gary McLain, had drug issues? Who knew this would be the last game without a shot clock? And, more importantly, who knew Villanova, a 9½-point underdog, had any chance at all?

There was, however, one rational explanation as to why so many millions of Americans would watch. What made Villanova-Georgetown must-see TV for them was its fascinating racial framework. With the possible exception of that historic Texas Western–Kentucky meeting, no NCAA title game has ever been so draped in race. While the black-and-white moral conflicts of the civil-rights era had turned a murky gray in a more ambiguous America, race remained close to the nation's soul in 1985. Coming less than three months after the second inauguration of Ronald Reagan, a president whose polices and politics had helped inflame racial differences, that NCAA title game epitomized the nation's growing polarization. Reagan, for all his posthumous popularity, was a despised figure in black communities. Philosophically opposed to the federal government's intervention in the ongoing push for racial equality, his administration pushed back. The fortieth president opposed a Martin Luther King, Jr., federal holiday, supported South Africa's apartheid regime, and soon was seen by many as an impediment to progress. In one poll that year, 56 percent of Americans said they believed Reagan was racist.

A Villanova–St. John's or a Memphis State–Georgetown

final would not have attracted an audience of thirty-one million. Six million fewer had watched the previous year's NCAA Championship, even though Georgetown took part in that one, too. But the Hoyas' 1984 opponent had been Houston. The high-flying, athletically gifted Phi Slamma Jamma Cougars epitomized a style of play much of America saw as black. As a result, for those unable to look past race, the 1984 title game was the kind of unappealing, black-on-black matchup they could watch any night of the week in the NBA.

Even though in 1985 both overwhelmingly white schools started five African-Americans, the pairing of big, bad, and black Georgetown versus Villanova, or "Vanilla-nova," had plenty of appeal. Though its fourteen-man roster was evenly split along racial lines—seven blacks, seven whites—it was easy for America to assign Villanova, or virtually anyone else in a pairing with Georgetown, the white hat. Anti-Hoyas sentiment ran so deep that, for many, the Wildcats' less-threatening black starters became surrogate whites.

For the previous few weeks, the country's sports fans had been watching Villanova, and they liked what they saw—or thought they saw. "They seem like nice kids," the refrain went in the days leading up to the title game. "At least they smile." The Hoyas didn't. They inspired love and loathing at unprecedented levels. "No program since John Wooden retired has left as deep an impression on basketball's collective psyche," Mike DeBonis would write twenty-two years later in *Slate*. The nation's fans were, to an unprecedented degree, either annoyed or delighted by them. Few were neutral. As would be the case with O. J. Simpson a decade later, how you felt about the Hoyas usually depended on your race.

As controversial as they were dominant, Georgetown had been the talk of college basketball for most of the decade, a trend that appeared to have as much to do with its blackness as with its ability. "The hot topic in Washington lately has been the Georgetown University basketball team," noted the *New Republic* earlier in 1985. "Not a hot topic is the fact that even though Georgetown's student body is disproportionately white, the basketball team is entirely black."

The Hoyas had plenty of fans, particularly in America's inner cities. There, the team's merchandise outsold that of the professionals. Young black men proudly wore blue or silver Hoyas jackets and hats, as well as the hard, practiced glares Thompson's players exhibited in public. So prized was Hoyas gear that seventeen months earlier, in Baltimore, a fourteen-year-old had been killed in a junior high hallway when he refused to surrender a Georgetown jacket. For the victim and his assailants, the Hoyas held a special significance. "[Georgetown basketball] has been adopted by black youth as a symbol of belligerence, hostility," *Sports Illustrated*'s basketball editor John Papanek told the *Washington Post*. The Hoyas lived up to that image. "Their swagger," a Big East rival noted, "is so much better than anyone else's."

Though he typically denied it, Thompson appeared to use race to his team's advantage. Derided as the Idi Amin of college basketball by a Utah columnist, the big coach was at best an enigma. Depending on who was asked, he was a racist, a compassionate educator, a bully, an African-American ideal, a manipulator, or a bluntly honest man. Thompson's Hoyas were an unsmiling, intimidating, defensive-oriented, in-your-face juggernaut, one that in addition to regularly beating the tar out of its opponents frightened the bejesus out of them, too.

"Georgetown has the panzer divisions and the swift tanks and the Luftwaffe and the long bombs," said St. John's coach Lou Carnesecca. "They just completely destroy people and, yeah, they scare the hell out of you." Point guard Michael Jackson would later contend that it was all an act. Others were never so sure. Sportswriters labeled it all "Hoya Paranoia," a phenomenon that a quarter-century later *Wikipedia* would describe this way: "Georgetown in the 1980s was viewed as a team of Twelve Angry Men—or, to be very specific, twelve angry black men. They had a cadre of intimidating players, who happened to be African-American, their reputations enhanced by the stifling press defense and aggressive offense which Thompson employed and encouraged." In fairness, Georgetown's attitude was as much a shield as a weapon. During an era when Reagan's actions gave shape to their mistrust of affirmative action, welfare, and other civil-rights staples, many whites saw Thompson's team as the enemy. For them, the Hoyas and their coach were arrogant, thuggish, threatening, all too quick to cry racism. "In a society accustomed to assigning race as a reason for both the successes and failures of its citizens, the blackness of Thompson and his team could not be treated as incidental to their achievements," wrote author and former University of Pennsylvania basketball star John Wideman.

As a consequence, the Hoyas, and especially Ewing, continued to endure heaps of racial-flavored abuse. Ever since he'd arrived at Georgetown in the fall of 1981, the gifted center had been chided cruelly, as much for his sharp features as for his perceived lack of brains. In nearly every road arena in which Georgetown played, someone was bound to hold up a sign mocking Ewing's intelligence or blackness. In Philadelphia's Palestra, before a game—ironically against Villanova—in his sophomore year, one fan unfurled a banner that read, EWING THE APE, as another tossed a banana peel unto the floor. "Not surprisingly, Patrick Ewing, 20, has had a few fights this year," *Time* magazine had written in 1984. "Racism is not surprising. It pervades sports and life. But the overtness of ape banners and bananas on the floor is chilling."

Thompson used the emotional, racially charged ammunition to motivate. If one of his kids were playing soft, the coach would call him aside and inform him that it looked as if he'd been "homogenized," a message the Hoyas took to mean they were "playing white." They responded to it all with a furious intensity on the court. It took a special opponent to hang with them, an extraordinary one to beat them. In Ewing's four seasons, the Hoyas would win 121 of 145 games. And nearly everyone had expected them to win his last one. "I don't think there was a living ass in the country," Thompson later said about 1985's NCAA title game, "who didn't think we were the better team."

Two-plus decades later, Villanova's upset, like Reagan's presidency, is still recalled as something transformative. But just as

Reagan's second term would be tainted by the Iran-Contra scandal, Villanova's marvelous victory is now remembered as much for Gary McLain's subsequent drug revelations as for its sheer implausibility. In the March 16, 1987, issue of *Sports Illustrated*, in a tale so gripping that it was one of the few the magazine ever started on its cover, McLain offered a startlingly frank account of his behavior before and after the game that made him famous. "I was standing in the Rose Garden," it began, "wired on cocaine." The tell-all instantly soured the feel-good vibes that had enveloped Villanova's upset. It embarrassed Massimino and the university and made McLain a pariah on campus for decades. The sordid story spoiled the triumph's fairy-tale purity and, for Massimino at least, triggered a remarkably rapid descent.

Now, so much later, McLain's story fits easily into a revised view of the 1980s. Casual drug use, like leveraged buyouts, street crime, and bad fashion, was a touchstone of the "Me Decade." Drugs were pervasive. Crack had been introduced, with devastating effects, into the inner cities. Cocaine and marijuana, it often seemed, were as socially acceptable as alcohol. Athletes in all sports were using cocaine liberally. Later in 1985 some of baseball's biggest stars featured prominently at the Pittsburgh trial of a cocaine dealer. In basketball its misuse became tragically evident in 1986 when Len Bias, the No. 1 pick of the Boston Celtics just days earlier, died of a cocaine overdose in a University of Maryland dormitory room.

Like America's relationship with drugs, college basketball was badly in need of reform in the 1980s. The growing popularity of four-corner offenses and other stalling tactics cried out for a shot clock. And if there was going to be a clock, maybe there should be a three-point line, too. Coaches, though neither Massimino nor Thompson, had been complaining for a decade about the need for both. While some leagues, including the Big East, had experimented with a clock that season, none was used in the '85 tournament.

Recruiting and academic standards were a mess, much as they always had been. Three years earlier, a former Creighton basketball star, Kevin Ross, had admitted on national television that he couldn't read. Sensitive to accusations that colleges were exploiting impoverished black youngsters, the NCAA responded in 1983 by enacting Proposition 48, an effort to create minimum academic standards for recruits. But since many of those recruits were blacks who might not otherwise have an opportunity to attend college, the proposal touched off a firestorm of criticism, particularly from black coaches like Thompson. The Georgetown coach railed that Prop 48's effect—if not its intent—would be to limit the number of blacks in college.

That was the backdrop for the astonishing events of April 1, 1985, a night when the basketball world was turned upside down. Villanova-Georgetown would be a perfect little microcosm of the 1980s.

And it would be much more.

CHAPTER ONE

We must control the tempo of the game.

—final comment in Villanova's title-game scouting report

on Georgetown

One vote.

That, at least for those who understood college basketball, was Villanova's real margin of victory.

If an April 4, 1984, NCAA Rules Committee vote to add a forty-five-second shot clock beginning the following season had been 9-4 in favor instead of 8-5, the Wildcats' 1985 championship might never have happened. Had a shot clock been utilized in the 1985 NCAA Tournament, the number of land mines on Villanova's already perilous path to history would have increased dramatically. Maryland, North Carolina, Memphis State, Georgetown, all teams that arguably had more talent but less patience, would not have been as constrained, as susceptible to Massimino's machinations. The Villanova coach was a chess master. Thompson knew that as well as anyone. The Georgetown coach had cautioned those who early on doubted 19-10 Villanova's ability to compete in the tourney. "Bet the jockey," Thompson said, "not the horse."

Though Massimino valued preparation and fundamentals and was a defensive wizard, the aspect of basketball that most concerned and fascinated him was pace. He loved to milk the clock for his purposes, to control his team's tempo and disrupt his opponent's. "We don't ever intentionally hold the ball," Massimino said before the Georgetown game. "But we're going to try to control the tempo of the game. We're going to make the extra pass. We're going to try to get the ball inside." That was how he constructed and instructed his team. Villanova had a more than capable point guard, an experienced core that didn't easily panic or turn the ball over, and a matchup-zone defense few opponents ever really deciphered. Massimino's defensive and offensive strategies were intertwined. The fewer possessions opponents had, the less likely they were to solve the defense. "When they score in the 70s and 80s," Massimino said, "we don't win."

Villanova, of course, had played with a shot clock. The Big East had experimented with one in conference games during the 1984–85 regular season, including Villanova's two losses to Georgetown. In retrospect, the use of a clock might explain why the Wildcats never found their stride until the tournament. But even in games with one, Massimino's approach changed very little. So when the device was removed for the postseason, his Wildcats' adjustment was an easy one. Without a clock, the Wildcats were able to frustrate opponents. During Villanova's national semifinal victory, in fact, Memphis State's players clearly were unnerved by their opponents' lengthy possessions. Their equally annoyed fans filled Rupp Arena with chants of "BOR-ING . . . BOR-ING . . . BOR-ING." The result was an ugly Villanova victory. When afterward it was suggested to Dana Kirk that the Wildcats were the tournament's Cinderella, Memphis State's coach huffed, "Cinderella must wear boots."

In CBS TV's opening to its championship-game coverage, Brent Musberger, while lauding Georgetown as a dynasty about to be coronated, also made note of what would be a key element. "No team has taken advantage of the lack of a shot clock in this tournament," the broadcaster said, "more than Villanova." Actually, the Wildcats would hold the ball for forty-five seconds or longer only twice, the most significant a nearly two-minute possession near the end of the first half that resulted in them exiting the floor with a 29-28 advantage. But they hurried no shots. The 'Cats, without any time constraints, knew they could be patient in finding holes, especially in the scary heart of Georgetown's gambling defense.

Yet it might all have been different if, at that NCAA Rules Committee meeting twelve months earlier, a single vote had gone the other way. With a shot clock, Villanova might have been eliminated in the early rounds, even in its opener against Dayton. And Ewing and Georgetown might have won a second consecutive championship and been recalled today as one of the college game's great dynasties instead of as its version of golf's Greg Norman—a towering figure denied legendary status by cruel fate.

* * *

A 9-4 vote was required because regulations governing the NCAA Rules Committee mandated a two-thirds majority for any change to the game's guidelines. That thirteen-member panel was comprised of veteran coaches and athletic directors from all three NCAA divisions. Vanderbilt coach C. M. Newton was its chair, Springfield College rules guru Ed Steitz its secretary. Other members included coaches Eddie Sutton of Arkansas and Jerry Krause of Eastern Washington. Junior colleges were represented by Bob Sechrest, the coach of Missouri's Mineral Area Community College. For them and their committee predecessors, change was an ongoing process. Through the years, the committee had tinkered constantly with basketball, reacting to new problems, correcting old mistakes, anticipating trends that could threaten to tilt the competitive balance. As a result, by the mid-1980s, basketball's pioneers would not have recognized the sport. The cages that once surrounded many courts had been removed. Walls that once were in play were made out-of-bounds. Originally restricted to one, players were permitted unlimited dribbles. The center jump after every basket was eliminated. A lane, a three-second rule, and a ten-second violation were added.

The committee, which always included a representative from Springfield College, the Massachusetts school where Dr. James Naismith had been teaching when he invented the sport as a winter diversion in 1891, tended to be overprotective. When, for example, it became obvious that behemoths like Bob Kurland, George Mikan, Wilt Chamberlain, Bill Russell, and Lew Alcindor could use their height in ways Naismith never anticipated, the committee acted. Consciously or not, race occasionally appeared to play a role in the committee's decisions. As with America in general, it was an inescapable issue in basketball. And the more blacks came to dominate the game, the greater the reaction. The committee, some suggested, seemed more inclined to rewrite the rules when its concerns were about large black men. To counter Chamberlain's enormous impact, for example, the committee shifted into overdrive. It banned offensive goaltending and inbounds passes over the backboard, mandated that players had to remain stationary on free throws, and that the defensive team had to have at least two men beneath the basket on those shots. The lane, originally six feet when it was added to stifle Mikan, was widened to twelve feet in the era of Chamberlain and Russell.

But the alteration that drew the most suspicion came in 1967, when the rules panel prohibited dunks. Given the timing, it was hard to argue that the arbitrary decision was not racially motivated. The ban was enacted the same year the spectacularly gifted Alcindor enrolled at UCLA, a year after David "Big Daddy" Lattin's emphatic dunk had punctuated Texas Western's surprise NCAA title-game triumph. "Dunking typified what a lot of people felt about blacks in basketball," said Perry Wallace, who in 1966 became the first African-American to play in the Southeastern Conference (SEC). "It was threatening." A decade later, after professionals like Julius Erving and Michael Jordan had transformed the dunk into an iconic American artistic expression, one whose appeal was an integral part of basketball's resurgent popularity, the committee finally lifted its ban.

*   *   *

By the time Villanova and Georgetown met in 1985, many of the questions surrounding the participation of blacks in basketball were moot. African-American coaches like Thompson, Temple's John Chaney, and Arkansas's Nolan Richardson headed prominent programs. Black players had starred at the collegiate level for more than two decades, and at every position. Even the old segregated conferences had opened their doors wide for them. In the Deep South's SEC, forty-two of the league's fifty starters in 1983 were black. So were all twenty starters on the four Southern schools that comprised that year's Final Four: Houston, Louisville, Georgia, and North Carolina State. When Villanova and Georgetown met in the 1985 championship game, in which all ten starters were black, the average men's team included 5.7 black players, double the 1966 figure.

But despite those encouraging trends, America and the mostly white men who ran basketball were far from color-blind. The focus of the racially obsessed in the 1980s merely had shifted to concerns about style and attitude. Dunking, speed, athleticism, improvisational flair, and, to some extent, up-tempo play were seen as symbolic of black basketball, a style often portrayed as "undisciplined." "That means 'nigger,'" Georgetown's Thompson told *Sports Illustrated* in 1984. "They're all big and fast and can leap like kangaroos and eat watermelon in the locker room. . . . It's the idea that a black man doesn't have the intelligence or the character to practice self-control." Conversely, despite countless examples to the contrary, self-control was viewed as a hallmark of white basketball, along with long-range shooting ability and a slower pace. A shot clock, its critics suggested without ever saying as much, would punish the diminishing pool of white players and reward more athletically blessed blacks. "[A clock] is also a boon to coaches who prefer to assemble great athletes and let them run and gun rather than think," wrote columnist Pete Axthelm, encapsulating the prevailing wisdom for his *Newsweek* readers in 1985.

For the most part, college basketball continued to be played without a clock, not because coaches wanted to hold the ball for minutes on end, but because when an opponent had superior talent, or a tenuous late lead needed protecting, they took comfort in knowing there was an option. But sentiment was changing fast. A 1980 National Association of Basketball Coaches poll found that by an overwhelming margin members opposed the implementation of a shot clock. Two years later, 42 percent favored adding one. And by 1983, nearly half—49 percent—wanted a clock. At 1984's Final Four, when the competing coaches were asked for their opinions, only Thompson opposed a clock. "Based on inconsistency during the regular season in conferences, I would prefer it the way it is," he said.

While there's no indication race was a factor in the shot clock's eventual implementation, it is interesting to note that in 1985, nearly two decades after Texas Western's groundbreaking triumph, all thirteen members of the rules committee were white men. When in 1984 those white men came together in Seattle for their annual post–Final Four session, on the day after Georgetown had won the championship at the nearby Kingdome, it was expected that they would approve a shot clock for all collegiate games, beginning with the 1984–85 season. In fact, a *Washington Post* story a week before had suggested the change was a fait accompli. "The [only] question to be determined," the *Post* story predicted, "is whether the clock will run the entire game or be turned off in the final four or five minutes."

The best argument against a shot clock, for many, was North Carolina, where the widely respected Dean Smith had revolutionized end-of-game strategy with his much-imitated "four-corners offense." Its concept was simple: Spread your players, have them pass the ball constantly to open teammates, and if the trailing team wanted to challenge the setup, wanted to risk fouling or leaving someone open beneath the basket, so be it. But while purists applauded the strategy, most casual fans hated it. During a March 7, 1982, nationally televised matchup with No. 3 Virginia, No. 1 North Carolina held the ball the last seven minutes and six seconds to protect a one-point lead. Despite loud boos from the sold-out Greensboro Coliseum crowd, the strategy proved successful. Criticized sharply, Smith, who had learned the game at Kansas under Phog Allen, a protégé of Naismith's, pointed out that the ultimate object of basketball was to win, not to win pretty. And there could be little question about the four corners' effectiveness. Between 1966 and 1972, Smith's Tar Heels had used the tactic in 107 games and won 105 of them. The four corners soon warranted a page in almost every team's playbook. "There probably wasn't a coach in the country who didn't teach an end-of-game stall," said Don Casey, who coached then at Temple.

Even John Thompson. Thompson had learned it while serving as Smith's assistant on the 1976 U.S. Olympic team. In a March 1984 NCAA victory over Southern Methodist, just a week before the shot clock vote failed, Georgetown successfully stalled throughout the second half, countering the widely held but mistaken notion that his was a run-and-gun team. Like so much of what Thompson and Georgetown did, his strategy was instantly criticized. It was one thing to protect a lead in the final minutes, but holding the ball early or in the midst of a game seemed antithetical to the sport's intent.

Proponents of a clock liked to point to a game on December 15, 1973, when Temple faced host Tennessee in the final of the Volunteer Classic. Temple's Don Casey, hoping to pull Ray Mears's Volunteers out of the packed-in zone they favored, had his underdog Owls hold the ball whenever they got it. "We thought it would give us the best chance to win," Casey explained. "So we took two guys and put them out by the twenty-eight-foot line, had them standing about five feet apart. We had them pass the ball back and forth, back and forth."

Mears wouldn't fall into the trap. With Tennessee's defense content to sit back, Temple guards Rick Trudeau and John Kneib just kept ping-ponging the ball. *Basketball Digest* would later describe the two as looking "like Easter Island statues in their Chuck Taylors, passing the ball back and forth for minutes at a time." The two did so, unchallenged, for the final eleven minutes of the first half, after which underdog Temple trailed the home team by just two, 7-5. When the Owls continued to stall in the second half, the sold-out crowd and Mears grew angrier, more vocal. "What are you doing? Play basketball!" Tennessee's coach shouted repeatedly at his counterpart. "If you don't like it," replied Casey, "come out and get us!" Frustrated fans began booing and hurling ice at the Temple bench. Seven Tennessee state troopers had to be positioned between the Owls and the increasingly hostile crowd. Incredibly, not a single field goal was made in the second half. Tennessee won what remains the lowest scoring game of the modern era, 11-6. Afterward, statisticians determined that the Owls had held the ball for thirty-two minutes and five seconds of the forty-minute contest.

Mears wasn't any happier when the game was over. "The people had come to see basketball," he said. "We invited teams from East and West so they could see different styles of basketball. Temple had an Eastern style. I told Casey, 'I gave you $10,000 to come in here to play and I'm disappointed. I'll never invite you back.'" So concerned were Tennessee officials about the irate fans that, to appease them, university president Ed Boling ordered Mears to have his Volunteers come out afterward and play an intrasquad scrimmage. The school delayed sending Temple its $10,000 check for more than a year.

The kind of negative reaction Temple provoked became increasingly problematic in the 1980s as a boom in cable television brought more college basketball games to TV and more revenue to athletic departments. Sponsors and spectators wouldn't spend money, the conventional thinking went, to watch two teams play catch. When in 1983 a nationally televised Kentucky-Cincinnati game deteriorated into a stall-ball match, which Kentucky eventually won, 24-11, ESPN was bombarded with complaints. And those gripes were quickly redirected to NCAA headquarters. Fans wanted to see more points, more action. Instead, by 1982, scoring in NCAA games had dropped for seven consecutive seasons and, at a combined 135 points a game, was at a thirty-year low. "We're in the entertainment business," said South Alabama coach Cliff Ellis, a shot clock proponent, "and that's not entertainment."

As the '80s progressed, the calls for a clock ratcheted up. "College basketball," *Sports Illustrated*, then the conscience of American sports, pointed out in 1982, "is becoming a study in tedium." The Sun Belt had been using a clock for several seasons, after its 1978 postseason tournament concluded with a 22-20 game. Both attendance and competitiveness had increased. And even though the clock was turned off during the last four minutes, Sun Belt games produced an average of twenty more points than those in the Atlantic Coast Conference and Big Ten. Still, the purists, particularly those on the stodgier East Coast, weren't convinced. By eliminating the ability to stall, they argued, the rules makers would be eliminating the possibility of David-and-Goliath upsets. "It'll just be run-and-gun like the NBA and the little guy will no longer have a chance," said Casey. Besides, why tamper with a sport that had never been more popular? Ever since Magic-Bird in 1979, the television audiences for all college basketball games, but especially those in the NCAA Tournament, had been exploding. Why mess with success?

When it finally became clear that change was inevitable, some coaches philosophically opposed to a clock conceded they could swallow one if it were turned off late in the game. "A team should be able to hold the ball then," said Boston College coach Gary Williams. Others said it needed to be paired with a three-point shot that would force teams out of their zone defenses. "There are some who believe it has to be a package deal," said Steitz, the longtime rules committee power and the man behind the three-pointer's eventual adoption. Besides, supporters liked to point out, look at what a shot clock had done for the National Basketball Association. In 1954, the eight-year-old NBA was struggling to survive. Its games, marked by an increasing physicality, tended to be slow, plodding, and low-scoring. Unless tempted by double-headers or pregame performances by the Harlem Globetrotters, fans of the league's nine teams simply weren't buying enough tickets. In the 1953–54 season, average attendance for NBA games was barely 3,500.

Syracuse Nationals owner Danny Biasone, a nervous little bowling alley proprietor who craved action, understood the discontent. So he set about handicapping it. Whenever he particularly enjoyed a game, Biasone dissected it. What he found was the more shots that were taken, the more points scored, the better he liked it. He charted how many shots the two teams took in those games. "I noticed it was usually about 60, or 120 for the two teams," he said. Biasone then divided 120 into the number of seconds in a forty-eight-minute game—2,880—and came up with roughly twenty-four. Why not, he thought, guarantee that teams shoot the ball at least once every twenty-four seconds? After the 1953–54 season, he proposed a twenty-four-second clock and the NBA owners—

desperate for any crowd-pleasing gimmick—adopted it. The next season, team scoring jumped from an average of 79 points a game to 93. By 1958 it hit 107. Per-game attendance showed a similar bounce, reaching 4,500 in 1955–56 and continuing in an upward direction. "The shot clock," said Celtics Hall of Famer Bob Cousy, "saved the NBA."

The NCAA, meanwhile, hoping to spice up a sport it only recently had sanctioned, added a thirty-second clock for women's basketball in 1970. By the early 1980s, men's leagues like the Sun Belt were experimenting with one, some forty-five seconds, others thirty or thirty-five. And even though the 1985 NCAA Tournament would be played without one, twenty-three leagues had used a clock during that regular season. Three—the Atlantic 10, Pacific Coast, and Big Sky—also tried a three-point shot.

But on April 4, 1984, to almost everyone's surprise, the rules committee announced it hadn't been able to reach an acceptable compromise. By an 8-5 vote, the shot clock proposal had been rejected. Iowa coach George Raveling, who was not a member, summarized the point of contention: "There are a couple of people on the rules committee who believe it should be off the last two minutes of the game because it rewards poor defense and promotes zone defense." (At that meeting, however, the committee did adopt a change confining coaches to a twenty-eight-foot-long box. At the time, many believed it was aimed at Thompson, who liked to roam and get close to the officials he generally towered over and intimidated.) So when the 1985 men's tournament began with games on March 14, the clock, like Cinderella's pumpkin at midnight, disappeared. It was a decision that struck many coaches as ridiculous. "For the tournament, we've gone from a forty-five-second clock," said Dave Bliss, whose SMU team played with one that season, "to a forty-minute clock."

CHAPTER TWO

Impeach the president, pullin' out my Ray-gun
Zap the next one. I could be your Sho-gun.

—Public Enemy, "Rebel Without a Pause"

There were 1,650 students at Baltimore's Harlem Park Junior High on the afternoon of November 18, 1983. DeWitt Duckett was one of them. A fourteen-year-old African-American boy who raised pigeons and had plenty of friends, Duckett proudly wore his new blue-satin Starter jacket to school that day. He wore it proudly because of the single word in big block letters across its back—GEORGETOWN. Sometime around 1:30 P.M., three older boys, two from another school, confronted Duckett in a crowded Harlem Park hallway. They wanted his jacket. When the boy hesitated, one of the aggressors pulled a gun and demanded that he surrender it. When Duckett still refused, he was shot in the neck. As he lay dying on the cold linoleum floor, one of his attackers, Ranson Watkins, ripped the jacket from his back. Police later found it in Watkins's bedroom. The "Georgetown jacket murder" was one of a spate of similar crimes in the nation's inner cities during an era when athletic gear—the expensive sneakers that few could afford but everyone craved, the hats and Starter jackets that bore the names or logos of popular teams—had become incredibly important artifacts.

And no merchandise was as popular in those places as Georgetown's. By the middle of the 1980s, Georgetown basketball had developed a real street cachet in urban communities. An all-black team with a take-no-prisoners style and a take-no-crap black coach who seemed to relish poking a finger in white America's eye, the Hoyas became a potent symbol of black unease and rebelliousness. According to Darryl McDaniels of the popular and controversial rap group Run DMC, wearing the Hoyas' hats, jackets, and distinctive footwear indicated "that you was down like Georgetown. It also meant that you had attitude [and] that you was bad." Georgetown had supplanted the NFL's Oakland Raiders as the sports world's most notorious and popular bad boys. So coveted was their merchandise that in 1984 the Washington, D.C., university became one of the first schools to trademark its athletic logo. Georgetown's mascot, aptly enough, was a snarling, drooling, spike-collared bulldog in a school beanie.

The '80s would be the decade when sports licensing and sports marketing became formidable and profitable industries. Until then, only children and obsessed fans had worn sneakers, baseball caps, or team jackets. But, thanks to Alabama's devotion to Bear Bryant, all that began to change in 1981. Seeking help in dealing with all the commercial entities that wanted to use his name or his houndstooth-hatted image, the Alabama football coach contacted a former player, Bill Battle.

Battle would prove so successful in licensing Bryant and his image that soon Alabama and other big-time football schools were hiring him to do the same for them. As a result, Battle founded the Collegiate Licensing Company that same year and soon had a few hundred colleges as clients. "Our pitch," he explained, "was that this wasn't going to cost the schools anything." Through shrewd marketing techniques that appealed to the fans' desire to associate themselves as closely as possible with their favorite teams, the trend took off. By 1985, overall sports-licensing transactions would for a first time top $250 million. By 2010, it would be at $4.3 billion business.

By the end of the 1980s, no college sold more licensed goods than Georgetown. Even without a football team to speak of, the university moved more merchandise than football superpowers like Alabama, Michigan, Texas, Penn State, or Notre Dame. While the 8 to 10 percent licensing fee it earned on every sale enriched the university, it also occasionally caused it embarrassment. During the 1992 Rodney King riots in Los Angeles, the round-the-clock television coverage revealed so many young rioters in Georgetown paraphernalia that the school felt the need to issue a disclaimer: "In today's world," the statement explained, "sports clothing . . . is certainly a highly visible choice of many, many people." Nike wanted in on the phenomenon and in 1981 specially designed a shoe for the basketball Hoyas, the Dynasty. In 1984, a new model, the Terminator, was released and soon the expensive gray-and-black sneakers worn by Thompson's team were ubiquitous in America's inner cities. "The distinctive shoes went quite well with the [Hoyas'] roughhouse persona," author

Todd Boyd pointed out in his book *Young, Black, Rich, and Famous*. At the same time, a Connecticut firm, Starter Clothing Line, founded in 1971 by an ex-basketball player, began to manufacture and market team jackets. Georgetown's quickly became its bestseller.

Reporters, curious about this intimate connection between young blacks and Georgetown basketball, went to Thompson for his reaction. In an interview with the *Washington Post*'s Dave Kindred, the coach defended the craze, saying it reflected some deep yearning in African-American youngsters. "Young black kids have identified with us and strongly," Thompson said. "I see it in a positive light. Everybody needs inspiration from somewhere. It's like me rooting for Joe Louis and [a white man] rooting for Joe Louis. It's the same, but it's different. I *need* Joe Louis to root for. And sometimes now I see touches of that need when people of color are rooting for Georgetown." And yet the overriding question about the Georgetown phenomenon remained unanswered: Did it signify hope or defiance?

On November 12, 1984, just six days after he trounced Democrat Walter Mondale to win a second term, President Ronald Reagan's daily calendar included a 4:15 P.M. photo shoot with *Sports Illustrated* in the White House's Map Room. Just before 3 P.M. there was a commotion at one of the gates to the executive mansion. Thompson and Ewing had just arrived for the same session with one of the popular sports magazine's best-known photographers, Lane Stewart. The Georgetown center, attired in his familiar uniform, gray and pocketless, had not remembered to bring his wallet on the short trip from campus. And while, at 7 feet and 230 pounds, Ewing possessed one of the most recognizable physiques and faces in America, a cautious but clueless White House guard was demanding identification. Soon, however, one of the guard's colleagues intervened and the two large visitors were admitted. But their journey to the Map Room wasn't yet complete. In a ground-floor hallway 100 feet from their destination, Ewing, Thompson, and an SI employee were stopped again. They were told they needed a White House escort to proceed further. One would not arrive for twenty minutes.

Black people liked to talk about the burdens of what they termed "the black tax," the painful social cost their color often exacted in a race-conscious society. Taxi drivers often ignored black businessmen. Black youngsters in white neighborhoods were stopped and harassed by police. Black shoppers were frequently mistaken for shoplifters. Now Ewing and Thompson were paying their share of the tax in the nation's most famous building. Reaching the Map Room at last, the two men were posed for a series of test shots by the meticulous Stewart. "Patrick," Stewart said at one point, "you're scaring me to death." Ewing, perhaps still uneasy after his entry troubles, glowered at Stewart as he had been glowering at his camera. "I'll smile when I'm ready," he said.

At exactly 4:15 P.M., a smiling and affable Reagan joined them. The Georgetown star and his coach had met the president before, at a Rose Garden ceremony the previous April to commemorate the Hoyas' 1984 NCAA title. Now, as the three men prepared to pose together, the 6-foot-1 Reagan jokingly reached for a chair, suggesting he'd need help if he wanted to appear in the same frame with the two giants. With that, Ewing smiled. The photo that two weeks later appeared on the cover of SI's 1984–85 college basketball preview issue showed Reagan clutching a ball with two hands as if he were displaying the set-shot form he'd used nearly a half-century earlier on the Dixon, Illinois, Junior High varsity. The president stood in front of and between Thompson and Ewing, each of whom also held a ball, but with one hand. Ewing was in his uniform, emblazoned with the name of his school and his number, 33. Beneath the top, he also wore a gray T-shirt, another Hoyas fashion first that he unwittingly had popularized. "Patrick had a cold one day at practice, and he wore the gray T-shirt under his uniform top," said Georgetown assistant Craig Esherick. "Pretty soon everyone was wearing them." The normally serious Thompson, dressed in a gray suit, white shirt, and blue-and-red striped tie, was smiling so widely he was virtually unrecognizable. The president wore his customary uniform—dark blue suit, white shirt, red tie. The words accompanying the cover photo were both clever and superfluous. THERE THEY GO AGAIN read the headline in big green letters above the president's head. It was a reference both to Reagan's famous 1980 debate retort to President Jimmy Carter and the widespread expectation that Georgetown was going to win a second straight national championship. And inexplicably, as if they were directed at the White House guard who hadn't recognized Ewing, captions identified the three men.

It was a clever and appealing cover for a magazine that specialized in them. But for many Americans the image on the November 26, 1984, issue was also a disturbing one. For opposite reasons, blacks and whites found it to be a jarring mix of the revered and the reviled.

In 1985 America, there was considerable anger and frustration in black communities, where the government's sudden disinterest was creating as much havoc as a new pharmaceutical scourge, crack cocaine. "The war on poverty," wrote the liberal sociologist Michael Harrington that year, "has become a war on the poor." The resulting anger that festered in those communities spilled over into the popular culture, particularly the raw and red-hot lyrics of hip-hop, a relatively new music form that Bill Stephney, a founder of the group Public Enemy, would characterize as "a fuck-you to white society." Although Public Enemy's often violent and misogynistic lyrics disturbed many whites and blacks, the group became a potent and popular symbol of urban discontent. While the city's police officials decried the group's antiauthoritarian slant, in predominantly black West Philadelphia, a little more than ten miles from Villanova's Main Line campus, Public Enemy was honored with a parade down Market Street.

Much of the rage would be channeled toward Reagan. In Public Enemy's wildly popular anthem "Rebel Without a Pause," the Republican president was referred to as "Raygun," and the lyrics urged his impeachment and, perhaps, worse. His White House, many blacks believed, was openly hostile to their plight and had shifted the long march toward racial equality into reverse. Black leaders liked to point out that Reagan's "Morning in America" had not yet dawned in their communities, where 22 percent of the population was unemployed in 1985 and 36 percent lived below the poverty line.

Philosophically opposed to the federal government's significant involvement and investment in most social programs, the Republican administration seemed to push back especially hard on civil rights. Race became a useful wedge issue. Piggybacking on President Nixon's Southern Strategy, Reagan's successful 1980 campaign had included thinly veiled appeals to the fears of white voters. He spoke of "welfare queens," "young bucks," and those who "bought vodka with food stamps." He gave a speech hailing "states rights" at Philadelphia, Mississippi, where the bodies of three murdered civil-rights workers had been found in 1964. Such references were, as *Time* magazine noted, "coded messages to lure disaffected blue-collar and Southern white voters away from the Democratic party." It worked. Rural and blue-collar whites flocked to the Republican Party, remaking the solidly Democratic South and the entire electoral map. Fifty-five percent of white voters had backed Reagan in 1980. That figure ballooned to 63 percent four years later. Meanwhile, nine in ten blacks in 1984 voted for someone else.

Reagan also opposed a national holiday for Martin Luther King, Jr., and, virtually alone in a world that was then aggressively targeting that nation's apartheid policies, his government stood by South Africa as an economic and trading ally. At the time, states and cities across America, including Washington, D.C., and Philadelphia, were shedding their investments in companies with ties to the African nation. In the nation's capital, protesters daily blocked the entrance to the South African embassy. Rallying students took over Columbia's Hamilton Hall in New York and rechristened it Mandela Hall, in honor of the imprisoned South African opposition leader. Touting a policy of "constructive engagement," the president called South Africa's apartheid regime "a reformist administration." "They have eliminated the segregation that we once had in our own country," Reagan said, despite the fact that between 1984 and 1986, 30,000 South Africans would be detained as political prisoners, and 2,500 killed. But even if that nation's government were racist, suggested United Nations ambassador Jeanne Kirkpatrick, it was better than being Marxist.

At home, philosophical and fiscal concerns made targets of many social programs from FDR's New Deal and LBJ's Great Society. In one Reagan budget, 70 percent of the $35.2 billion in proposed trims came from programs for the poor. Subsidized housing and school lunches were diminished or eliminated. More than 675,000 households were removed from the rolls of Aid for Families with Dependent Children in the decade. As if it were going out of its way to antagonize, the administration also sought to restore the tax-exempt status of Bob Jones University, even though that private South Carolina Christian college flaunted federal regulations by prohibiting interracial dating. Other tax-code changes benefited the wealthiest Americans. "The 1980s began a massive redistribution of wealth back to the wealthy," wrote Jeff Chang in his book *Can't Stop, Won't Stop: A History of the Hip Hop Generation*.

The recoil among blacks came quickly. Hip-hop's defiance

soon was finding other cultural expressions. In *Boyz 'n the Hood*, John Singleton's film about growing up in South Central L.A. during the 1980s, young boys walk past a trash-strewn murder scene. One of the youngsters approaches a leftover Reagan campaign poster that is hanging on a wall above the crime site and shoots his middle finger at the smiling president. "[Reagan] made greedy white men feel good about being greedy white men," black comedian D. L. Hughley would say in 2009. "He was the kind of Moses of leading them."

Thompson's political views were never as transparent as his critics believed them to be. Whatever his views on Reagan, he kept them mostly to himself. But when in 1983 the NCAA passed new regulations regarding admission requirements for athletes, he erupted publicly. With black athletes increasingly in the college sports spotlight, the scrutiny of them intensified. People saw interviews with young basketball or football stars, on scholarship at prestigious colleges like Georgetown, and wondered why they so often were incomprehensible. After the 1984 NCAA title game, the Hoyas' Reggie Williams stumbled badly through a nationally televised postgame interview and the critics howled. That and the *60 Minutes* segment with Ross in '82, in which the former Creighton star admitted he couldn't read, seemed to be confirmation that the NCAA's oft-stated concept of the student-athlete was farcical. "We've raped and exploited a generation of black athletes," said Penn State football coach Joe Paterno, an advocate for tougher academic standards.

Suddenly calls for reforms were as plentiful as questions

about the system. How and why were these academically defi-
cient athletes being admitted to colleges? Were they receiving
preferential treatment simply because of their athletic talents?
What kind of courses were they taking? Why weren't colleges
educating them properly? Were they merely disposable talents,
discarded onto society's scrap heap after their eligibility ex-
pired? These were delicate subjects. While no one wanted
to see the athletes exploited, limiting their access to college
promised serious consequences. If the cycle of poverty and il-
literacy were ever going to be broken, it seemed essential that
the door be opened wider. If sports were a way to ensure that,
Thompson and others said, then so be it. "Just exposing these
people to that [college] environment helped in the next generation," said Perry Wallace, the lawyer and professor who had
been the first black athlete to integrate the SEC. "Bill Russell
might not have gone to college without basketball, but his
daughter was admitted to Harvard." And, Wallace might have
added, had not Providence accepted Thompson, the coach's
oldest son might not have been admitted to Princeton.

Reacting to the criticism, the NCAA in 1983 passed Proposition 48. The amendment to NCAA bylaws, which was to
take effect in the 1986–87 school year, had two essential elements: To be eligible as freshmen, athletes must have scored
700 or better on their SATs (or 15 of 36 on the ACT test) and
had at least a 2.0 average in high school core curriculum
courses. It threatened an earthquake. According to an NCAA
study, six of seven black basketball players at the nation's top
colleges and three of four black football players would have
been ineligible as freshmen under Prop 48's mandates.

Thompson, most of his black colleagues, and many white coaches who had come to rely on black talent immediately cried foul. Limiting blacks' access to college, they said, would only make a bad system worse. "This system we have, I do think it's bad," said Thompson. "But I know far more [now successful] guys who have come from the system than have been exploited by it." His relentless stridency on the issue— Thompson eventually would call for a boycott by black coaches—only increased the perception that he saw every-thing in stark racial terms. For those who viewed that as a fault, it meant he was a "reverse racist," a "troublemaker," a "bigot." America in 1985 clearly preferred a more benign view of race relations, something of the sort most popularly ex-pressed by the nation's No. 1 television program, *The Cosby Show*, in which two black professional parents raised a family of happy, successful children in Brooklyn Heights affluence. Why didn't Thompson have white kids on his teams? Why did he shield his players from the media? Why did they play with a chip on their shoulders? Why didn't they smile? In short, why couldn't John Thompson be more like Cliff Huxtable?

CHAPTER THREE

There is a divide between the old and the new.

——Roy De Caro, 1971 Villanova graduate

If Villanova's 240-acre campus had a metaphorical heart, it almost certainly would be the compact area that contains its two wildly divergent basketball arenas. The old field house, built in 1932, at the apex of the Great Depression, is brick, rectangular, utilitarian, comfortable. The new facility, meanwhile, constructed with a donation from perhaps the ultimate American aristocrat during the height of the "Me Decade," is a crazily spired, oddly shaped structure, an intrusive element amid classical campus architecture. Their juxtaposition is telling. Geographically and spiritually, the mellifluously named university is an odd mix of past and present, as the title of its official 1999 pictorial history so aptly indicates: *Villanova: Ever Ancient. Ever New.*

Villanova's past lies to its east. Just down Montgomery Avenue sits the Merion Cricket Club, whose turreted, Frank Furness–designed clubhouse, manicured cricket pitch, and emerald-green tennis lawns speak of an age that has vanished nearly everywhere else. Farther east, its border just twelve miles from campus, lies Philadelphia with its centuries-old history, its stifling traditions, its civic cautiousness. Between the city and the campus are the stuffy communities and now subdivided estates of the Main Line, where the forces of old and new have battled for more than a century.

The present is to Villanova's west, symbolized by I-476, the super highway that bisects Lancaster Avenue just blocks from campus. Locals call 476 the Blue Route because for several decades it was just a blue line on a map as Main Line wealth and recalcitrance successfully delayed its intrusion. Finally finished in 1990, it has made the area west of Villanova a twenty-first-century hub, affording its corporate parks and go-go subdevelopments easy access to the Pennsylvania Turnpike, I-95, and the bustling business and retail center of King of Prussia.

On a late spring morning in 2007, more traffic than usual exited the Blue Route at Lancaster Avenue. From there, the cars traveled east to St. Thomas of Villanova, the campus church whose Chartres-like spires, topped by sparkling gold crosses, make it the university's signature structure. The day was sunny, the pleasant weather contrasting with the gloomy faces of the men in the two distinct groups that had gathered on the old church's steps. Many in the gray-haired, paunchier pack had played basketball there in the 1960s and early 1970s for Jack Kraft. The younger group had been coached by Massimino or his artless successor, Steve Lappas. Shuttling between the two packs, like some extremely well-groomed diplomat, was Villanova's current basketball coach, Jay Wright. All were there for the funeral of Howard Porter, the forlorn star of the Kraft team that had lost to UCLA in 1971's NCAA title game.

Perhaps the most gifted player in school history, Porter had been the star of that overachieving team, which also included future NBAers Chris Ford and Tom Inglesby. Soon after the sweet-shooting, 6-foot-8 forward went to the NBA, it was discovered that while still in college he had signed with an agent, an older Villanova graduate named Richie Phillips, and with the Pittsburgh Condors of the now defunct American Basketball Association. The NCAA eventually stripped the '71 Wildcats' name and accomplishments from its record book. Harder yet to bear for Villanovans, its unprecedented national runner-up status was vacated. Porter fell hard, out of pro basketball following a few injury-plagued seasons and into a life of drugs. But not long before his death he had remarried, seemingly turned his life around, become a respected parole officer. Thanks to Wright, Porter even had reconnected with Villanova, where the player always believed he'd remained an outcast. Instead, three and a half decades later, he found he was beloved. And then one night his wife called the police to report him missing. They found Porter a week later, in the trunk of a car in a Minneapolis alley, beaten to death.

A lot of people believe the old Villanova died with 1971's embarrassment. Massimino and the new Villanova he envisioned arrived two years later. He was from North Jersey and had come to Philadelphia just two years earlier as an assistant to Penn coach Chuck Daly. When he was hired, Massimino had very few connections to the parochial city and its insular basketball community. Very soon he started to steer Villanova basketball away from its Philadelphia heritage. Mirroring a trend among its students in general, more and more basketball players were arriving from northern New Jersey, New York, and Connecticut. The growing demand for new revenue sources even moved the university to reassess its historic ties to the Big 5—the fiercely competitive Philadelphia-area basketball affiliation it shared with Penn, LaSalle, St. Joseph's, and Temple. The battle lines were drawn between old and new, Philadelphia and New York, Big 5 and Big East.

The fights Massimino picked were especially intense because they involved basketball, the alpha sport at Villanova, even when legendary track coach Jumbo Elliott was winning national titles and molding Olympic gold medalists. On one side were older alums, Philadelphia-area natives mostly, who had attended in an era when Villanova was the college of choice for graduates of the area's many Catholic high schools. These people wanted to honor the school's basketball past, preserve its old rivalries and heritage, particularly its long association with the Big 5. "The tradition," said Father Ed Hastings, an ex-basketball player and a 1972 graduate, "is bigger than any of us." For them, Villanova was a uniquely Philadelphia concept, a significant part of a milieu that encompassed local parishes, and local priests, local taverns and local summer leagues, local traditions and local legends. An end to any of it would invalidate their pasts as much as the school's.

On the other side were younger and more geographically diverse graduates, the bulk of whom came from New York

City's sphere of influence. They tended to view Villanova in a regional, even national context. For them, the Big 5 was little more than a curious relic, an afterthought compared to the potential of a conference like the Big East. Whenever losses to Penn, Temple, St. Joseph's, or La Salle threatened Villanova's NCAA chances, these people howled. To old-school Villanovans who were accustomed to watching the Wildcats play in their cozy field house or in Philadelphia's historic Palestra, this new breed would be epitomized by the Pavilion, the Wildcats' ugly on-campus arena. Widely despised since its opening in 1986, its modern design seems out of place amid the campus's Gothic fieldstone buildings. The acoustics are lousy. It holds only 6,500. And it was named originally for John E. DuPont, the mad, wealthy dilettante who eight years later, on his nearby estate, shot and killed U.S. Olympic wrestler Dave Schultz.

"It's a no-win for us," Wright said about the divide. "If we lose two [Big 5 games], that might knock us out of the tourney. . . . On the other hand, I tell the people who complain about the Big 5, 'Hey, I live here. I like living here. I have to walk down the street each day and talk to those people. How could I do that [end the affiliation] and still live here?' " It was a conundrum Massimino never solved. Or cared to solve.

Like so many wealthy merchants in post–Revolutionary War Philadelphia, when John Rudolph wanted to build his country estate, he looked west. Rudolph purchased nearly 200 oak-and-hickory-rich acres along the old Lancaster Turnpike in

Radnor Township. The handsome property was twelve miles from Philadelphia's western border, close by a railroad connection and, by the standards of the time at least, easily accessible to the city. By 1808, Rudolph had constructed a two-story stone mansion with a mansard roof and christened it Belle Air, a name he borrowed from his father's northern Maryland estate. A Catholic in a still overwhelmingly Protestant nation, Rudolph originally had to make the long journey to Philadelphia for Sunday Mass. Occasionally, priests from the city, including those from St. Augustine's—the first church in the nation founded by the tiny Augustinian order—traveled to Belle Air and said Mass there.

Rudolph died in 1838, and three years later his financially strapped children auctioned the property. On October 13, 1841, the land, mansion, and outbuildings were sold for $18,000 to the same Philadelphia Augustinians who had so often visited there. The priests soon founded a parish, St. Thomas of Villanova, on the site and in 1842 added the first Catholic college in Pennsylvania, the Augustinian College of Villanova. Shut down briefly during Philadelphia's anti-Catholic riots in 1844, the college, populated almost exclusively by Irish-Americans, graduated its first class in 1847. A year later, it was accredited by the state. Starting in 1890, Villanova, as locals were then calling the school, began a slow but steady expansion. And as was the case at so many Catholic colleges, sports would be an integral part of its growth.

By the late 1800s in America, athletics were seen as an essential component of the collegiate experience, a way to produce the well-mannered, well-rounded gentleman who was that Victorian age's ideal. Organized intercollegiate competition was the logical outgrowth, beginning as early as 1852 in such sports as baseball, football, rowing, track and field, tennis, and ice hockey. When in 1895 Minnesota State School of Agriculture beat Hamline, 9-3, a new game called basketball joined the list. While football would help transform tiny, remote Notre Dame into the most famous Catholic institution in the country, the sport proved to be a financial burden for many other Catholic colleges. Big stadiums, fifty-man rosters, and costly equipment were out of their reach. Still, many of those schools attempted to maintain football programs through the first half of the twentieth century, before several were moved to drop or downsize the sport in the years after World War II. At those places, basketball had been or soon became the sport of choice.

Most urban colleges already possessed gymnasiums, so basketball's costs—backboards, a few balls, and uniforms—were minimal. The potential rewards, however, were great. DePaul in Chicago burst into the national consciousness in the 1940s, thanks in large part to 6-foot-10 George Mikan, one of basketball's first renowned big men. Others would soon mimic DePaul with great success. Between 1947 and 1963, Catholic schools would win five NCAA titles—Holy Cross (1947), LaSalle (1954), San Francisco (1955 and 1956), and Loyola of Chicago (1963). The connection between Catholics and basketball would reach its apex in 1985, when three of the four Final Four teams—Villanova, Georgetown, and St. John's—were Catholic institutions. Of the forty teams that made it to the Final Four in the 1980s, seven were Catholic—Georgetown three times, plus Villanova, St. John's, Providence, and Seton Hall. (Since then only three have gotten that far—Marquette in 2003, Georgetown in 2007, and Villanova in 2009.)

At Villanova, basketball debuted in 1920 with a 43-40 victory over visiting Catholic University. The team's home court, the cramped gym inside Alumni Hall, was so tiny that occasionally games were moved to West Catholic High School in Philadelphia. In 1946, Paul Arizin, a 6-foot-4 Marine veteran from South Philadelphia who had been cut from the basketball team at LaSalle High, enrolled at Villanova to study chemistry. When he tried out for basketball in his sophomore season, coach Al Severance wondered what had taken him so long. The player sportswriters would soon dub "Pitchin' Paul" had an unstoppable weapon, a still rare jump shot that his leaping ability allowed him to get off whenever he wanted. Though Arizin always preferred the jumper, he could drive hard—and often acrobatically—to the basket and was a dogged rebounder. According to his biography on NBA.com, he was "an early version of Michael Jordan or Sidney Moncrief."

On February 12, 1949, in a game against an overmatched Naval Air Material Center team, Arizin scored 85 points in a 117-25 victory, still a record for a Villanova player or any Philadelphia-area collegian. As a senior, he collected 735 points, five off the then national record, and averaged 25.3 points a game, the second highest ever at the time. Villanova went 25-4, and the Sporting News named him its College Player of the Year. Eventually, the school retired his number 11 jersey, the number he also would wear as a professional. Arizin's 1949 team made it to the NCAA tournament, where they were beaten by eventual national champion Kentucky. With players like Larry Hennessey and Bob Schafer, Severance would again produce NCAA teams in 1951 and 1955.

Though Villanova found players in Philadelphia, New Jersey, and elsewhere in the Mid-Atlantic region, all were white until the late 1950s. Even well into the 1980s, the campus itself remained almost exclusively white. As was also the case at Georgetown, Villanova yearbooks and other student publications reveal few black faces that didn't belong to track or basketball team members. "Villanova," the *New York Times* noted in 1985, "is attended largely by the children of the East Coast affluent, most of whom are white." The stark racial makeup of its campus would cost Villanova the services of an early black superstar. Sherman White, a Philadelphia native who was raised in Englewood, New Jersey, was a scholastic sensation, a center-sized big man who could score from inside or outside. In 1947, on the recommendation of his high school coach, a Villanova alum named Tom Morgan, White agreed to come to the Main Line school. He played freshman ball, but soon, with no other blacks on campus, he wearied of the lonely life there and transferred to LIU. There, tragically, he would become a key figure in the game's worst point-shaving scandal. Sentenced to twelve months in prison for his role, White's promising career ended abruptly and prematurely.

The well-publicized travails of his former recruit provided a cautionary tale for Severance. And when Villanova was looking to move some of its more attractive matchups to

Philadelphia, the coach refused to consider the most logical site, Convention Hall. It was, after all, the gamblers who frequented another big-city arena, Madison Square Garden in New York, that had ensnared White and several other collegians in the betting scandal. Severance knew gamblers also frequented Convention Hall and virtually every other large civic arena at the time. Though LaSalle, St. Joseph's, and Temple played there, Severance sought what he termed some place with "a more collegiate atmosphere." At the time, that meant the University of Pennsylvania's 9,000-seat Palestra or nowhere. Fortunately for the coach, Penn administrators allowed Villanova to share the on-campus arena where the first NCAA game had taken place in 1939. Throughout the early 1950s, Villanova and Penn staged popular Palestra doubleheaders, while the other three Philadelphia-area schools that in 1955 would form the Big 5 continued on at Convention Hall.

After the unfulfilling experience with White, Villanova basketball would not include another black player until Kenny Harrison in the 1956–57 season, a year before future college coach George Raveling became the program's first African-American star. Before Raveling graduated in 1962, he would help the Wildcats get selected for back-to-back National Invitation Tournaments (NITs) in '59 and '60 and be instrumental in persuading two fellow African-Americans from Washington, D.C.—Tom Hoover and George Leftwich—to attend. Later, as a Wildcats assistant, Raveling would establish a Florida recruiting pipeline that produced such players as Johnny Jones, Clarence Sims, and, most notably, Porter.

Severance retired in 1961 and was replaced by a little-known Philadelphia-area high school coach named Jack Kraft. Aided by the growing basketball passion the Big 5's founding had created on campus and by talented local players like Wally Jones, Hubie White, Jim Washington, and Bill Melchionni, Kraft would enjoy immediate and sustained success. The Wildcats went 21-7 in his initial season and made it to an NCAA regional final, where they fell to Wake Forest. His next ten teams all reached the postseason—five NCAAs and five NITs. In 1966, Raveling, by then a Kraft assistant, was on a recruiting trip to Florida when, at a high school game in Sarasota, he first saw Porter. "I had never seen a guy in high school do what he could do," Raveling said. The assistant called Kraft immediately and told him that if they could land him, "we can win a national championship."

Porter was a more physically refined, 1960s version of Sherman White. At 6-foot-8, he could shoot from distance, break a defender down in the low post, and leap out of the building. By Porter's senior season, joined by Ford, Inglesby, fellow Floridian Sims, and Philadelphian Hank Siemientowski, it seemed Raveling's prediction might come true. The Wildcats finally broke through that regional-final barrier with a 90-47 demolition of Big 5 rival Penn and were headed to the Final Four at Houston's Astrodome.

Entering that East Region final, Dick Harter's Penn team had been unbeaten and ranked No. 3 in the nation. They also had beaten Villanova three consecutive years. One of those victories, a 32-30 Penn triumph the previous season, had been the result of stalling tactics that upset Kraft. So when the Wildcats moved out to a big early lead against Penn in their tournament meeting in Raleigh, North Carolina, Kraft kept his foot on the accelerator, not removing his starters until the closing moments of the rout. A furious Harter would not forget.

Villanova went on to beat Western Kentucky in a riveting Final Four semifinal, earning the right to play UCLA in the NCAA Championship game. If John Wooden's UCLA dynasty ever had a vulnerable year it was 1971, a brief interlude between the reigns of Alcindor and Walton. But before 31,275 fans at the enormous Astrodome, the Bruins held off stubborn Villanova for a 68-62 triumph.

Kraft's next team made it back to the NCAA tournament. Then the results of an NCAA probe that focused on Porter nearly collapsed the program. Investigators had determined that Porter not only had signed with an agent while still in school but had affixed his name to a pro contract. "I was told it wasn't binding and wasn't a contract," Porter said decades later. "I was in a fog." Soon enough, so was Villanova basketball. The Wildcats' 1971 accomplishments were expunged from the record books. The grimier underside of the program's pristine public image was exposed. Questions arose about recruiting tactics and the academic qualifications of Porter and others. Engulfed in turmoil, Kraft's 1972–73 team went 11-14. Afterward, the coach, fifty-two at the time and concerned about the program's sudden U-turn, sought a longer contract than the year-to-year deals he'd always had. When Villanova administrators balked, Kraft went looking for another job. He found one at Rhode Island, which granted him a more secure four-year deal. In November of 1973, in a tersely worded news release in which the chastened university seemed almost embarrassed to be calling attention to itself, Villanova announced that it had hired a Penn assistant, Rollie Massimino, to be its next basketball coach.

CHAPTER FOUR

The academy at Georgetown . . . will be of great service hereafter, if well conducted. —Archbishop John Carroll 1792

Maybe it's not surprising that Georgetown basketball got all mixed up with race. After all, the university's most famous president was a former slave. Patrick Francis Healy was born in Georgia in 1829 to Michael and Mary Eliza Healy. His mother—half-black, half-Irish—had been a slave on his father's plantation. Though she eventually became Michael's common-law wife, antebellum state law held that the mixed-race couple's children were slaves. Since slaves were not permitted to attend Georgia schools, Healy sent his fair-skinned children north to be educated at Irish-Catholic schools. Patrick would attend high school and college at Holy Cross in Massachusetts, graduating in 1850 and soon afterward entering a Jesuit seminary. He then traveled to Belgium, where he became the first person of African-American ancestry to earn a doctorate. Ordained in 1864, Healy became Georgetown's twenty-ninth president in 1873.

America's first Catholic college, Georgetown had been

founded by America's first Catholic bishop. Maryland Archbishop John Carroll had purchased land along a high bluff
of the Potomac, just across from Northern Virginia, with the
intentions of starting a college there. In 1789, work would
begin on its initial buildings. Two years later the first student, a future congressman named William Gaston, enrolled
there. The school's instructors were Jesuits, the Catholic in-
tellectuals who had fled Europe and, encountering anti-Catholic
sentiment here, established clandestine schools throughout
the colonies. Georgetown's creation was the culmination of a
more-than-century-long battle by Maryland Catholics to create a college in the New World. Once established, its early
progress was slowed by financial troubles and by the era's
often virulent anti-Catholic sentiment. But when the federal
government awarded it a charter in 1815, the college's expansion began in earnest. During Healy's nine-year tenure as president, the tiny college, which would derive its name from the
Washington neighborhood in which it was located, began its
transformation into a modern educational institution. Healy
added sciences to the classical curriculum, made vast im-
provements to its schools of law and medicine, and oversaw
the construction of several neo-Romanesque buildings surrounding Dahlgren Quadrangle, one of which still bears his
name.

Basketball had taken root early in Washington, and by
1906, fourteen years before the sport would surface officially
at Villanova, Georgetown had a team of its own, though
throughout much of its first six decades many must have wondered why. The Hilltoppers, as they were known then, played

their first basketball game on February 9, 1907, a 22-11 rout of Virginia at the armory on 15th Street. The armory and other downtown facilities were utilized because Ryan Hall, where the team practiced, had little room for spectators. Later coaches found ways to squeeze fans into Ryan, using the claustrophobic conditions to their teams' advantage.

By the late 1920s, newspaper headlines were referring to the basketball team as the Hoyas. The origins of the unusual nickname remain murky, even at Georgetown. Some point to a nineteenth-century baseball team there that referred to itself as the Stonewalls. Since all students then took both Latin and Greek, one combined the Greek word "hoya" and Latin "saxa"—"what rocks"—to create what he thought to be a clever cheer at baseball games. Another theory suggests "hoya saxa" more likely was the common graffiti scrawled onto the stone walls that surrounded a campus field. When the baseball team began playing there, the phrase, so closely associated with the site, was adopted as a cheer and the Hoya half of it became the the team's nickname.

Unlike their unique moniker, Hoyas basketball teams were, until 1943, rather mundane. But in that war year, following a 20-4 regular season, Georgetown earned its first bid to the young, eight-team NCAA tournament. On March 24, at Madison Square Garden, the Hoyas upset NYU, 55-36, to earn a national semifinal date with DePaul and its bespectacled, all-everything center, the 6-foot-10 Mikan. By today's standards, Mikan was slow and clumsy. But in the 1940s, No. 99 was an unstoppable force at both ends of the court. In DePaul's first-round NCAA win, for example, his shot-blocking presence beneath the basket had caused Dartmouth to miss its first thirty-four attempts. Many of those blocks would today be goaltending violations, and recognizing an inherent unfairness, the NCAA Rules Committee soon took steps to prevent such defensive maneuvers.

Overnight, literally, Georgetown coach Elmer Ripley devised a strategy to stymie Mikan. He would glue bulky, 6-foot-3 center Henry Hyde, the future Republican Congressman from Illinois, to the Blue Demons star. But on offense, Ripley instructed his Hoyas to do the opposite, to stay clear of the DePaul giant. The result was a 53-50 upset victory for the Hoyas, after which a Georgetown student reportedly stood up and yelled, "Believe it or not . . . by Ripley!" The glory was short-lived. In the March 30 NCAA final, also at the Garden, Georgetown was defeated by Wyoming, 46-34. The title-game loss initiated a run of mediocre basketball that wouldn't really end until Thompson arrived three decades later.

In the boom years that followed World War II, Georgetown was attracting most of its basketball players, as well as its students, from New York City and its environs. Though it was located in a city with a sizable African-American population, the university remained segregated. It wouldn't get its first black basketball player until 1966, by which time even many teams in the South had integrated. Great black hometown talents like Elgin Baylor, Dave Bing, George Leftwich, Tom Hoover, Ollie Johnson, and Thompson himself would be ignored by the school. As a result, in an era when several other small Catholic colleges were prospering, even capturing NCAA titles, Georgetown usually struggled to win as many games as it lost. Between 1948 and 1972, the Hoyas finished at or below .500 fifteen times. Only once in that dismal stretch would they get to a postseason tournament, losing in the 1970 NIT's opening round to Pete Maravich's LSU. "By 1971–72," wrote Thompson biographer Leonard Shapiro, "the basketball program was in disarray, and an embarrassment as well."

Following that season, coach Jack Magee and athletic director Jack Hagerty were fired in tandem and a search committee created to find a new coach. With its new Community Scholars program, Georgetown at last had started courting black students, especially those from the district. Now student groups and even some administrators urged the committee to continue the outreach by hiring a black coach, preferably one from Washington. "It didn't take a genius to figure out that finding a coach who would be appealing to the Washington community and who would be able to bring black athletes to Georgetown would not only help the Community Scholars program but also might help the basketball program," said Deacon, the Community Scholars program director. Deacon would inform the committee that there was an extremely successful candidate, the coach at St. Anthony's High School, in its own backyard. His name, the educator informed the panel, was John Thompson.

CHAPTER FIVE

Yes, he's fiery, competitive, driven. But he's a genius preparing for a game.

—Villanova guard Harold Jensen on Rollie Massimino

Salvatore Massimino was sixteen in 1914, when, on the eve of World War I, he left his native Sicily. The promise of America was a magnet for multitudes on the island as well as those in Southern Italy. Between 1880 and 1920, four million of them would immigrate to the United States, the great majority settling in the crowded cities of the Northeast. Massimino ended up in Newark, a factory and port city that was separated from glamorous Manhattan by the swampy Meadowlands and the Hudson, Hackensack, and Passaic rivers. There he would meet and marry Grace Alberti, another Sicilian immigrant, and the couple would have four boys.

Sal had been apprenticed as a shoemaker in Sicily, and in America he found work repairing shoes, eventually opening his own shop. He and Grace were simple people, their Catholic faith as strong as their work ethics. Those beliefs would provide some comfort for them in the great sorrows of their lives, the accidental deaths of two young sons, tragically both named Tom. Their first son, Tom, was killed in a freak gas explosion at the family's Newark apartment when he was six years old. Another boy, Carmine, came next. When a third son was born, his parents named him after his deceased brother. Incredibly, this Tom also would die in an accident at age six, struck and killed by an automobile while playing in the street near his family's apartment. Their fourth and last son, Roland V. Massimino, was born on November 13, 1934. By then, the family and many other Italians had departed Newark's crowded First Ward and made the move to neighboring Hillside. Located in Essex County, Hillside bordered Newark's predominantly Jewish Weequahic neighborhood. "All my childhood friends were Jewish," Massimino recalled. The author Philip Roth, a Weequahic native born just months before Massimino, described the area decades later in his novel *The Plot Against America* as "industrial plants, shipping terminals lining Route 27 and the Pennsylvania Railroad viaduct east of that . . . and the very edge of America east of that—the depots and docks of Newark Bay where they unload cargo from around the world."

The youngest child, Rollie would be the favorite of his understandably overprotective parents. While Carmine learned his father's cobbler's trade in the shop, the family would not permit Rollie even to enter the establishment. Rollie, the Massiminos vowed, would have a better life. Grace in particular filled the boy's head with dreams almost as determinedly as she filled his stomach with the spaghetti she cooked every night but Monday. She sent him to piano lessons, monitored his schoolwork as best she could, and made sure he didn't aimlessly roam the streets. Even at twenty-one, he had an 11 P.M. curfew.

As a boy, Massimino immersed himself in the American sports his father, who died at seventy-seven, in 1975, never played or fully understood. Rollie played football, baseball, and, despite his diminutive stature, basketball in the playgrounds at the nearby Jewish Community Center. He would grow only to 5-foot-8, but he was smart and clever, and he enjoyed using those qualities to outwit bigger opponents, particularly on the basketball court. At Hillside High, he would be a three-sport standout, good enough to be named the school's outstanding athlete as a senior.

His parents insisted he attend college. "There was never a question about that," Massimino said. But having little experience in the process, they turned it over to their son's basketball coach, Joe Silver. Massimino, who graduated from Hillside in 1952, was an apt enough point guard to have earned several scholarship offers. He settled on one from the University of Vermont because, while it was seven hours by car from Hillside, it was still the closest to home, Mom, and her pasta. In Massimino's three varsity seasons in Burlington, Vermont had a combined record of 25-34. A self-described "ordinary player . . . with a set shot," he was no star. Whatever his contributions were, they weren't notable enough to have been recorded by the school's sports-information office, which in 2011 said it had no individual statistics on the man who in 1983 was inducted into the university's Hall of Fame.

His parents had imparted their religious zeal to their son,

who while at Vermont attended 6 A.M. Mass most mornings. For a time, like many Catholic boys in the '50s, Massimino even considered becoming a priest. "But I wanted to get married, have kids, coach," he said. After graduating from Vermont in 1956 with a bachelor's of arts in education, Massimino returned to New Jersey looking for work as a high school teacher and coach. His first job came at Cranford High, where, for $3,600 a year, he was a basketball and football assistant as well as a business instructor. Cranford's head basketball coach at the time, Bill Martin, had once had future NBA coach Hubie Brown as an assistant. He saw some of the same eagerness and potential in Massimino and carefully nurtured the young man's ambitions. A photo in Cranford's 1957 yearbook shows the first-year assistant coach with a youthful smile, a trim waistline, and a full head of hair. Over the next twelve years, at Cranford and two other high schools, the hairline would recede as the waistline and the résumé expanded.

In October of 1958, a fellow teacher asked a mutual friend for a ride to the nearest train station. Massimino accompanied them, and by February he and the teacher, Mary Jane Reid, were engaged. A few months later, in August, they were married. With new responsibilities and a salary that by then had reached only $4,000 a year, Massimino decided to further his education. He took courses at Rutgers University that in 1959 earned him a master's degree in health and physical education. That same year, the couple purchased a $12,000 home in Cranford, thanks to a loan from Massimino's father. At Martin's urging, Massimino applied for and got the basketball head coaching job at his alma mater, Hillside High. There he twice led his old team to the New Jersey Group IV state finals, where they lost both times to Newark's powerful Central High.

Massimino quickly realized that his coaching talents went beyond Xs and Os. He also had a knack for psychology. He understood which players needed to be stroked, which required a harsher hand. "His greatest quality as a coach, I think, was that he knew what motivated you," said Jensen. "He understood how to get at you. He didn't focus a lot on individual skill development. But he was a genius in molding a team." Still, the intricacies of the game held their own fascination for the young coach. He was constantly jotting down ideas, especially for his defenses. Massimino picked the brains of older coaches and attended as many clinics and summer camps as a young father and husband could manage. Before long he had built a minor reputation as a defensive wizard. That reputation spread at least as far as Hanover, New Hampshire, where in 1963 Dartmouth coach Doggie Julian contacted him and asked him to speak to his team on the subject. Later that same year Julian called to let Massimino know there was an opening at a prestigious Massachusetts high school, in Lexington, the leafy Boston suburb where the Revolutionary War had begun. Massimino quickly applied for and got the job at Lexington High, spending the next six years there. One of his teams, featuring future University of Oregon star Ron Lee, won a state title. Another finished with a 20-1 record.

But by 1968, despite the success he'd enjoyed at Lexington, Massimino, like young people all across America in that turbulent year, was restless. He'd coached 221 high school games and won 160. But he was married, with four children now, and his ambition rivaled his appetite. He wanted more. Over the years, thanks to all the networking he'd done at those summer clinics and camps, he'd become enmeshed in the incestuous coaching world, where who you knew often was more important than what you knew. He had met and befriended such young and promising college coaches as Chuck Daly and Bob Knight. Those friendships whet his appetite for life at the next level. So when the State University of New York at Stony Brook started a basketball program in 1969, Massimino was hired as its first coach, for $19,000 annually. As was almost always the case for him, success came immediately. That first Stony Brook team went 18-6 and earned a berth in the NCAA's small-college tournament. Then, after his 1970–71 squad finished with a 15-10 record, Massimino got a call from Daly.

When Daly had been Boston College's coach, he had seen and scouted Lexington High often. He'd been impressed, especially by the team's matchup-zone defense. Daly told Massimino he'd been hired to coach the University of Pennsylvania and he wanted Massimino to come with him to Philadelphia as an assistant. There was just one problem. The Penn job paid only $13,000, $6,000 less than he'd been making at Stony Brook. Daly convinced Massimino to look beyond the dollars. The move, he insisted, would be a sizable career upgrade. Who knew where it could lead?

Ivy League Penn was then an Eastern powerhouse. The two men who had preceded Daly as the head basketball coaches there, Dick Harter and Jack McCloskey, would both move on to long NBA careers. So would Daly, of course, as well as the man who succeeded him, Bob Weinhauer. Between 1969 and 1971, Harter's Quakers had gone 53-3. Entering the 1971 East Regional final with Villanova, they were 28-0 and ranked No. 3 in the country. Harter would leave for Oregon after that season, his last game a blowout loss to Villanova in the NCAA tournament, and Daly would be hired. "We've got a lot of talent coming back from that ['71] team," Daly told Massimino. "We can't screw this up." Finally, Daly convinced him. Massimino piled his wife and kids into a 1960 Pontiac and headed for Philadelphia. There both men were outsiders. Neither had the kind of Philadelphia connections that always had been virtually mandatory for getting a job at a Big 5 school. But Daly was extremely likable, and Massimino was tough enough— many would add "abrasive"—to survive in the rough city, possessed of the kind of aggressive personality that would serve him well anywhere on the East Coast. And besides, both could coach. It didn't take long for the city to embrace them.

During their first victory at Penn, a 94-74 rout of Navy on December 4, 1971, as the sold-out Palestra rocked with noise, Daly turned to Massimino. "Now, Rollie, isn't this worth $6,000?" The Quakers went a combined 46-10 in Daly's first two seasons, won a pair of Ivy League titles, and reached the NCAA's Sweet 16 twice. But again Massimino grew restless. Daly was a great coach and a great friend, but Massimino was in his late thirties, too old, he felt, to still be an assistant. So when in 1973 the owner of a professional team in Bologna, Italy, contacted him about becoming his coach, Massimino was sorely tempted. And then one morning that same year he picked up the *Philadelphia Inquirer* and read that Jack Kraft was leaving Villanova. The Wildcats had just endured an awful season. The campus and the college community were still reeling from the Howard Porter scandal that had forever marred the magical '71 season. Whoever got that job, Massimino thought, was going to have his hands full. He wondered who that might be. "Wait a minute," Massimino thought. "Why couldn't it be me?"

It would be. The same day he read about Kraft's departure, Massimino was contacted by Villanova's administrators. They met for three hours in a Holiday Inn in downtown Philadelphia. For Massimino, it was clear the scandal-scarred school wanted him badly. On November 13, 1973, with remarkably little fanfare, Villanova introduced Massimino as its new basketball coach. "I took the job without ever having been to Villanova," Massimino said. "But it was my dream job." He was just the third man to fill the position since 1936. "That stability is what impressed me," he would say. Initially things were every bit as difficult as he'd imagined. Villanova was still an independent, but its schedule was better than its talent. His first two teams went a combined 16-37. The 1973–74 Wildcats managed just seven victories, the school's lowest total since World War II.

The lessons came hard and fast. The 1971 mess had poisoned the recruiting well for Villanova. With very few ties to Philadelphia's basketball community, Massimino had little chance to land the city's best players. Always prideful of their program, Villanovans were embarrassed. And, in at least one way, the program Kraft had left him was even worse than Massimino had imagined. Villanova's vengeful 90-47 rout of Penn in the '71 NCAA East Region final had so galled Dick Harter that the Quakers coach, before he left for Oregon after that season, vowed he would "get back at those guys." His chance came on December 23, 1973, when Villanova played in Eugene. Massimino knew all about Harter's hurt feelings, but mutual friends had assured the Villanova coach any ill will from "90-47"—as the game would forever be recalled in Philadephia—had dissipated. They were wrong. A gleeful Harter poured it on the visiting Wildcats nonstop, pressing throughout, keeping his starters—including Massimino's old Lexington star, Ron Lee—in the game long past the point where the eventual 116-77 humiliation was competitive. Harter was so delighted by this retribution that he later recounted that on his drive home that night, he pulled his car off the road and "laughed for twenty minutes."

But Massimino's memory would prove to be just as long, his competitiveness just as fierce. So in 1980, when Harter, by then coaching at Penn State, brought his Nittany Lions to Villanova, he would get some payback. The Wildcats purposefully rolled up the score in a 98-53 rout. Late in that game, Massimino punctuated a Stewart Granger dunk by leaping off the bench and repeatedly pumping a fist in the air. Granger, curiously, would become a symbol of the turnaround Massimino eventually enacted at the school. Realizing the trouble he was having getting Philly kids, the coach brought in a fellow North Jersey Italian, Mike Fratello, as an assistant and told him to look for talent in the New York City area. Brooklyn's

Granger would be one of the first national names signed by the Wildcats new staff.

Massimino's first winning season came when the Wildcats went 16-11 in 1975–76. A year later they were asked to join the Eastern Eight, along with Pitt, Penn State, and five other schools. Villanova finished second that initial season, with an overall record of 23-10. The 'Cats would win the next three league titles, earning two NCAA tourney bids in the process. After the 1979–80 season, athletic director Ted Aceto got a call from Dave Gavitt. The Wildcats athletic director then summoned Massimino to his field house office. "Rollie," Aceto told him, "Dave Gavitt just phoned. He wants to know if we'd be interested in joining the Big East. What do you think?"

CHAPTER SIX

*There were many times . . . when I wondered if this thing was
really going to work.*

—Dave Gavitt, founder of the Big East

In the last week of March 1985, Dave Gavitt couldn't stop
thinking about the wonderful absurdity of it all. Three Big
East teams in the Final Four. It seemed every newspaper,
every magazine, every television network in the country was
doing a story on how this young league had pulled it off. It
had been a remarkably swift maturity. The Big Ten was ninety
years old, the Big Eight seventy-eight, the Pac-10 seventy, the
ACC thirty-two. Yet none of those conferences had ever gotten three teams to an NCAA Final Four. And yet his league,
just six years old, had managed it.

And it was *his* league. Virtually alone, Gavitt had recognized the value in a basketball conference that would stretch
from Boston to Washington, uniting the large cities in the East
Coast's megalopolis. He thought about all the talent in those
places, all the big arenas and newspapers, all the natural rivalries that would emerge. Mostly he thought about its potential

for enormous TV audiences. "He built it around media markets," said John Marinatto, one of Gavitt's successors as Big East commissioner. "That was a very different concept back then."

Just as important as the millions of viewers in those markets were the young basketball players there. Great basketball had long been a hallmark in East Coast cities like Philadelphia, New York, and Washington. In urban playgrounds, parks, and parish gyms, a unique level and style of play had developed. But with no showcase league to attract and keep them, the region's best players, for decades, had been taking their talents elsewhere. Philadelphia's Wilt Chamberlain emigrated to Kansas, New York's Lew Alcindor to UCLA, Washington's Elgin Baylor to Seattle. Countless other urban superstars followed, opting for the kind of exposure and atmosphere they couldn't get in a region without a super conference, in cities dominated by professional sports.

Gavitt's timing couldn't have been better. In that year of 1979 there was an abundance of high school talent on the East Coast. In particular, Patrick Ewing, a seven-footer from Cambridge, just across the Charles River from Boston, already was being compared to the best centers ever. A strong eastern basketball conference might help keep him and others close to home.

Before the Big East would start up in 1979 there would be disputes to settle, meetings to endure, contracts to sign, and details, lots of details, to sort out. But in the end it would be two events separated by ninety-nine days and seventy-nine miles that made all the difference. On May 31, 1979, the athletic directors from Providence, Syracuse, Boston College, Connecticut, St. John's, Seton Hall, and Georgetown met in a boardroom at the Providence Civic Center. Gavitt had hoped for a larger gathering. He wanted a Philadelphia presence for the league, too, but Temple, his first choice, declined, and Villanova was committed to the Eastern Eight for at least one more year. Though most of the ADs remained skeptical of the plan he'd outlined, Gavitt continued to push and prod them. He trusted his ability to sell the concept. A Rhode Island native and a Dartmouth graduate, the thirty-five-year-old was extremely smart and personable. He'd been Providence's basketball coach for ten years, getting the Friars to five NCAA tournaments. He'd already been chosen to coach the U.S. Olympic team in 1980. He knew what the future looked like. "This thing is going to be as big as the ACC," he promised. "We're going to fill the largest arenas. We're going to get a big TV contract. And we're going to have a postseason tournament in Madison Square Garden every March."

The idea had come to him a year earlier in Hershey, Pennsylvania, during the annual meeting of the East Coast Athletic Conference. A loosely affiliated and unwieldy amalgam of forty large and small schools segmented into several indistinct groupings, the ECAC recently had been given a mandate by the NCAA: Realign into divisions whose members must play each other twice a season. For some, that arrangement meant eliminating profitable matchups with the bigger ECAC schools for home-and-homes with smaller ones. It all made little sense to Gavitt. That's when he asked the ADs of several of the larger ECAC colleges to join him for the meeting in Providence the following spring. The topic would be the formation of a new basketball-only conference.

Seven ADs showed up. At least three of the original invitees, Temple, Rutgers, and Holy Cross, declined and would live to regret it. Gavitt's powers of persuasion prevailed. That day the seven-team league was formed. Naming it wouldn't be so easy. "Big" followed by the number of member schools had been done often. Besides, the number was likely to change frequently if Gavitt's dreams came true. Someone suggested the President's Conference. Others the Seabord Conference or the Super Seven. When the discussion got more elemental, and the ADs realized it was going to be both big and in the East, they at last had a suitable name. Villanova would join the new conference a year later, Pitt in 1982. Those schools had been members of another East Coast league, one assembled in 1975, primarily around football. The founders of the Eastern Eight—later the Atlantic Eight and Atlantic 10—hadn't thought much about TV, perhaps because some of its members were located in such small markets as State College, Pennsylvania; Morgantown, West Virginia; and Amherst, Massachusetts.

Now, with cable TV exploding and television money becoming an increasingly important and profitable pursuit, Gavitt understood the essential role the medium would play in college sports. And what TV network wouldn't want to have an entrée into the Big East's markets—New York, Philadelphia, Boston, Washington, Hartford, Pittsburgh? Surely that lineup would be irresistible. But to whom? The initial reaction from the established networks, Gavitt said, was lukewarm. "When you guys grow up," one executive told him, "call back." Eventually, the commissioner made deals with independent stations in several cities. Then, at 7 P.M. on September 7, 1979, broadcaster Lee Leonard, seated behind a desk on a blandly decorated set in Bristol, Connecticut, welcomed viewers to a new cable sports network. "If you love sports," Leonard told the approximately 30,000 viewers who were watching ESPN debut that night, "if you really love sports, you'll think you died and went to heaven."

It didn't take long for the two young New England–based entities—one desperate for a regional TV outlet, the other for sports programming—to find each other. And in 1980, before the start of the second Big East season, in a trailer outside ESPN's ramshackle headquarters, Gavitt signed a contract uniting the Big East and ESPN. The marriage between TV and the Big East, which soon would appear to have been made in heaven, had to endure a little hell in its early stages. In that first season, for example, a Seton Hall–Princeton telecast started late because, after one of the referees failed to show up, the power went out in Seton Hall's Walsh Gymnasium. Electricians eventually restored the lights and an official who had worked an earlier women's game at Walsh was pressed into duty, his blue shirt and white sneakers contrasting with his more traditionally attired whistle mate. "There were many times, and that certainly was one, when I wondered if this thing was really going to work," said Gavitt, who died in 2011. "But I knew basketball could work in prime time."

A more serious existential threat came in 1982. Penn State football coach Joe Paterno wanted to start a powerful all-sports East Coast league that would have football as its keystone. Penn State would be pulling out of the Eastern Eight and Paterno wanted Rutgers, Temple, West Virginia, Pitt, and Big

East members Syracuse and Boston College to join him. Gavitt sensed that Pitt, the number two football program in the East, was the wild card. Knowing there was some long-standing antagonism between that school and Paterno's Penn State, he made his move. Not long afterward, Pitt announced it would be joining the Big East. Paterno's plans went up in smoke, his program having little choice but to look west, where it eventually merged with the Big Ten.

Basketball-wise, the Big East's turnaround probably came when Ewing announced he would be attending Georgetown. Suddenly East Coast stars were staying at home. Ewing and nine others among the east's top thirteen graduating seniors in 1981 committed to conference schools, a lineup that also included Chris Mullin, Pinckney, Pearl Washington, and Walter Berry. "When Patrick came to Georgetown, it did for the Big East what [Joe] Namath's signing with the Jets did for the old AFL," said Bill Raftery, the broadcaster who was then Seton Hall's coach. "It gave us instant credibility." And just about the time all those players arrived in the league, Syracuse opened its Carrier Dome, which held 32,000-plus for basketball. In 1981, the Big East signed a long-term deal with Madison Square Garden to serve as permanent host for its postseason tournament beginning in 1983. There were no more doubts about the Big East. "That was the last piece of the puzzle," Gavitt said of the Garden deal. "We were on Broadway. We'd made it in only our fourth year."

The baby conference was playing with the big boys. Gavitt recalled the night he realized that. It was at the 1982 East Regionals in Raleigh. Villanova was ahead of Memphis

State when the announcer revealed that in the Midwest Regional Boston College had beaten Kansas State. At the news, the Villanova students started chanting, "Big East! Big East! Big East!" "As a coach, I had heard the chant of 'A-C-C' so many times over the years," Gavitt said. "I said to myself, 'My God, we've made it.' "

The Big East and ESPN would help foment a basketball renaissance in the 1980s. The first sign of that revival had appeared in 1979 when the Indiana State–Michigan State NCAA title game attracted the largest audience ever for a basketball game. March Madness quickly became an annual sports ritual, the tournament's final typically attracting ratings numbers that the NBA could only dream about. From 1979 until the end of the century, every NCAA final would have an audience of more than twenty-five million. Most topped thirty million. Over that same span, average attendance at NCAA tournament games jumped from 12,619 to 21,197.

Meanwhile, when Indiana State and Michigan State were playing in Salt Lake City, the NBA was in a funk. Its only regular-season national TV contract was for a Sunday afternoon game on CBS. That network's ratings for prime-time NBA playoff games had been so bad that executives pushed to have the games tape-delayed and aired at 11:30 P.M. Two-thirds of the league's franchises were losing money. There was talk of folding the weak teams and downsizing to a twelve-team league. The NBA's best player, Kareem Abdul-Jabbar, not only was a Muslim but was reserved, private, and aloof—hardly a marketer's dream. Drugs, fights, and—though few wanted to confront the topic—the league's changing racial makeup had combined to diminish the pro game's appeal. The most notable negative occurred in 1977 when, during a Lakers-Rockets brawl, a punch from L.A.'s Kermit Washington shattered the jaw of Houston's Rudy Tomjanovich. The fact that Washington was black and Tomjanovich white only exacerbated the racial stereotypes that were dogging the league.

But there was something about the Bird-Johnson rivalry— and race probably had a lot to do with it—that electrified the public. When the duo graduated to the NBA, their popularity went along with them. Bird was the first white superstar to emerge since Bill Walton, whose politics and manner hadn't particularly endeared him to whites or blacks. And the effervescent Johnson had an appeal that crossed racial barriers. Those two would win six MVP Awards between them, become nationally known figures, and lead the Celtics and Lakers to three memorable—and highly rated—NBA finals in the 1980s.

The NBA added a three-point line for the 1978–79 season and, particularly after David Stern was hired as its commissioner in 1984, started to market the remarkable athleticism of its players. Its showboating All-Star Game and slam-dunk contest turned into wildly popular events that drew casual viewers as well as fanatics. When North Carolina's Jordan, whose jump shot had defeated Georgetown in the closing seconds of 1982's NCAA championship game, arrived in Chicago in 1984 and soon teamed up with a youthful athletic-wear company called Nike, the sport's popularity, as well as its cultural and commercial influence, ballooned. Before Nike signed Jordan as its symbol and introduced the Air Jordan sneaker in 1987, the Oregon firm had sales of $900 million. Within a decade, that figure would jump 1,000 percent, to $9 billion. By 1985, basketball was cool again.

CHAPTER SEVEN

Do I contradict myself?
Very well then I contradict myself.
(I am large, I contain multitudes.)

—Walt Whitman, "Song of Myself"

A harsh February wind cracked across the Potomac River hillside that Georgetown University had occupied for nearly two centuries. Temperatures that night, February 5, 1975, had fallen below freezing and were expected to dip into the low 20s. Like turtles seeking comfort in their shells, spectators en route to a Georgetown basketball game sank deep into their outerwear. As they entered the university's McDonough Gymnasium, the twenty-four-year-old arena that bordered Piney Branch Park, fans emerged and shivered in relief, unzipping parkas, removing hats, scarves, and gloves. On such a frosty night, it seemed odd that no one would notice that a window above the stage at one end of the old arena had been left open just a crack.

Georgetown was hosting Dickinson College, whose team had bused the ninety miles from Carlisle, Pennsylvania, in the kind of bland matchup that marked the soon-to-become-irrelevant East Coast Athletic Conference. John Thompson's Hoyas had followed up a promising 7-2 start by losing six of their next seven games. The slump was disappointing for those who had hoped for an awakening of a program that had slumbered through most of its existence. After mediocre 12-14 and 13-13 records in Thompson's first two seasons, better things had been expected in this, his third. But a variety of impediments had conspired to scuttle those hopes. Merlin Wilson, the team's leading rebounder, had back problems. Another Hoya had missed several games after Thompson discovered he'd cut classes. A third was sidelined with academic problems.

The classroom issues, in particular, fed into the bigoted fears some Hoyas fans had voiced after the school had hired Thompson, its first black coach, in 1972. Georgetown, these people believed, apparently would now be willing to lower its standards in order to improve its basketball fortunes. The frustrations ran so deep that in recent games at McDonough, some spectators had felt emboldened enough to heckle the thirty-three-year-old former high school coach with cries of "Go back to St. Anthony's" or "Bring back Magee," the latter a reference to the unsuccessful coach Thompson had replaced. As Georgetown's pep band hit the opening notes of the national anthem, the modest crowd lazily rose to its feet. It was at that moment when the bedsheet first became visible. Just above the American flag that most eyes were focused on, it was being pushed through the open window. Unfurling as it tumbled down the wall, the white sheet contained a scrawled six-word message: "THOMPSON, THE NIGGER FLOP, MUST GO."

Oh say can you see, indeed. An incensed spectator grabbed the sheet and yanked it to the ground. Apparently, neither Thompson nor his players initially had seen the hateful message. But virtually everyone else had, including several black youngsters who were seated behind the home team's bench as part of the "Coach's Corner" outreach Thompson had initiated. "It'll be in their memory banks forever," Thompson said afterward.

It wasn't the first time a Georgetown basketball crowd had embarrassed itself and the university with an overt display of prejudice. Nine years earlier, when the Hoyas were playing NYU in New York, a young student in a Nazi uniform led the Georgetown student section in mock chants of "Sieg Heil!" When many at predominantly Jewish NYU complained, a Georgetown official suggested it was all a harmless parody. "We have friends who are Jewish people," the Rev. Anthony Zeits, director of student personnel, told the *New York Times*. As a concession, Zeits promised that the Nazi-garbed student would be banned from future Georgetown-NYU games. The rest of the time, however, he could continue to cheerlead. A day after the anti-Thompson sign's appearance, the campus was alive with outraged reaction. Had it been students? Outsiders? Security guards futilely hunted the perpetrators. Meetings were held, impassioned telephone calls made, news conferences scheduled, player boycotts threatened. At one session with reporters, Floyd Yeoman, who was black and a freshman on Thompson's team, read a lengthy statement from the players: "We have no intention of boycotting. GU is our school," Yeoman read from the statement's conclusion. "We will continue to play for Mr. Thompson, the flop—the nigger flop. But let us caution a certain element that our patience is growing short. Let me say that all of us have only one regret— that our names weren't listed with Mr. Thompson's on that sign."

As hurtful as the episode must have been for Thompson, in a curiously unintended way, it made things easier for him. All but his most ardent critics now rallied around him. Once wavering columnists and editorialists supported him. The administration, which loudly denounced the incident, stood more firmly than ever in his corner. On the court, meanwhile, his players responded by winning five games in a row, seven of their last eight. And when Derrick Jackson hit a 20-footer with two seconds left in the ECAC tournament final, Georgetown had a 61-60 triumph and its first NCAA tournament berth in thirty-two years. As the joyful Hoyas celebrated in their locker room, Thompson entered, quieted his players and changed the subject. "I said it was a great win, mostly for me," Thompson would recall in 1980. "I was going to get a lot of publicity. Maybe I'd get a raise, even a better job offer. Then I said, 'What are you guys getting out of it?' And I walked out. I didn't want them ever to forget the bargain they'd made, the real reason they were at Georgetown."

The locker-room speech was the kind of enigmatic be- havior people would soon learn to expect from Thompson. Georgetown's coach, 6-foot-10 and close to 300 pounds, was an enormous mass of complexities. Anyone who thought they had a handle on him usually was quickly disabused of the notion, often by Thompson himself. Nobody understood him. And he preferred it that way. He could provoke anger and laughter, understanding and befuddlement, hatred and love. He could employ an elemental profanity and a thoughtful eloquence. He could be brutally blunt and yet shroud his coaching motives in mystery. He could be defiantly obtuse as well as gently instructive. He could demand absolute adherence from players off the court and yet seem to ignore their questionable behavior on it. He could uncover racism where it had festered unseen and see it where it didn't exist. "America's coach," a Colorado sportswriter noted when Thompson was named to head the 1988 U.S. Olympic team, "is America's puzzle."

Though many have attempted to parse his behavior over the years, Thompson has rarely felt the need to explain it. In Catholic grade school, when the nuns couldn't understand why he acted as he did, he wouldn't tell them. When he gave up an NBA career after two years with a championship team, he didn't explain why. When he and his team continued to defy the conventional images of a successful college program, he didn't offer excuses. When the media thought they understood what drove him and his players, he enjoyed telling them they were wrong. "I hear that bull, that 'us-against-them' stuff," he said. "I don't sit down and say, 'Fellas, they're against us. Let's go out and win.' I just think that people who have trouble with themselves usually find a lot wrong with other people."

In assessments of Thompson and his teams, for perhaps one of the first times in sports, psychological attributes were given more weight than physical ones. Georgetown's success, the thinking went, had more to do with its attitude than its athleticism. It wasn't that Patrick Ewing and his teammates played harder and smarter and better than opponents, it was that they intimidated, bullied, inspired fear. And, to some extent, both rationales were correct. Clearly there was something different about the Hoyas. They seldom smiled or acknowledged opponents. They rarely embraced other players before or after games. They performed with a passion that bordered on fury. "They didn't just want to beat you," Villanova's Pinckney said. "They wanted to destroy you." Perhaps only Thompson and his players knew whether it was real animosity or merely an act designed to create a competitive edge.

Much of how Americans saw Thompson's Georgetown teams, of course, had to do with how they saw race. Had the Hoyas been all white or even a little less black, it's possible their style would have been envied and emulated. But in 1980s America, whenever fear and aggression were combined with blackness, the resulting brew was a combustible one. "I'm sure race exacerbates those perceptions," said Esherick, who had played for Thompson and then joined him as an assistant. "Black people bring their perception of white people and white people bring their perception of black people to the table. You can't prevent that from happening among a small percentage of people no matter what."

Thompson's system appeared to stifle the improvisational skills that basketball fans had come to expect from black players. Stereotypes suggested all-black teams ought to be undisciplined, and yet Thompson's appeared to be governed by rigid guidelines on and off the court. As he liked to point out, whites tended to see in blacks what they expected to see. And they didn't know what to make of an all-black team that played as aggressively and as disciplined as his. "White men run the game," Thompson said. "A white coach recruits a good black player. He knows the kid's got talent, but he also knows—or thinks he knows—that because he's black he's undisciplined. So he doesn't try to give the player any discipline. He puts him in the freelance, one-on-one, hot-dog role and turns to the little white guard for discipline. Other black kids see this and think this is how they're expected to play, and so the image is perpetuated." Such talk, however accurate it might have been, made white America uncomfortable. As obsessed as the nation was with race, it preferred that the subject be discussed—if at all—behind closed doors, or in the shadows. Thompson was one of the first prominent sports figures to confront racial attitudes head-on. If America didn't understand his team, he said, maybe it was because they didn't understand themselves.

Understanding themselves was easier than understanding Thompson. The man defied conventional logic. You'd think becoming the first African-American coach in an NCAA championship game (1982), then the first to win a title (1984) would have made him proud and happy. Instead he chafed at any attempt to label him or his accomplishments. "I resent the hell out of that question," Thompson said in 1982 when a reporter asked him how he felt about achieving the milestone. "It implies that I'm the first black man accomplished enough and intelligent enough to do this. It's an insult to my race. There have been plenty of others who could have gotten here if they had been given the opportunity they deserved." You'd think that he'd have barked angrily at Fred Brown when the Georgetown guard, with no provocation, threw away the ball and the Hoyas' chance at an NCAA championship in the final seconds of 1982's title-game loss to North Carolina. Instead, he embraced and comforted the distraught player. "I could have reacted the other way," Thompson said. "I was lucky." You'd think that when Georgetown's 1984 national champions gathered for a twenty-fifth reunion in 2009, Thompson, long since retired, would have welcomed the chance to share in that past glory. Instead, as his players were being introduced to a wildly enthusiastic crowd at Washington's Verizon Center, he sat in the stands and watched dispassionately. "I am not trying to be anything other than what I am," he said. "And I'm really not certain what that is."

Whenever Anna and John Thompson, Sr., returned to visit family in southern Maryland, their young son was puzzled. Why, he asked his parents, did the black attendees at the Catholic church have to wait for the white parishioners to finish before they took Communion? "Don't get caught up in that," his mother counseled. "The world can be very mean sometimes. Just go ahead and ignore it." It was one mother's lesson he never learned. John Thompson, Jr., would never be much good at ignoring anything.

He was born in Washington, D.C., three months before Pearl Harbor, on September 2, 1941, the youngest and only boy among four children. His mother and father had moved from rural Maryland to the nation's capital, where Anna worked initially as a domestic and her husband toiled as a laborer in a tile factory. As a boy, Thompson's father had helped support his impoverished family by picking fruits and vegetables on nearby farms, foregoing his education after a few years of elementary school. "My father couldn't read or write," Thompson would say. "His name was John Thompson, too, but he couldn't spell it."

Until World War II's conclusion at last created some impetus for change, Washington was a predominantly segregated city. Employment, education, and housing were governed by race. There were separate public schools for whites and blacks. The Thompsons, Catholics amid the city's largely Protestant African-American community, enrolled their son at Our Lady of Perpetual Help elementary school. Taller than all his classmates, Thompson struggled both academically and socially through the early grades. The nuns who taught there thought a ruler across the knuckles might induce him to better behavior and grades. It only made him rebel harder. As an adult, Thompson would run a highly disciplined organization, but as a boy he chafed in that kind of environment. The befuddled nuns eventually placed him at the back of a row earmarked for "babies," an insult that because of his size stung even more. "I didn't like them," Thompson would say of the nuns, "and they didn't like me." Frustrated and ignorant about such things as learning disabilities, they told Thompson's mother that her son "was not educable." One nun even suggested he might be slightly retarded. Anna Thompson, who in her fifties returned to school to earn a nursing degree, refused to listen. By sixth grade, her son was attending public school. "Life was explained to me in a limited fashion," Thompson would say. "[When] you are young and black and growing up in a segregated situation, you learn to expect certain things."

Like most kids, white and black, growing up in the late 1940s and early 1950s, sports provided the great diversion. And baseball was then the sport of choice. Since the hometown Senators would be one of the last major-league teams to integrate, the city's large black population tended to ignore them. Thompson and his father often went to Griffith Stadium, not so much to see the woeful Senators as to watch visiting black stars like Cleveland's Larry Doby or Satchel Paige. By the time he got to Browne Junior High, where his interest in basketball developed, Thompson was over six feet tall. When he wasn't learning about the game from Browne's coach, Kermit Trigg, he was getting tutored on the court at the city's many rec centers and playgrounds. The quality of Washington basketball, then and now, was superb. Elgin Baylor was a few years older than Thompson, Dave Bing a year younger. The game there was tough and physical, possessed of an edge that it sometimes lacked in other places. According to George Leftwich, the future Villanova player and a Thompson friend, in Washington, unlike in New York and other big cities, rebounds in half-court games didn't have to be returned to mid-court. "[That] taught us to box out and gain body position and to play a more physical style." It was a lesson in toughness Thompson never forgot.

Before departing Browne, Thompson, 6-foot-6 and still growing, attracted the attention of Bob Dwyer, the basketball coach at Archbishop Carroll High, a Catholic high school. Dwyer, according to Thompson's biographer, Leonard Shapiro, was one of the first in the city to recruit black players to his private school. "He wasn't so much a crusader as he was a realist," Shapiro wrote. "The black players constantly worked at the game; their skills seemed at a much higher level." Dwyer asked Thompson to come to Carroll for a talk. While he was there, the coach took him to the gym and had the big youngster work out against Tom Hoover, a 6-foot-9 varsity player who later played at Villanova. "It was obvious," Dwyer said, "this kid Thompson was going to be a good player." After the coach assured him his $200 tuition would be covered, Thompson enrolled at Carroll for the 1957 school year.

The Catholic high school would mark his initial prolonged exposure to whites. "Some of my superstitions about white people were overcome," Thompson would say, "and I think they learned about black people, too." Thompson came of age, academically as well as athletically, at Carroll. The teams he starred on would go 86-3 against other high schools, 103-8 if you counted all their games against college freshmen teams and amateur clubs. They would win fifty-five in a row at one point and capture two city titles. Fully grown to 6-foot-10 when he averaged 21 points a game as a senior, he was named a high school All-American. Just as significantly for someone who had had such difficulty in elementary school, Thompson was ranked forty-eight in a senior class of almost three hundred students.

* * *

People still argue about whether Red Auerbach had anything to do with Thompson's decision to attend Providence College. Auerbach is dead and Thompson isn't saying.

Then the coach and general manager of the perennial NBA champion Boston Celtics, Auerbach was a Washington native who perhaps better than anyone in his generation knew and recognized talent. In the mid-1950s, old friends from the city had told him about Thompson, much as Auerbach would one day inform Thompson about Ewing.

The NBA then had a territorial rule in place for its drafts. Teams could forfeit their first-round pick and instead select a player who had gone to high school or college within fifty miles of their city. That, for example, was how Wilt Chamberlain ended up in Philadelphia, Bob Cousy and Tom Heinsohn in Boston, Oscar Robertson in Cincinnati. And Providence fell into the Celtics' sphere of influence.

Whatever his motivation, and it probably had as much to do with the school's Catholic affiliation or the fact that African-American Lenny Wilkens was the team's captain when he visited as it did the possibility of one day being a Celtic, Thompson signed with the Friars. Providence won the 1963 NIT in his junior season. As a senior, he averaged a school record 26 points and 14 rebounds a game, and the Friars earned their first bid to the NCAA tournament, losing, ironically, to Kraft's Villanova team in a first-round matchup.

In the 1964 NBA draft, two clubs exercised their territorial rights—the Cincinnati Royals took the University of Cincinnati's George Wilson, and the Lakers grabbed UCLA's Walt Hazzard. With the regular round's first pick, the Knicks selected Jim "Bad News" Barnes from Texas Western. Boston, with its initial choice, took a big center, but it was Mel Counts, a seven-footer from Oregon, and not Thompson. Auerbach didn't use his territorial pick for Thompson because he didn't have to. The Celtics got the Providence center with the ninth and last pick of a third round that had previously yielded such long-forgotten names as Brian Generalovich, Tom Dose, Art Becker, and Steve Courtin. Boston had taken Cincinnati's Ron Bonham in the second round. "As a player," Auerbach said of Thompson, "he was not spectacular at any phase of the game. . . . I used him to give Bill Russell a breather. He never complained. He just did his job. He was a coach's dream."

By then Boston had won seven world championships with Russell at center, including the last six, so Thompson's playing time, understandably, was limited. But from his vantage point on the bench as the Celtics won two more world titles in his brief NBA career, he learned much from Russell and Auerbach that he would apply later. Neither of those men cared how the public or opponents viewed them. Auerbach gloated over victories, bullied referees and opposing coaches, took whatever measure he felt necessary to get his team a win. Celtics opponents long complained about the frequent lack of hot water, heat, or air-conditioning in Boston Garden's minuscule visitors' locker room, problems many attributed to Auerbach's competitiveness.

"He ached when we didn't win," Russell would write of Auerbach. "His whole body would be thrown out of whack when we lost. . . . He was our gyroscope, programmed solely for winning, and it was difficult for any of us to deviate from the course he set for us." Auerbach also was a master psychologist who kept a tight lid on his team, threatening exile for any player who dared expose its inner workings to the press. He shook up racial perceptions, too, drafting and playing more blacks than anyone in the league. When he stepped down as coach in 1966, he named Russell as his replacement, making him the first black to head a major professional team. Russell, meanwhile, aside from all the mental and physical attributes that made him perhaps the most successful basketball player ever, possessed an extreme racial awareness. He gave his children African names and was, Thompson would note, the first person he knew who referred to himself as "black" not "negro." "He was black before it was fashionable to be black," Thompson said. The superstar center was not afraid to address racism when and where he saw it, and he'd seen plenty in Boston. Russell had an independent air about him, an aura that strongly indicated he was his own man. "[Thompson] acts the way he does because he does not want people getting too close," Auerbach said. "He learned that from me and Russell—be in control, put the other people on the defensive."

Thompson acquired the nickname "Caddy" in Boston because on the court that's exactly the role he played for Russell. In eighty-four games over two seasons, he averaged roughly 3.5 points and 3.5 rebounds. He played seventy-four games in his rookie season, but injuries and Auerbach's decision to use Mel Counts more frequently limited him to just ten appearances in the 1965–66 season. When, because he'd played so little that second season, the champion Celtics voted Thompson only half a $5,000 play-off share, he confronted his teammates.

Impressed by his guts if not his reasoning, they reconsidered and presented him with a full share. The following season the NBA would be adding a tenth team, the Chicago Bulls. Auerbach made Thompson, who had married Gwen Twitty that off-season, available in an expansion draft and the backup center was one of eighteen players the new team selected. When it became clear he wasn't going to earn much money or playing time in Chicago, he announced his retirement and returned home to Washington, D.C.

"I had no intention of becoming a coach," Thompson would say decades later. "It was only by accident that it happened."

Back in his hometown, Thompson instead hoped to teach or, his conscience inflamed by Russell, perform some sort of meaningful social work to better the lives of those in his community. He would do a little of both. His first job was with the United Planning Organization, a new federal program aimed at helping inner-city youngsters. He also headed up an urban 4-H program, educating those same youngsters in some of life's basic skills.

Basketball came back into his life through a side door. A few months after his return, Thompson learned from Dwyer and his parish priest that St. Anthony's High School was seeking a basketball coach. The school didn't have much of a legacy in the sport, and there wasn't a line of applicants waiting to take the job. When Thompson expressed interest, he was hired. The new coach immediately stressed discipline and, with the aid of Mary Fenlon, a former nun who had been teaching at another Catholic high school in the city, academics. Players had to call him "Mr. Thompson," and he and Fenlon kept a close eye on their classroom performances.

He found youngsters that none of the private schools wanted. He developed a basketball network around the city, and it sent him prospects and projects that more often than not he molded into productive players and teams. Very soon, D.C. opponents learned that few teams played harder or tougher than St. Anthony's. "His theory then and now is the same," said Leftwich. "We'll just keep coming at you and punching the ball inside. Finesse is not one of his ways."

Thompson transformed St. Anthony's into a city power. In six seasons, his teams would win 122 of 150 games. That success inevitably prompted calls that St. Anthony's play the area's premier Catholic school, Morgan Wooten's DeMatha High. But every time a game looked near, conflicts arose about where and when it should be played. Thompson, convinced DeMatha was ducking him, blamed Wooten and stewed. Finally, in the summer of 1970, as part of a local summer league, the two high schools were set to meet. Fans from all over the district flocked to the Boys Club facility where the anticipated matchup was to take place. They would leave disappointed, but with a better understanding of the man who would soon become an iconic figure in their city. Feeling that he and his school had been disrespected consistently by DeMatha over the years, Thompson now returned the favor. He stayed home and sent assistant Bob Grier to coach St. Anthony's. The team Grier brought with him consisted of seven nonvarsity players. DeMatha romped, 108-26, in a mismatch an angry Wooten would term "a travesty."

Not only could Thompson coach, but the guy had chutzpah. A lot of people took notice, including Charles Deacon, an African-American educator at Georgetown. And less than two years later, when that school was looking for a new basketball coach, he suggested giving Thompson a call.

Georgetown's seven-person search committee would contact fifty-one candidates and bring three of them in for more detailed interviews. Afterward, the panel had no difficulty recommending Thompson to the administration. "The other two [candidates]," the Rev. Robert Henle, the university's president, would admit later, "were white and frankly mediocre beside him."

Black coaches were still extremely rare at Division I colleges, and Georgetown's decision came under immediate scrutiny. Some critics, apparently unable to believe that a black man might be qualified on his own merits, felt that Georgetown was either appeasing those who claimed it was too white or taking a shortcut to basketball success. The university administration countered, then and now, that they merely hired the best candidate. "No one said, 'Let's get us a big, black coach to show we aren't segregationists and maybe he'll bring us some big, black players and we can win a few games,'" said the Rev. Timothy Healy, who succeeded Henle in 1976.

On March 14, 1972, Thompson's hiring was announced. That September, an article in the student newspaper more thoroughly introduced him to Georgetown. The writer, an undergrad named Bill Clinton—not the future president, who had also gone to Georgetown—asked the coach about the deflated basketball displayed prominently on his desk. It was there, Thompson explained, to remind him and his players that basketball was a means to an end and not an end itself. Their mission at Georgetown was not just to win games but to get an education and prepare for a productive life. "If my job consisted only of the mechanics of coaching a team," Thompson told Clinton, "I'd quit." Thompson, the young writer for *The Hoya* pointed out, was married and had two sons, though during his almost twenty-seven years there he would shield them from public scrutiny as doggedly as he did his team. The new coach, it quickly became evident, spoke a language unlike that of his colleagues. He was blunt and seemed to see the world much differently than the average college basketball coach. There was, Clinton wrote, "no innocent idealism in what he says about athletes."

Thompson meant what he said. His first hire at Georgetown was Fenlon, who stayed in the program throughout his long tenure. According to Thompson's son John III, the academic adviser whose stern visage would become a familiar sight on Georgetown's bench had considerable sway over anything that didn't happen on the court. Fenlon devoted herself especially to seeing that Thompson's players were properly educated and departed with a degree. She and the coach would be a successful team. Overall, 97 percent of those students who played four years for him at Georgetown—76 of 78—graduated, one of the highest percentages ever recorded at a big-time basketball school. She was relentless in her duties as an academic overseer. In 1985, one of those interviewed for a student-in-the-street feature in *The Hoya* was Michael Jackson.

When asked about a much-discussed problem with a campus building, the point guard professed ignorance. "I'm rarely here," the player said, "and when I am, Mary Fenlon keeps me so damn busy, I don't have time to walk around campus." But she concerned herself with more than schoolwork. "John also is very strict about things like haircuts, language, and how they dress," she said.

At home, meanwhile, according to John III, it was the coach's wife, Gwen, who ran the show. "Moms is the boss of the house," he said. "That tough-guy image is all a façade; if he gets out of line, she'll straighten him out."

On the court, things improved dramatically for Thompson and the Hoyas after that 1975 NCAA appearance. In nine seasons between then and 1984–85, Georgetown would fail to win at least twenty games only once and qualified for the postseason each year—seven NCAA appearances and two NITs. Thompson had no trouble finding talent, particularly big men, in Washington, Baltimore, Virginia, and the Carolinas. Before Ewing, he recruited such players as Craig Shelton, John Duren, Ed Spriggs, Sleepy Floyd, Gene Smith, and Fred Brown. Mike Riley and Esherick, two players who would become his assistants, also were early signings. He installed basically the same system that had been so successful at St. Anthony's: snug defense, full-court-pressure, relentless rebounding, and a pound-it-inside offense.

As the years passed and he and his Hoyas became better known nationally, Thompson's outspokenness and, in particular, the racial makeup of his teams won him praise in black communities and scorn from many whites. While he recruited several white players early, none ever became stars at Georgetown. Gradually, as the Hoyas' reputation as a "black" team grew more pronounced, there would be fewer and fewer white players. Yet his closest aides—Fenlon, recruiter Bill Stein, and Esherick—all were white. Thompson called "pure crap" the suggestion that by stocking his team exclusively with black players he was practicing a sort of reverse-racism. "Whether someone is white or black has nothing to do with it," Stein, Thompson's chief recruiter from 1972 to 1982, told Shapiro. "Whether a person can fit into his program, into the kind of style he wants to play, that's what matters. People can make a big deal about how he's a black coach with an all-black team. A white coach with an all-white team, that's acceptable. Nobody thinks much about it. A white coach with a black team, they'd say, 'What a great guy.'"

And the more success Georgetown enjoyed, the more popular it became among blacks, the more black kids wanted to play there. They sometimes recruited him. "If you are a good black player," Pitt coach Paul Evans would say, "where would you want to play?"

But, as with the message Thompson's players got when he warned them that by playing soft they were becoming too "homogenized," race obviously had something to do with the way he coached and the way he recruited. Very early on, there were whispers that he was telling black parents their sons would be better served playing for a black coach. "Remember one thing," former University of the District of Columbia coach Wil Jones once said, "He's going to win one way or another. If making white folks uncomfortable gets the job done for him, he'll get it done that way."

Increasingly, as Thompson walled off his program, his players found that fitting in meant foregoing a lot of typical college life. Georgetown's players lived on campus but in dedicated areas. They practiced, studied, and ate together, apart from their classmates. Thompson made sure the media, outsiders, and even fellow Georgetown students were kept at arm's length. After Ewing arrived, it seemed, the isolation tactics intensified. Few knew where the Hoyas stayed on the road. All practices and the periods before and after were closed. Interview requests were carefully screened and rarely granted, even when they came from Ewing's classmates. *The Hoya* tried for four years to arrange an interview with the school's big man on campus. It never got one. Acknowledging that big-time sports took up a big chunk of time, a perplexed and frustrated student sportswriter wondered why Ewing and his teammates weren't being allowed a more normal collegiate existence, weren't "interacting with one's peers and the outside world." These were all issues that by April 1, 1985, made Georgetown unlike any college basketball team before or since.

CHAPTER EIGHT

A caricature, a swollen shadow,
A stupid clown of the spirit's motive,
Perplexes and afronts with his own darkness.
—Delmore Schwartz, "The Heavy Bear Who Goes With Me"

Villanova's unlikely championship had its genesis in an unlikely location, at a summer camp that began its existence with an unlikely name. In 1966, New York basketball junkies Howard Garfinkel and Will Kleine started a basketball camp, one that they hoped would allow rising high school seniors an opportunity both to improve and market their skills. Garfinkel had gone to summer camps as a boy and believed he understood how to run one successfully. When he found an available site 115 miles north of New York City, Camp Orinsekwa in Niverville, New York, the Roy Rubin Basketball Camp was born.

Rubin was a friend, the then successful coach at Long Island University. Garfinkel figured Rubin's relatively well-known name would help sell his idea in the New York area, which is where his initial focus was. He couldn't have known, of course, that a few years later Rubin would graduate to the NBA. There, in the space of a single season, he destroyed his reputation and had an adjective permanently affixed to his name—Poor Roy Rubin. In the 1972–73 season, his first and last in the NBA, Rubin's Philadelphia 76ers set a still-extant record for ineptitude, losing 73 of their 82 games. Rubin's name soon yielded to the more generic Five Star, and the growing camp relocated to another remote locale, Honesdale, a Pocono Mountains community in the northeastern corner of Pennsylvania.

With the aid of coaches like Hubie Brown, Chuck Daly, and Bob Knight, Five Star quickly acquired a lofty status in the basketball community. By the late 1970s, at the dawn of a new basketball renaissance, it was attracting the absolute best players and instructors. What made Five Star unique, many now insist, was the quality of its teaching. Knight, for example, developed a system of learning stations. Players moved from one to another, tutored at each stop by some well-known coach in a different basketball fundamental or technique. The lessons were permanently etched in the minds of the campers. Pinckney, for example, never forgot Station 13, where, in a group with Ewing and future Louisville star Billy Thompson, he learned the intricacies of the jump-hook from Rick Pitino.

It was there in the remarkable summer of 1980—when Five Star's attendees also included such future Hall of Famers as Ewing, Jordan, Mullin, and Karl Malone—that Pinckney, McLain, and McClain first met. The three youngsters, their personalities as distinct as their talents, bonded immediately.

Early on at Five Star, they found themselves on competing teams. Each liked what he saw of the others. "Something clicked," recalled McClain. "Right then I knew I wanted to play with them." The trio's energy and enthusiasm derived from its smallest member. McLain had grown up on Long Island but followed his high school coach, Bill Donlon, to Methuen High in Massachusetts. He did so, in part, to escape the trouble he was beginning to find for himself.

The child of a broken home—his parents divorced when he was nine—McLain was smoking marijuana regularly by the time he was sixteen. He was, he would admit later, a hurt and insecure child, one who tried to mask his insecurity, at first with an outgoing demeanor and later with a more powerful remedy. As a youngster, he was mouthy, flashy, impulsive, a class clown always in search of an audience. Not surprisingly, he would be the first of the three new friends to decide on a college. It wasn't that difficult. McLain didn't have as many options as his taller buddies. Only Holy Cross and Villanova had expressed much interest. "He wasn't a great recruit," Massimino said. "He was just a player." Holy Cross was just too far removed from the spotlight for his taste. Villanova seemed more exotic. It wasn't North Carolina, but he'd have a better shot at glory there. He'd seen the Wildcats on TV a couple of times. He knew all about the Big East.

So he chose Villanova. And once he did, he pestered McClain and Pinckney to do the same. "I thought we could have a real chemistry," McLain said. His efforts focused first on McClain. He telephoned the Massachusetts youngster constantly in the late summer and fall of 1980. "You've got to come, too," he told his new friend. "We can make something happen there. They're in this new super league, the Big East. The coach is this little fat dude who looks like Louie DiPalma [Danny DeVito's character on TV's *Taxi*]. I'll put the ball in your hands there. We'll all be stars." He was right. But their real stardom, and ultimately their fame, would come as a unit. Pinckney and to a lesser extent McClain would enjoy only modest NBA careers. McLain would never get there. Yet in some perverse way, McLain would become the best known of the three—though not for the reasons he'd imagined that summer.

McClain, the silky 6-foot-6 forward from Holy Name High in Worcester had a personality that was a pleasant cross between the brash McLain's and the low-key Pinckney's. He was the first to relent to his smaller friend's nagging. After visiting the campus and hearing Oxenreiter's tape, he committed to Villanova. McLain and McClain then teamed up on Pinckney, a 6-foot-9 center from Adlai E. Stevenson in the Bronx who was being more heavily recruited. "What good is having a great point guard and a great power forward," McLain told him, "if we don't have some talent in the paint?" While Pinckney was amused by McLain, he was not yet convinced.

Pinckney would discover later that he and Ewing had more in common than basketball ability and their roles in one of the sport's most memorable games. Both were one of seven siblings. Both had several older sisters who doted on them. Both came from two-parent homes. Both had mothers who were employed in hospitals, hardworking fathers who did manual labor. Both grew up in apartments across the street from public playgrounds. Both left much of the college-recruiting process to their high school coaches. Both were mama's boys who wanted to go to college relatively close to home.

The Pinckneys lived in the Bronx's James Monroe Housing Projects. The youngest child and only son, Ed, was born in March 1963. Since his father, a construction laborer, often worked two or three jobs, his mother was the disciplinarian and teacher. The boy's older sisters waited on their little brother, dressed him, fed him, treated him like a delicate toy. "The fact that Ed was a very laid-back person probably came from him being the baby of a family with six older sisters," said Massimino. "He was the spoiled kid on the block." Though both his parents were tall, neither had ever played basketball. The boy would first drift to baseball, dreaming of becoming a New York Yankee until, at the urging of friends, he gave basketball a try.

The family's apartment on Story Avenue was directly across the street from PS 100, a public school whose playground contained several courts. Pinckney quickly was taken in by basketball, enjoyed it so much that he often rose early to play before school, at PS 100 or at nearby PS 131. A poster of Knicks star Walt "Clyde" Frazier hung in his bedroom. When the Knicks won a second NBA title in four years in 1973, the popularity of basketball in New York, already at a high level, skyrocketed. As it did, each borough developed its own style of play. "Brooklyn is like a more driving-to-the-basket, slashing style of ball," Pinckney would say. "A lot of flamboyancy, like the Pearl Washingtons, the Stewart Grangers. The Manhattan game would be the power. . . . And the Queens style was finesse. The Bronx is a combination of them all." When he was twelve and well over six feet, Pinckney accompanied a friend to Harlem, where he found the talent level "eye-popping." Gradually, he started to play there, too, making the journey by subway.

At Stevenson, coach Steve Post recognized Pinckney's potential early. "I knew right away Ed was special," Post said. "He was 6-2 or so and coordinated." He also had an easygoing personality that attracted other youngsters and earned him the nickname "Easy Ed," had a strong work ethic, and was extremely coachable. "What a difference it makes when a kid lives with a father and a mother," said Post. "Ed had an innocence about him. You wanted to help him."

When Pinckney was a tenth-grader, Fred Brown, the future Georgetown star, transferred to Stevenson and Post's team became a city powerhouse. Brown had a harder edge than Pinckney. Hoping some of that toughness would rub off on his mild-mannered center, Post had Brown go one-on-one with him after practice. "In the beginning, Fred whooped him," Post said. In a 1980 city championship matchup with Franklin High, Brown fouled out late. Post told Pinckney it was time he became a leader and took charge. The youngster did. Stevenson won and colleges everywhere noticed.

Their interest abated little when he hurt his ankle as a senior. Post, knowing Pinckney's parents were insistent about him getting a good education, eliminated several less prestigious colleges from the list, as well as those, like Louisville and North Carolina, that were too far from home. Pinckney liked Providence and was ready to sign there until coach Gary Walters inexplicably told him, "Ed, you'll be better off going to

Villanova." Pinckney was flabbergasted. Why Villanova? For him, the school was too far out in the country. But three things eventually swayed him—McLain's constant nagging, his mother's affection for Massimino, and McClain's good-looking sister. Massimino was one of the few coaches who visited the Pinckneys' apartment. He ate Ed's mother's cake and told her he would see to it that her son went to class and got educated. "You should go to Villanova," his mother urged Ed not long after that visit. "That little Italian coach, he'll make sure you graduate." On a recruiting trip to the school, Pinckney encountered McClain. Accompanying the Massachusetts schoolboy was his sister, who attended nearby Harcum Junior College. "She was beautiful," recalled Pinckney. And with that added inducement he was sold. Mitch Buonaguro, Massimino's chief assistant, had worked at Five Star that summer. But he claimed he had little to do with convincing the trio to come to Villanova. "They recruited themselves," he said.

Pinckney and McLain wound up as roommates in Sullivan Hall. McLain made life noisy and sometimes crazy, but Pinckney never wanted for laughs. Or dreams. One day that first autumn, the two of them were in McClain's room when the topic of their always rambling conversation shifted to what they hoped to accomplish before graduating. One of them suggested they list their ambitions on index cards. "For some reason," said Pinckney, "all the cards had 'Final Four' on them. . . . We made a pact then that we'd get there." The three were inseparable, on and off the court. "From their first day together, they had a feel for each other," said Buonaguro.

Their daydreams about shared future success became grander. In one, they would all be drafted by the same NBA expansion team. They liked that idea so well that they had business cards printed that included their new collective nickname, "The Expansion Crew."

The adjustment to college and Massimino's system wasn't easy for them or for any Villanova freshman. The coach, as the style his teams played indicated, was old-fashioned. He didn't like flash. He tolerated dunking, but told players that if they ever missed one, they'd find their butts on the bench before the ball hit the court. Then there was the matter of trying to fit in with the team's veterans. During one early practice, Pinckney went up for a dunk only to be knocked hard to the ground by John Pinone, the Wildcats' bulky and physical 6-foot-8 star. "You ain't dunking on me, kid," Pinone told him. Pinckney, a pencil-thin 160 pounds when he enrolled, soon discovered that weight-training would be essential if he ever hoped to play effectively in the Big East. And for a city kid who had never done much, Massimino's emphasis on running gave him difficulties. On the first day of practice, Pinckney was curious about the buckets that were lined up alongside the court. He asked assistant Steve Lappas about them. "Those," Lappas told him, "are for when you're going to puke. You're going to work harder than you ever have."

Despite their vivid imaginations, none of the freshman threesome was a starter when the 1981–82 season began. Massimino had Villanova heading in an upward direction by then. In 1977–78, his fifth season, he'd gotten the Wildcats to an East Region final, where they were defeated by Duke. It would be the first of four Elite Eight trips for Villanova in seven years. The Wildcats would finish the 1981–82 season with a 24-8 record, a Big East regular-season title, and two NCAA tournament victories. The three freshmen, especially Pinckney and McClain, saw some playing time early that season. But all three believed they ought to be starting. They watched other Big East freshmen, guys like Mullin and Ewing, become instant stars. The latter particularly impressed Pinckney, who figured he'd have to face the Georgetown phenom at least twice a season. "I said, 'Wow, I still have a lot of work ahead of me,'" he recalled.

Deriving fortitude from each other, they marched into Massimino's office one day and told him they all thought they should be starters. The coach would have a strange relationship with the trio. Their collective spirit, and McLain's outspokenness in particular, sometimes drove him crazy. But personally he would like them as well as any players he ever had. "They've made my hair stand on end," he would say. "And they've made me love and hug them." Surprisingly, the coach was receptive to their complaint and Pinckney and McClain soon found themselves in the lineup. McLain, stuck behind the talented Granger, had to bide his time, one talent he surely didn't possess. "Stewart knew Gary was right behind him," Pinckney said. "Gary really wanted that job. He was determined to push him in every way. The two of them competed in everything." Their freshman season ended just shy of the Final Four, with a loss to Michael Jordan's North Carolina in the East Region final.

The following season, a team Massimino would later call his most talented, was practically a mirror image of the 1981–82 squad. Another 24-8 record, a 12-4 mark and second-place in the Big East, and two tournament wins. It ended the same as well, again on the precipice of a Final Four, with a loss to Hakeem Olajuwon's Houston in the Midwest Region final. It should have been pretty heady stuff. Two twenty-four-win seasons, four NCAA victories, two regional finals against future legends. But it wasn't near enough for the ambitious Expansion Crew. "We were like costars," said McLain of their roles on those teams. "We were part of it but not really part of it."

They were all key contributors their junior season. But though it ended with another NCAA trip—the school's fifth straight—Massimino's club slipped a bit, finishing 19-12 and advancing only to the NCAA's second round.

By the time they were seniors, they weren't sure their Final Four vow would ever be fulfilled. And while each had improved tremendously at Villanova, Pinckney in particular wondered if his last season there was going to be the end of the basketball line for him. Was he good enough for the NBA? He just wasn't certain. For all his talent and success, he still had considerable self-doubt. "[He used to say] he didn't want to be a pro," Massimino recalled. "That was his out. It took the monkey off his back. He was always 'Easy Ed.' I've always tried to talk to him about the future, about what he wants. Does he want to drive a Volkswagen or a Mercedes? Does he want to struggle or does he want real comfort? If you want that kind of thing, you have to extend yourself, you can't hold back. You can't say, 'Later, it will come later.'" Pinckney would absorb the lesson at just the right time.

Not long after McLain got to Villanova, he graduated from marijuana to cocaine. This was the 1980s, and the drug was ubiquitous at Villanova, as at practically every other school in the country. He snorted it, smoked it, sold it. He got it from guy friends and from girls. He did it alone in his dorm room, in bathrooms at nearby bars, and sometimes, he would write in an infamous 1987 *Sports Illustrated* article for which he earned a reported $40,000 and the enmity of his former coach and teammates, in basketball arenas just before games.

What attracted McLain to Villanova, he would write, was the basketball program's growing national reputation and, not insignificantly, its women and parties. "Gary was a ladies' man," Pinckney would say. It was one way of reaching out for the affirmation he needed so desperately. Drugs were another. On his first visit to Villanova, McLain went to a Philadelphia disco with a Wildcats player and the two of them got high in the club's parking lot.

Massimino had an inkling of McLain's drug problem before the youngster agreed to play for him. When he visited the then high school senior, his mother and high school coach were also there. Donlon told Massimino that McLain had smoked marijuana. "We won't tolerate that at Villanova," the coach warned. "You're not going to ruin our program. We work too hard." Perhaps, in an era when casual drug use was much more commonplace, Massimino can be excused for not being more vigilant with McLain. The coach had no reason to believe the marijuana use was a sign of worse to come. "Would I take a guy with a problem? No way," he would say. While at Villanova, McLain was confronted at least twice by the coach, who had heard rumors about his drug use. Each time Massimino threatened to boot him off the team if the reports were ever confirmed. At one point, the coach also talked about instituting drug testing, a threat the player believed was aimed at him.

But, in the end, McLain would continue to smoke marijuana, use cocaine—both the powder and the cooked free-base solution—and even sell drugs throughout his Villanova days. And, either because no one in authority knew or because no one wanted to know, nothing was ever done. "I am convinced," Massimino said later, "I did everything I could."

CHAPTER NINE

You hated to see those signs. It must have been a terrible four years
for him.

—Ed Pinckney on the fan abuse directed at Patrick Ewing

As John Thompson took his seat behind Boston Garden's scorer's table that winter's day in 1979, he gazed around the familiar arena. The old dump hadn't changed much. The uneven parquet floor. The smell of spilled beer and steamed hot dogs. The claustrophobic aisles and hallways. The smoky haze that clung like a fog to the rafters of the fifty-one-year-old building in Boston's North End. Thompson knew it all well. He'd had plenty of time to survey the place during those two seasons in the early '60s when he was Bill Russell's seldom-used backup on the Celtics.

Russell was the greatest player Thompson ever saw. His shot-blocking and rebounding abilities, his defensive instincts, his determination and absolute lust for victory helped transform those Celtics into an NBA dynasty. As Thompson sat there watching the Massachusetts high school state-championship game, the Georgetown coach was thinking about Russell again. The big kid for Cambridge Rindge and Latin, the center he'd come to see, reminded him a little of his old teammate. Just a high school sophomore, the sixteen-year-old was raw. But Thompson could see his athleticism, feel his intensity, sense his potential.

Sometime early in the second half of the Cambridge school's victory Thompson turned to Bill Stein, his chief recruiter at Georgetown. "Bill, if you get him for me," he said, "I'll win the national championship."

In retrospect, despite all the drama that attended his choice of a college, Patrick Ewing was destined to play at Georgetown. The connections that would lead him to Thompson were too numerous, too powerful.

Though he'd been born and raised in Washington, Thompson had strong ties to New England basketball. He'd played there both collegiately and professionally, for Providence College and the Celtics. One of his closest friends on the Celtics had been Tom "Satch" Sanders, the erudite forward from NYU. Sanders had played until 1973, then taken the job as Harvard University's basketball coach. He hired as one of his assistants a young Cambridge native named Mike Jarvis. Jarvis, who had been an assistant coach at Northeastern, in Boston, stayed there several years before leaving to head the basketball team at a high school just a few blocks away from Harvard's campus, Cambridge Rindge and Latin. The school had been created in 1977 through the merger of Rindge Technical School and centuries-old Cambridge Latin, Jarvis's alma mater. It was there that the coach first encountered Ewing, as tall and promising as he was skinny and raw.

Another of Thompson's Celtics connections surfaced in the fall of 1979. That's when Auerbach, who had been his coach in Boston, telephoned him with a tip. Thompson respected Auerbach, another native Washingtonian. Not only was he one of the world's most savvy talent evaluators, but like Thompson he didn't care what people thought of him or his tactics. "John," Auerbach told Thompson on the phone that day, "I've just seen this kid who reminds me of Russ. His name is Pat Ewing. You've got to see him. You've got to get him."

Ewing would average 14 points a game that year, as a sophomore. That number would jump to 18 his junior season, 23 when he was a senior. Rindge and Latin would win 94 of 99 games during his time there, capturing three consecutive state championships.

Now, not long after Auerbach's phone call, Thompson was sitting in Boston Garden, watching the sophomore center lead his team to the 1979 Massachusetts championship. Auerbach was right. This kid reminded him of Russell. He had to have him.

Eight years before Thompson would first see her son play, Dorothy Ewing came to Boston from her native Jamaica seeking to improve the circumstances of her large family. Reluctantly, she had left her seven children in Kingston with her mother and husband, Carl, promising to send for them when she found a suitable residence and employment. "Ultimately, the dream of all island people is to come to America and accumulate something," she explained in 1983. A sturdy, determined woman, she soon found a job in the busy kitchen at Massachusetts General Hospital and began saving her money. At the same time, she was taking nursing courses. One by one, her family joined her. On January 11, 1975, her son Patrick, the fifth oldest of the seven children, arrived in Massachusetts. "I was excited about coming to America," he recalled, "but I was sad about having to leave my grandmother and my older sisters."

The Ewings would settle in a five-room apartment on River Street in Cambridge. A satellite community of Boston, its population just under 100,000, Cambridge was in the early stages of transitioning from middle-class to upscale, a change that would better reflect the two world-class universities located there, Harvard and MIT. The Ewing residence, in the city's Cambridgeport neighborhood, sat just across the street from a playground. Patrick, already six feet tall at age twelve, used to watch from his bedroom window as the local kids played basketball there. A shy boy with no experience in the sport and little with American teenagers, it took him months before he could muster the courage to join in. "They needed an extra guy one day, so they took me," Ewing said. "I got teased a lot at first for being so big and so bad. . . . They told me I would never be anything. They said I would never learn the game. At first, I couldn't understand why they said those things. But I got used to it. And I learned not to let what anyone said affect me."

That basketball naïveté and his tentative nature were exacerbated by a growth spurt that saw him shoot up to 6-foot-6 by the time he entered eighth grade. He towered above friends and schoolmates. In winter, Ewing wore an oversized rain coat and pulled a wool cap down to his eyes, as if he were trying to hide inside his clothes. He looked, spoke, and felt like an outsider. "Everyone looked at me like I was some kind of freak," he said.

The move to Massachusetts, his size, and his development into a basketball prodigy weren't easy transitions for Ewing. His circle of friends stayed small. As his basketball talents emerged, interviews, which might have helped the public understand him better, were so painful that Ewing rarely did any. As a result, it was easy for those who didn't know him to believe they did. His inhibition and sensitivity were mischaracterized as surliness or, worse, stupidity. This mistaken reputation would dog him for years.

"He's somebody people completely misperceive," said Esherick, Thompson's chief assistant at Georgetown. "Patrick is one of the nicest people you'll ever meet. Patrick is one of the most pleasant people I've ever been around as a coach and one of the easiest and most fun kids to coach. He was very private. Very private. And by being private he gave some people the wrong impression. But being private doesn't mean you have something to hide. It means that maybe you don't feel like sharing things. Some of the misperceptions about him were just outright silly. I coached the guy, knew they guy, and he is just a very nice man and a very smart man. Maybe if he had to do it all over again, he'd be less private. But that's the way he did it."

The lanky youngster was welcomed onto Rindge and Latin's seventh-and-eighth-grade team by coach Steve Jenkins. Jarvis provided the raw but promising youngster some additional tutelage. By the time Ewing was a ninth-grader, it was clear to Jarvis that, though the boy still had much physical and basketball maturing to do, the nation's colleges were soon going to be pursuing him avidly. He was going to require help in the recruiting process. Jarvis also realized Ewing was far from stupid. He was curious, hardworking, and determined to learn. With the right kind of academic assistance, he could prosper. "If Patrick was being taught something and he didn't understand it, he would raise his hand and let you know," said Jarvis. "If you told him and he still didn't get it, he would raise it again. He might raise his hand two or three times, but as soon as he stopped, you could be sure Patrick knew it."

Basketball-wise, Ewing would soon shed his awkwardness, hone his innate quickness and competitiveness, and develop remarkable timing. He also possessed an inner reserve of talent and resolve that, then and later, could be summoned when needed. "He had that second gear that great players have," said Esherick. "All of a sudden, when he had to, he could run faster, jump higher."

The more opponents focused on neutralizing the young phenom—bumping him, elbowing him, hacking him—the more he learned to counterpunch, literally and figuratively. He could take it and he could dish it out, too. On the basketball court at least, Ewing would learn to overcome his self-consciousness.

Following his junior season, he had become such an adept player that he was invited to try out for the 1980 U.S. Olympic team, a squad that disbanded prematurely when the U.S. boycotted the Moscow Games. But while it was together, Ewing displayed a new assertiveness. During a shoving match with Bill Laimbeer, for example, he retaliated by punching the older NBA bad boy in the face. "When you're tall and black, you're a big target, a very big target," said Jarvis. "You've got to stand up for yourself. Basketball gave Patrick the opportunity to relieve his tensions and frustrations. And sometimes he took it out on opponents."

As more and more college coaches noticed Ewing, Jarvis realized he had to develop a screening system. He suggested that he, Jenkins, and Ewing's parents form a committee to deal with all the interested coaches. Hoping to facilitate the process, Jarvis drafted a letter that would be sent to colleges across the country. A well-meaning effort at communication and promotion, it turned into a monumental mistake. Mailed to two hundred schools, the letter introduced Ewing to those coaches who, unlike Thompson, were not yet familiar with him. It outlined his size, his skills, his accomplishments, and then got to the special academic assistance they believed the player would require from any school that signed him.

Ewing was an average student in the classroom who, because of a learning disability that would be detected later at Georgetown, did not test well. Despite that, the letter noted, he was an eager learner who, with the right tools, could do well academically. "In order for Pat to be successful in a regular college curriculum," the letter advised, "he will need the following:

1. Conscientious guidance in course selection.
2. Daily tutoring (the services of the tutor must include covering reading material with Pat, some level of explanation of new material, proofreading of papers, and help with construction of papers).
3. Permission to use a tape recorder to tape lectures, and at times testing. (Pat's slowness in writing does not give him ample opportunity to express himself.)
4. If there are basic Skills Development Programs, Pat should take these.
5. Constant monitoring of his program. Pat is quite motivated to do well and is conscientious in getting his work done. He learns a great deal through listening, a skill that he has developed to compensate for his reading deficiency. The Ewing family, Pat, and all those concerned are interested in a positive educational experience, a diploma, and the necessary skills that are needed after graduation."

They were, in retrospect, reasonable requests. But many coaches, especially those from schools that ended up being spurned by him, saw it differently. To them, the letter suggested Ewing was stupid and demanding help that wasn't available to the average student. Eventually, eighty schools responded to the Jarvis letter. That number was soon culled to sixteen, a total that included some of the biggest names in the sport: UCLA, Kentucky, North Carolina, plus Boston College and Boston University, Georgetown, and Villanova. Kentucky, which would recruit another seven-footer in Sam Bowie, soon dropped out. The much-publicized sweepstakes came down to a final six of Boston College, Boston University, UCLA, North Carolina, Georgetown, and Villanova. Between mid-October and the end of November, Ewing would visit each campus.

Though his parents almost certainly would have balked, there was another option available. Ewing had shown NBA scouts enough that, if he'd wanted to, he could have gone professional right out of high school.

For most of its first quarter-century, the NBA had barred players from the draft until four years after their high school class had graduated. If they attended college, as almost all prospects did, they couldn't leave early for professional basketball. But in 1971, University of Detroit sophomore Spencer Haywood, who had led the NCAA in scoring that year, challenged the restriction. Later in 1971, the U.S. Supreme Court, by a 7-2 vote, sided with Haywood and invalidated the NBA's rule. Four years later, in 1975, two high school centers, Darryl Dawkins and Bill Willoughby, were selected in an NBA hardship draft. Ewing was, by most any evaluation, superior to both.

There were a couple of reasons—one philosophical, one physical—why Ewing decided to go to college instead. First, his mother insisted he get a degree. Also, during those Olympic tryouts in 1980, he had been pushed around by older, more physical players like Laimbeer. "He picked himself off the floor the first six times [he got knocked down at the Olympic tryouts] and decided he needed four years and some more weight," said Jarvis.

Finally, with speculation about his college decision becoming a national obsession, Ewing announced that he would be revealing his choice at a news conference on February 2, 1981. Anyone paying attention understood that very little mystery remained. Ewing already had crossed UCLA off his list since it was too far from home. Something about North Carolina left him uneasy, he said. And he really had no intention of staying in Boston. He'd visited Villanova and neither Massimino nor Alby Oxenreiter's tape recording had altered his conviction that Georgetown was the place for him.

There really hadn't been much doubt from the moment he'd met Thompson. Ewing, Jarvis said, was impressed and excited by "the chance to learn the center position from a man who played it." His attraction to Georgetown's coach went deeper. Here, thought Ewing, was a strong, eloquent black man, one so tall he could actually look him in the eye. As attached as he was to his family, Ewing decided that it would be better for him to go to school somewhere beyond—but not too far beyond—Boston. "To grow as a person," he would say, "I needed to get away from home." Much later, however,

Thompson suggested there were other reasons Ewing turned his back on his hometown.

Boston had a reputation for being hostile to blacks. The Red Sox had been the last big-league baseball team to integrate. Black Celtics like Russell, Sanders, K.C. and Sam Jones, and even Thompson himself had encountered racism, both subtle and overt, in their early years there. Even while those Celtics were a championship machine throughout the 1950s and 1960s, it was the all-white Bruins of the National Hockey League who sold out Boston Garden game after game. Beyond sports, the notorious battles over forced busing in the late 1970s, when Ewing was coming up, had generated considerable racial animosity and negative publicity. "Patrick has a perception of Boston—and I don't think he would discuss this openly—as being a very prejudiced place," Thompson said later. "[At a Rindge and Latin–Boston College Prep game] that I went to when he was a senior, there were ugly chants. And the administrators just sat there."

Ewing's news conference took place at Satch Sanders's restaurant on Standhope Street in Boston. With Jarvis and his parents at his side, and with at least two hundred cameramen and reporters crowded in front of him, the clearly ill-at-ease high schooler, wearing a dark pinstriped suit, began to read from a prepared statement. He thanked all the coaches who had contacted him, though none of the final six were present and none had been told officially of his decision. His obvious discomfort in the spotlight appeared to confirm what Jarvis had written in his letter. This was an intensely private person for whom public speaking held all the appeal of a root canal. At one point in the news conference, when Ewing appeared especially tense, Jarvis reached over and attempted to calm him. Finally, the high school senior got to the day's denouement: "After considering all the facts," he read, "I have decided to attend Georgetown University." The revelation was met by shouts of joy from Georgetown fans and graduates who, anticipating the news, had come to the event. Others who had gathered in the restaurant applauded loudly. An obviously relieved Ewing smiled and, as if retreating from something radioactive, instantly jerked away from the microphones. At that moment, someone nearby, possibly Jarvis, can be heard telling him, "Good job!"

As dramatic and important as the announcement may have seemed, it technically wasn't binding. According to NCAA recruiting regulations, players had until April 8 to sign a letter of intent and Ewing had not yet done so. Some speculated that some of the scorned coaches were planning shady last-minute maneuvers to get Ewing to change his mind. Jarvis, who knew him better than anyone but his parents, didn't buy it. "There's no doubt in my mind," Jarvis said of the player's decision, "that this is it."

When reporters asked Patrick's father, Carl Ewing, about the possibility of the youngster's opting for the NBA early, he assured them his son would be staying at Georgetown for four years and that he'd be coming home with a degree. Ewing, Jarvis told reporters, would be entering into the university's liberal-arts program and then, if everything went as planned, would switch to business management. "He is considering the possibility that some day he will have a lot of money," Jarvis said, tongue-in-cheek, "and he wants to manage it himself."

His hometown was crushed . . . and bitter. Several weeks after the big announcement, the *Boston Globe* obtained a copy of Jarvis's original letter. The newspaper reported that Boston College, Boston University, and Villanova each had been prepared to accept Ewing even though those schools hadn't yet viewed his academic record or even received an application. "To this day," Massimino told the paper, "I don't know his grades or College Board scores. He didn't apply with us. It's never happened that way before with us. Usually we make them apply first."

The revelation only reinforced what so many Americans felt about college athletics. Academics were a smoke screen. If a kid were a good enough athlete, grades didn't matter. Most schools were all too eager to bend their rules to accommodate a talent as large as Ewing's.

More specifically, the *Globe* story exacerbated the notion, unsubstantiated though it was, that Ewing was an unqualified student who was being admitted to an outstanding university merely because of his basketball ability. Actually, while still in high school, Ewing had been a part of the MIT-Wellesley Upward Bound Program, a college-prep course for economically disadvantaged high school students. And as Georgetown administrators tried to point out at the time, their university since the late 1960s had been actively seeking to attract more African-American students. A Community Scholars program had been established to help the university achieve that goal.

Motivated inner-city kids with potential—kids like Ewing—could now gain entry under a more generous and practical set of academic standards. Ewing, the administrators of that Georgetown program determined, had taken solid courses at an excellent high school, had a strong desire to learn, and came from a good family that wanted him to succeed. He was, they felt, an excellent risk. "Patrick Ewing was one of the easiest people to deal with that we've ever had," Charles Deacon, the Community Scholars director, would tell Thompson biographer Leonard Shapiro.

Georgetown president Rev. Timothy Healy portrayed the Boston-based brouhaha over Ewing's academic background as a case of sour grapes. "As long as Patrick Ewing went to one of the Boston colleges, he was fine," Healy said. "The Boston newspapers wanted him to stay in Boston. But as soon as he went to Georgetown, he became an illiterate to them. Well, if he was an illiterate, then why did the Boston papers want him to stay in Boston in the first place?" The resentment soon spread elsewhere, especially to places that had been spurned. Before he'd even played his first game as a Hoya, the misperceptions about Ewing had hardened into accepted wisdom. And very soon they would morph into something else, something uglier.

The history of basketball was, like the history of race relations in America, marred by prejudice and ignorance. Early on, when urban Jewish players proved particularly adept at the game, ridiculous racial stereotypes were dredged up to try to explain the trend. "The Jew [was good at the game because he] is a natural gambler and will take chances," noted a 1930s *New York Daily News* sportswriter. Later, when it became clear that blacks, too, could play, the rationales were equally inane. Dean Cromwell, Jesse Owens's coach in the 1936 Olympics, explained that the black man excelled at sports like basketball and track because "he is closer to the primitive than the white man. It was not that long ago that his ability to spring and jump was a life-and-death matter to him." Famed Kentucky coach Adolph Rupp, who was as misguided on subjects of race as he was astute about the Xs and Os of basketball, would later expound on Cromwell's theory. "[In Africa] the lions and tigers caught all the slow ones," Rupp said.

As long as blacks competed separately, as, with rare exceptions, was the case for most of the first half of the twentieth century, it was easy for whites to sneer at the brand of basketball they played. Even when the barnstorming, all-black Harlem Renaissance enjoyed success against the best white teams, few were convinced the results had any significance. "They have a great bunch of players," Dutch Rennert of the white Original Celtics said patronizingly of the Rens, "but we generally succeed in outsmarting them one way or another and they are inclined to let down when you get ahead of them."

But by 1955, when Russell, heady and athletic, led the University of San Francisco to consecutive NCAA titles, it was getting more difficult to make those hare-brained arguments. Russell's San Francisco team had six black players, a remarkable total for that era. It made for a racial mix that, not surprisingly, made the Dons a target. Before the 1955 NCAA championship game in Oklahoma City, for example, fans there yelled "Globetrotters" and worse at them as they warmed up, while others tossed pennies onto the court. Even then entire conferences in the segregated South remained lily-white. And those northern schools that had a black player or two on their starting units seldom had room for any on their benches. If coaches were going to risk alienating fans and alumni by suiting up blacks, those players had better be stars. It wasn't until Texas Western, with its all-black starting unit and two black substitutes, defeated Kentucky in 1966's NCAA title game that the unwritten numerical quotas started to evaporate.

Later, when blacks showed up in colleges in ever-increasing numbers, questions about their intellectual abilities persisted. When in the 1971 NCAA tournament, Western Kentucky, which had an all-black starting five, thumped Rupp's Kentucky, which started five whites, the Baron could hardly conceal his displeasure. Told by reporters that Western star Jim McDaniels had complained beforehand that the NCAA bracket appeared to favor Kentucky, Rupp boiled over. "I doubt that he has the intelligence to comprehend how the NCAA brackets are made," he snorted.

Athletic integration finally came to the South in the late 1960s, a positive development unless you were one of those racial pioneers who had to travel to Mississippi or Mississippi State. "It was," Vanderbilt's Perry Wallace, the SEC's first black athlete, said of his initial visit to Starkville, Mississippi, "depraved, nightmarish."

* * *

No one ever knew who was responsible that night. No one ever did. But on January 31, 1983, before Georgetown met Villanova at Philadelphia's Palestra, someone unfurled a bed-sheet message that labeled Ewing an "ape." Later, when George-town's center was introduced, a banana peel was hurled onto the court.

Both insults had their origins in the Villanova student section, a few thousand youngsters—almost all of them white—huddled together in the dark, intimate, and noisy confines of the famed basketball arena. Villanova athletic director Ted Aceto eventually confiscated the banner—and several others containing similar sentiments. For Aceto, it was a constant struggle at these Palestra games. Insulting banners and chants were a tradition in the Big 5, but often they crossed a line. Students, deriving a bravado from their numbers, liked to pick on any opponent with a quirky style, a cocky attitude, or an imposing scoring average. But this was different. Even if the racist banner directed at the seven-foot Georgetown star could be excused as prankish, the hurled banana peel seemed unspeakably cruel. With his ebony skin, pronounced features, long arms, and reported academic struggles, Ewing would frequently be derided as an "ape" or "gorilla."

The Palestra incident was not the first. Such abuse had become a regular feature of Georgetown games. According to *Time* magazine in 1985, bananas or banana peels had been thrown at the Georgetown star on at least a dozen occasions during the 1984–85 season. The total in each of his three pre-vious years might even have been higher. And then there were the signs: EWING KANT SPELL DIS, PATRICK CAN'T READ, EWING

CAN'T SPELL ESPN, THE HOYAS MIGHT NOT HAVE SLEEPY [Floyd, the star who graduated in 1983] BUT THEY'VE STILL GOT DOPEY.

Ewing rarely commented on the insults, though they almost certainly stung and caused him to compete more fiercely.

"It was hard," Esherick recalled of the insults and abuse. "It was very hard. There were times when he got so upset that he would cry."

In fact, he rarely commented on anything. From the moment he arrived at Georgetown as the nation's top recruit, he had been shielded from the press and the public. In the few postgame interviews he did, his responses tended to be guarded, unrevealing.

While much of the media viewed the incidents with a "boys-will-be-boys" shrug, Thompson did not stay silent about the race-flavored abuse of his star. Earlier in the 1983–84 season, the coach had pulled his team off the floor at Providence, demanding the removal of several inflammatory signs. "It's been evidenced throughout history that keeping quiet about things doesn't help the situation," Thompson said. "People probably said that about Hitler, too. 'Keep quiet and he'll go away.' I won't continue to sleep in peace and ignore it."

After the Palestra incident, Thompson would complain formally to the Big East. "It's up to the individual schools to keep the situation as tidy as possible," conference commissioner Dave Gavitt told the *Washington Post*. "I don't know how to prevent the signs from going up. It's unfortunate people choose to do it. The game administrators must keep control. Really, there is nothing the conference can do to control the signs in nine different buildings." Administrators at the league's schools never condoned the signs, of course, and sometimes even tried to remove them. More typically they suggested the banners were merely a reaction to Ewing's great abilities and not meant to disparage his intelligence or race. Harry Edwards, the sociologist who had helped organize the threatened boycott of black athletes at the 1968 Olympics, called the hatred Ewing endured "unconscionable."

Thompson, not programmed to sit by silently in the face of such racism, seethed. "Sooner or later," the coach said in 1983, "I'm going to tell my players to go up in the stands and get the sign." During a game at Syracuse in his junior season, as Ewing stood on the foul line, an orange hurled from high in the hostile crowd that packed the spacious Carrier Dome, struck the backboard. Thompson again pulled his team off the court. "All that stuff was just so offensive, but all he'd do is go out and kick our ass," said Villanova's Everson. "All that did was piss him off. I always wanted to have a conversation with him and tell him how much I respected how he played the game. To have had to go through all that nonsense and still play at the level he did, that makes me respect him even more."

The bananas, oranges, and signs weren't happening in Mississippi. The incidents occurred in supposedly sophisticated Northeastern cities like Philadelphia, New York, Boston, Providence. And they hadn't just popped up out of nowhere when Ewing got to Georgetown. Boston fans had once pelted Rindge and Latin's team bus with bananas and on another occasion a brick shattered one of the vehicle's windows.

But the most worrisome incident occurred during the 1982 Big East tournament. A few weeks after it had been called in to a Georgetown operator, Thompson revealed to reporters at the Final Four that there had been a death threat against his All-American center. The university operator, he said, had taken a call from a man who wanted to know where Ewing would be staying in New York during the tournament. When asked why he needed the location, the man replied, "Because I want to kill him." Security precautions were taken and when the team got back to its campus to prepare for the NCAA tournament, Ewing was sent across the Potomac, to a Marriott hotel in Arlington, Virginia. When later that same week the Hoyas traveled to Utah to play their NCAA opener, a burly Georgetown student came along as a bodyguard. "It scared the hell out of me," Thompson told the stunned sportswriters, regarding the threat. "You can say it's pretty common. But it was pretty common when the president of the United States was shot [in Washington in 1981 as the Final Four was taking place in Philadelphia], wasn't it?"

The abuse continued right up through the final game of his collegiate career, the loss in Lexington to Villanova. Ewing later said he resolved that however hurtful things got, he wasn't going to allow it to affect his game or his team. And he didn't. As one of the most dominant players in college history, Ewing, a three-time first-team All-American, would lead Georgetown to three Big East titles, four NCAA appearances, fifteen NCAA tourney victories, three Final Fours, and the 1984 national championship. He was an Olympic gold medalist in 1984, the winner of virtually every player-of-the-year award in 1985. He shot 62 percent for his career, scored 2,184 points, and had 1,316 rebounds and 493 blocked shots.

Interest in Hoyas basketball grew so intense thanks to Ewing that, during his freshman season, the school announced it no longer would play its home games at tiny, on-campus Mc-Donough but instead would move them to the 18,756-seat Capital Center in suburban Landover, Maryland. After the Hoyas won their only national championship in Ewing's junior season, there were few challenges left. Speculation increased that he might enter the 1984 NBA draft, where he would have joined Michael Jordan, Hakeem Olajuwon, Sam Bowie, and Charles Barkley at the top of that now-legendary class. "I probably thought he should have gone because of the money," Thompson said during the 1985 season. "From a purely dollar standpoint, I think it was a stupid decision. But now, seeing him laughing and enjoying college and seeing him grow as a young person, I'm glad he stayed."

There was a point, though, early in his junior year, when it appeared Ewing might not be back for the 1984–85 season, might never get that college degree he'd promised his parents. On an afternoon in September 1983, Ewing got a message that Thompson wanted to see him in his office. When the coach told him to call home, the youngster knew something was wrong. Back in Cambridge, his sister answered the call and tearfully told him their mother had died of a heart attack. Dorothy Ewing was fifty-five. "I wanted to quit school," Ewing said later. "I couldn't get excited about basketball or my classes anymore. "But my family convinced me that my mom would have wanted me to finish and get a degree." (He stayed, of course, earning a bachelor's degree from the College of Arts and Sciences in four years.) As with almost everything else in his life, Ewing internalized his grief. "He never said one blessed word," Thompson recalled. "He went about fulfilling his obligations in the classroom and on the basketball court."

CHAPTER TEN

We were just happy to see our name go up on the board.

—Villanova's Steve Pinone

By the standards at Villanova, which a *New York Times* reporter would characterize later that same year as a "banzai
party school," it was a pretty pathetic party. On Sunday, March
10, 1985, Villanova's players and staff were crowded into the
coaches' room inside the small brick field house they would
soon abandon for newer quarters. Someone had provided
sodas, salty snacks, and TastyKakes. Rows of chairs were
crowded in front of a borrowed television set that was tuned
to CBS's NCAA tournament selection show.

Sitting close to the TV was Jake Nevin. The nearer the old
trainer was to the set, the Wildcats players believed, the better
their odds of getting into the tournament. Almost alone among
Villanova's anxious basketball family, the ailing trainer had
been certain of a bid. Three days earlier, the Wildcats had
atoned for an ugly regular season-ending loss to Pitt by defeating the Panthers in their Big East tournament opener. But a
night later in the semifinals, St. John's blew them out. Having

believed they needed at least two Big East tournament victories to insure an NCAA berth, the Wildcats were downcast on the bus ride back to Philadelphia that night. Except for Nevin. His faith couldn't be shaken. "You guys," he kept saying in a voice reduced to a whisper by Lou Gehrig's disease, "are in."

Though the players knew to trust Nevin's upbeat instincts, they found themselves astride an emotional tightrope that Sunday afternoon. Some couldn't eat. Some couldn't sit. Some couldn't watch. "It was agonizing," said Jensen. "You had guys that worked hard for four years and they wanted to make some noise in the NCAA tournament. Now we're sitting on the fence wondering whether we're going to get in or not."

Villanova had been to the previous five NCAA tournaments, advancing to the Elite Eight twice in that stretch. Massimino wanted desperately for the small Catholic school to get to the next level. Not because he liked the spotlight, which he did, but because he wanted to test himself and his team against the best. Except for the two years it was held in Philadelphia (1976 and 1981), he hadn't even attended a Final Four. He wasn't one of those coaches who traveled annually to the event just to schmooze or job hunt. If he went to another, he vowed, he was going to bring his team, not his résumé. And with his three key players graduating that spring, who knew when or if he'd ever get another chance?

As uneasy as the Wildcats were that Sunday, their situation was actually better than they imagined. For a first time, the NCAA tournament field would be at sixty-four teams. Massimino knew there weren't half that many teams better than his. Still, he had doubts about the selection process. How much did the men on the NCAA committee know about his team? Eight days earlier, Villanova had played perhaps its worst game in his twelve years there, the horrible loss at Pitt. Worse, that embarrassment had been nationally televised. If committee members who previously hadn't seen Villanova play had been watching, they couldn't have been impressed.

The Wildcats' numbers didn't look that impressive on paper—a 19-10 record, 9-7 in conference. A year ago, they'd been 18-11 and made it into a fifty-three-team field. But that counted for little now. Who knew which teams they were competing with and what their relative strengths were? If a strong schedule meant anything, they had a shot. No league was tougher that year than the Big East. Yes, Villanova had ten losses, but five were to league rivals Georgetown and St. John's, if not the two best teams in the country then certainly two of the top three. "Some of us thought we'd get in. But we couldn't be sure," said reserve Steve Pinone. "It wasn't like it is now. There was no 'bracketology' for six weeks before the field was announced. People didn't really study it closely back then." Though nobody talked then about "bubbles," either, Villanova clearly was sitting on one.

One hundred six days earlier, a season that would end so memorably on a Monday night in Kentucky had dawned rather unremarkably on a Saturday night in Vermont. The Wildcats had traveled to New England because a year earlier the University of Vermont had inducted Massimino (class of '56) into its Hall of Fame. Unable to attend that ceremony, he'd agreed to schedule a Wildcats game there early in the 1984–85 season so that his alma mater could honor him properly. So early on Saturday, November 24, 1984, Villanova boarded a USAir commercial flight at Philadelphia International Airport bound for Burlington. Accompanying the usual traveling party was Al Severance. If as expected the Wildcats won, it would be the program's one thousandth victory. Severance, who had been the coach for 413 of them between 1936 and 1961, wanted to be there to celebrate the milestone.

Though they had almost all their key players returning from an NCAA team, the 1984–85 Wildcats somehow weren't even ranked in the AP's preseason top twenty. The sportswriters who voted in the poll might not have recognized it, but the players who that morning were scattered throughout the plane's coach section—Villanova, like most college teams, didn't yet fly charter, a practice they would adopt a few years later—had considerable potential. Four starters returned from the 19-12 team that had made it to the second round of the 1983–84 NCAA tournament, losing there to Illinois. In Pinckney, McClain, and McLain, the 'Cats had a solid senior core. Junior forward Pressley was inconsistent but possessed of considerable ability. Guard Happy Dodds had graduated, but junior Dwight Wilbur and sophomore Jensen were better than adequate replacements. On the bench, Massimino could call on two seven-footers, Everson and Wyatt Maker. And a pair of freshmen, forward Mark Plansky and guard Veltra Dawson, figured to help. "If they had a weakness," Dayton coach Don Donoher would say, "it was their lack of depth." And if they had a strength, it was their cohesiveness.

Perhaps because of the affable personalities of the three

senior starters, all fourteen players got along remarkably well. Each knew and accepted his role. Massimino's system, both on and off the court, was so established by then that everyone understood what was expected. There were no cliques, no bitter battles over playing time. His players genuinely liked one another and, though he often got under their skin with his foot-stomping, sputtering outbursts, they respected their coach. They'd bonded even more tightly when they learned the previous April that Nevin, their beloved trainer, had Lou Gehrig's disease and might not survive the forthcoming season. Wanting to make a gesture that represented the depth of their feelings for the little man, the players decided to dedicate the 1984–85 season to Nevin. Suddenly, a formless schedule acquired meaning. A somewhat murky ambition had become a clear goal. It was the first indication they had that something special might lie ahead.

After a summer in which some players had stayed at school to take courses and others returned home, the team reunited on campus in mid-August. On Mondays, Wednesdays, and Fridays, they all rose at 6 A.M. and, under the supervision of Massimino's third assistant, Lappas, ran as a unit. On Tuesdays and Thursdays, they'd run in the afternoon. Gradually, they increased the distances they tackled. "Running was kind of a team-building, discipline-type thing to get us focused, get us all together," said Pinone.

It was more than that. Running was something to be taken seriously at Villanova. The university's track program had an international reputation. Longtime coach Jumbo Elliott had been a legend in the sport. A 1935 graduate, Elliott, between 1949 and his death in 1981, would guide Villanova to eight national titles. His runners, some from Ireland and Africa, would capture eighty-two NCAA individual events and set sixty-six world records. Twenty-eight of Elliott's pupils had gone on to the Olympics and five had won gold medals—Ron Delany ('56, 1,500 meters), Charlie Jenkins ('56, 400 meters), Don Bragg ('60, pole vault), Paul Drayton ('64, 4×100-meter relay), and Larry James ('68, 4×100-meter relay). Elliott stressed stamina. And Massimino told his players that stamina would be essential if the Wildcats were to survive and prosper in the physical Big East battles that lay ahead. The coach wouldn't even permit players to practice until they could run a mile in under six minutes. The basketball team's time challenges each October became so embedded as a Villanova ritual that they drew spectators. As each player began to run, students held up signs that forecast an anticipated time. When Everson, the lumbering backup center, hit the track, those signs sometimes were replaced with calendars.

Before October's official start of practice, there also would be weight lifting and, depending on what kind of summer the players had, weight losing or weight gaining. If someone wanted to lift or ride an exercise bike or take one hundred shots or work on his ball-handling, he simply walked over to the gym and did it himself. "You didn't have anyone monitoring you," said Pinone. "There wasn't the structure there is now."

There were no athletic dorms, either. A few seniors lived in St. Mary's, one of the newer residence halls out on an edge of the school's property. But most were in Sullivan Hall, a then thirty-one-year-old building near the heart of campus. Since football had been dropped in 1981, the basketball players were the campus celebrities. But all were fully enmeshed in the life of the relatively small school. There were few places to hide at Villanova. Sooner or later everyone encountered everyone else, whether it was at meals, in the library, at weekend parties, or at Kelly's or any of the other popular student pubs along Lancaster Avenue.

Academically, all the players took a full load of fifteen credits a semester. Massimino had lost some kids along the way, but all thirty-eight of those who had reached their senior year had graduated. Between proctored study halls, workouts, and two and a half hours of practice every afternoon, there wasn't much time for socializing. "Nobody complained," said Pinone. "We were close. If it was good for the team, we did it. There were no little cliques. The seniors weren't off doing their own thing. They hung around with the sophomores and the freshmen."

Before the start of its schedule, Villanova played an exhibition game against a Brazilian team. Massimino had to watch from the stands. He'd recently been stricken with diverticulitis and spent three days in the hospital.

The actual opener at Vermont was a breeze. Massimino, honored in a pregame ceremony, got to clear his bench in the 80-54 win. Curiously, in what would be a precursor to how this season would end, Jensen was perfect from the field, hitting all ten of his shots.

Villanova followed up that one thousandth victory with

seven more in succession, four of them over Temple, LaSalle, Penn, and Drexel, all Philadelphia-area schools and all but the last Big 5 rivals. As Villanova's ties to the Big East strengthened, its historic Big 5 connections frayed. All those dangerous intracity rivalry games were problematic for a coach and a program with national ambitions. Each Big 5 game was a war and Massimino hated each one. Suppose, as had happened the previous season, Villanova lost a couple? It could mean no NCAA bid. How would all those alums who were so devoted to the Big 5 feel about that?

Until Massimino arrived in 1973, Villanova traditionally had loaded up its roster with players from Philly's Catholic League and Public League. Slowly, as the school widened its horizons, talent-rich Philadelphia began to be ignored. Whatever the reasons, outstanding local players like Dallas Comegys, Andre McCarter, and Rodney Blake, who in the past might have been expected to go to Villanova, headed elsewhere. By the 1984–85 season the trend had become so pronounced that except for the coach's son, R. C., the Wildcats didn't have a single player from the Philadelphia area or, for that matter, the entire state of Pennsylvania. Yet those were issues to confront down the road. Villanova would sweep its four Big 5 games that season and beat Drexel as well. Though they couldn't have known it at the time, a loss in any might have kept the Wildcats out of the tournament.

They improved to 8-0 when they routed BYU, 91-61, in the opener of Georgia's Christmas tournament in Athens. Despite its unbeaten status, Villanova still hadn't moved into the top twenty. If anyone were then forecasting a Final Four, three of the teams that eventually made it there would have been easy choices. Georgetown, Memphis State, and St. John's were at that time ranked first, third, and fourth, respectively. But Villanova? A Final Four team? Few could have predicted that at the end of 1984, or even until the moment, three months later, when it happened.

On December 29, in the Georgia tournament's title game, the Wildcats led the host Bulldogs by seven with four minutes to go. But in what the coach and his players would attribute to home-cooking, they were whistled for offensive fouls on four late possessions and wound up losing, 75-68. Their next game, their first of 1985, and their first on the Big East schedule, would be in four days, at home against a very good Syracuse team.

Thanks especially to a marvelous senior class, the Big East that year was loaded: Georgetown had Ewing, Williams, and David Wingate; St. John's had Mullin, Walter Berry, and Marc Jackson; Syracuse had Pearl Washington, Rafael Addison, and Rony Seikaly; Boston College had Michael Adams and Domenic Pressley; Pitt had Charles Smith; and, of course, Villanova had its trio of seniors, Pinckney, McClain, and McLain. Analyses suggested the league was essentially three-tiered: Georgetown, St. John's, and Syracuse were on one level; Villanova, Pitt, and Boston College not far below on another; and Providence, Seton Hall, and Connecticut on a lower rung. Despite all that individual talent, it remained a coach's league. Thompson, Massimino, Carnesecca, Jim Boeheim, Gary Williams, and their colleagues were hands-on teachers who demanded discipline, defense, and a sensible tempo.

Perhaps more so than the other Big East schools, Villanova

was a slave to its sets. The Wildcats' matchup-zone defense often forced turnovers that rarely were converted into fast-break points. The 'Cats preferred to walk the ball upcourt, signal a set play, and run it. If it failed to produce a good shot, they'd run another, and another.

The philosophy was sound. With no extra point yet awarded for twenty-foot jumpers, there was no practical incentive to take them. Why heave up a long shot after a pass or two when you got the same two points for a layup at the end of a twelve-pass possession? And the longer you held the ball, the fewer offensive opportunities your opponent got. Massimino realized that his front court was his strength, and he drilled Villanova on working the ball inside to Pinckney, McClain, and Pressley.

The Wildcats beat Syracuse, then Connecticut at home, before losing to St. John's in New York. Then came their first meeting with Georgetown.

Villanova by then had emulated Georgetown and moved its more attractive matchups to a large civic arena in South Philadelphia, the 18,000-seat Spectrum. The program had long since outgrown its fifty-three-year-old, 3,200-seat campus arena. Now, thanks to a $10 million contribution from Main Line wrestling maven John DuPont, a $25 million, 6,500-seat replacement arena was being built just behind the existing field house. The 'Cats planned to move there for the 1985–86 season.

But on January 12, 1985, a sellout crowd jammed the South Philadelphia facility to watch the matchup between the

Wildcats and the defending national champions. Earlier that week, Villanova had finally entered the top twenty, at No. 16. Remarkably, that left it as only the fifth-best team in the Big East. Four other teams in the conference were ranked higher— Georgetown (1), St. John's (3), Syracuse (7), and Boston College (12).

Clearly uncomfortable against Massimino's ever-shifting defenses, the Hoyas fell behind early. They shot just 28 percent in the first half and went to the locker room down by eight. Even with a shot clock, Villanova had set a slow tempo and the halftime score, 27-19, reflected it. This time there was no magic for Villanova. The same Wildcats who would shoot 90 percent in the second half of the title game made just 6 of 32 shots after intermission on this day—4 for 25 in the second half, 2 for 7 in overtime. At one point, continually trying to force it inside to Pinckney, the 'Cats turned the ball over on five consecutive possessions. Georgetown would rally and hold on for a 52-50 overtime win. The competitveness of the game would be largely overlooked in April. And, though no one would know it until his 1987 article, McLain had gotten high before the game. "They're the No. 1 team in the country," an obviously disappointed Massimino said afterward. "I thought our kids hung in there real well. But if you don't put the ball in the basket, the game's going to swing."

By the time the Wildcats traveled to College Park on January 27 to face another future tournament foe, Maryland, they were 13-3 and had stepped up to No. 14. If the polls and changing public perceptions were an accurate reflection, the six-year-old Big East had eclipsed the Atlantic Coast

Conference as the country's best basketball league. Such praise for the nouveau riche conference galled Maryland coach Lefty Driesell. So did the fact that recruiting in the East suddenly was much more difficult for him. Driesell was determined to make a statement against Villanova. "We got in the huddle before the game and coach said to us, 'I'm tired of hearing this Big East stuff,'" Maryland's Keith Gatlin said.

That day Villanova had no answer for Len Bias, who collected 30 points and 13 rebounds in a 77-74 Maryland victory. Bias had so worn down Pressley that Massimino was forced to try the 6-foot-6 freshman Plansky against the 6-foot-9 Terrapins stud. "As soon as I came into the game, Lenny drops to the low block and starts screaming, 'Mismatch! Mismatch! Give me the rock!'" recalled Plansky.

Humbled, seemingly questioning themselves, the Wildcats would go 6-6 the rest of their schedule, falling out of the AP poll. A 57-50 road loss at Georgetown on February 11, which featured another blown halftime lead, was sandwiched between losses to St. John's and BC. The schedule concluded with the demoralizing twenty-three-point loss at Pitt. There they trailed 40-23 at halftime. Massimino, angry and looking for a motivational ploy before the start of a Big East tournament he now knew would be crucial to his team's postseason hopes, told his starters they had three minutes to turn things around. "If you don't start playing," he yelled in the locker room at halftime, "I'm taking you all out." Minutes later, following an easy Pitt basket, Massimino yelled, "Get 'em out of there!" and Villanova's veterans headed for the bench. Pinckney was depressed. A regular season that had begun with an 8-0 record and high hopes was ending with an 18-9 mark and a bad loss. There was still the Big East tournament, but what hope did they have against St. John's and Georgetown? "It's over," Pinckney told himself.

Unheralded, unsure of themselves and their future, the Wild-cats arrived in New York City on March 6. The Big East tour-nament, an effort to ape the tremendously successful and pioneering ACC tourney, had debuted in 1980. Initially, it al-ternated among some of the conference's big arenas. The first, in 1980, took place at Providence's Civic Center. Hartford hosted in 1981, Syracuse in 1982. But Gavitt had always wanted Madison Square Garden for its permanent home and in 1982 he'd signed an agreement to that effect.

New Yorkers, whose infatuation for the Knicks had di-minished the popularity of the college game there, suddenly were captivated by the Big East and its tournament. Just as im-portantly, so was the New York media. The Knicks had slipped as programs like St. John's and Syracuse ascended. By 1985, the Big East tourney atmosphere reminded many of New York basketball in prewar years, back when the NIT was the post-season king and Garden doubleheaders the sport's major showcases. "This is like it was here in the 1930s when Ford-ham, St. John's, NYU, CCNY, and Manhattan all had good teams," Providence coach Joe Mullaney said at a pretournament news conference.

The city was particularly abuzz about the 1985 event. It would be the last for Ewing and Mullin. Who knew how it might play out? There could be brawls, last-second heroics, upsets. But what excited everyone was the possibility of a rubber match between Georgetown and St. John's in the March 8 title game.

Those two teams, Nos. 1 and 2 in the conference and the nation, had split their two regular-season meetings. The most recent, played at the Garden a week earlier, had generated massive media attention. Georgetown handed the Redmen their first conference loss then, but with a 15-1 record St. John's still took the regular-season championship.

Afterward, most conceded the postseason tourney title to 27-2 Georgetown, which was riding a ten-game winning streak and had taken two of the previous three league tournaments. Syracuse's Boeheim made a point few seemed willing to consider, one that in a month would be recalled as prescient. If anyone was going to be able to beat the Hoyas the rest of the way, he predicted, it was probably going to be another Big East team. "Teams here know them, and really think they have a good chance to beat them," he said. "When they get to the NCAA tournament [nonconference opponents] are going to be scared to death of them."

For all the hype it generated, the Big East tourney actually meant very little to its top seeds. Georgetown, St. John's, and Syracuse had long ago locked up NCAA spots. With no one quite certain of how a sixty-four-team field might be composed, it was Villanova, Pitt, and Boston College who appeared to be playing for something. Of those three, only Villanova made it through to the semifinals, turning the tables on Pitt in a 69-62 quarterfinal triumph that, in retrospect, might have been the long season's most pivotal victory. That win set up the Wildcats' third meeting with St. John's. Though their two earlier losses had been relatively close games—76-71 and 70-68—it wasn't a good matchup for them. Mullin, Berry, and seven-footer Bill Wennington gave them fits. "St. John's just seemed always to get the better of us," said Everson. "They had our number."

The number would be 15 in the Garden semifinal, with St. John's cruising, 89-74. Pinckney scored 27 points, most after the outcome had been decided. The 'Cats had limited Mullin to only 14, but Berry got 22. "They just have too much personnel," McClain said. Afterward, reporters asked Massimino which of the nation's two best teams he thought might capture the Big East title the following night. "I can't say one team will win, because they're both terrific," he said diplomatically. "I hope they [St. John's] and Georgetown advance and meet each other in the NCAA finals." With that, the coach walked down a dimly lit Garden hallway to his locker room, gathered his downbeat Wildcats together, and boarded a chartered bus for the ninety-mile ride home. There was nothing to do now but wait for Sunday.

If the Wildcats' Selection Sunday party was a drag, the NCAA tournament committee's get-together in Kansas City wasn't much livelier. On that afternoon, the nine committee members were in their third day of deliberations in a fortieth-floor conference room at the Hyatt Regency, the high-rise hotel where four years earlier a lobby walkway collapse had killed 114 people. Their work had been conducted with such secrecy that before a phone call would be patched through to the room, two code words had to be conveyed to the hotel operator. There would be no exceptions, the operators were told, not even for wives.

For the committee, chaired by Vic Bubas, the former Duke coach who had become Sun Belt Conference commissioner, picking the NCAA's first sixty-four-team field was a new and challenging experience. There were no accepted parameters. The panel had been criticized in the past for loading up with five teams from a single conference. How many could they possibly take now and still maintain the event's egalitarian feel? Should they strive for a geographic balance? How much weight should be given to strength of schedule? And what about those teams that won their conferences, only to lose in the winner-take-the-bid league tournaments that were now commonplace?

As of late Sunday afternoon, twenty-nine teams had already earned a spot in the field. Some, like Georgetown, had done so by winning conference tournaments. Others, like Michigan of the no-tourney Big Ten, got in by virtue of a regular-season title. That left thirty-five at-large entrants to be chosen from a pool of ninety-three teams that the panel felt warranted attention. "It was like picking the thirty-five best corned-beef sandwiches," Virginia athletic director and committee member Dick Schultz would say. "Only when you're dealing with basketball teams, when you get to the last ones, they don't all look and taste the same."

The committee members finally emerged from their cocoon at 4:40 P.M.. CBS, which had been airing the selection show since 1982, got an advance look at the brackets so that, before going on the air at 5:30 P.M., it would have time to fill in the slots on the big board in its New York studio. Conceived almost as an afterthought in 1982, the selection show had quickly become must-see TV for college basketball fans. It was perfect television, fraught with mystery, suspense, and a built-in audience. Even those schools who knew they were in had no idea who, when, or where they'd be playing, how they'd be seeded. The drama was so intense and widespread that the network typically dispatched camera crews to the campuses of several bubble teams, eager to record the joy or disappointment when players and coaches learned their fates.

As that '85 show came on the air, host Gary Bender began to run down the tournament field region by region. Georgetown, of course, was the No. 1 seed in the East and overall. As such, the Hoyas would open against the tourney's lowest seed, Lehigh. The Engineers had been 9-18 before three victories in their East Coast Conference tourney earned them an unlikely berth. Asked later that day if he'd seen the top-ranked Hoyas play yet, Lehigh coach Tom Schneider said, "I've watched enough of them maybe to not watch any more." The three other regions' top seeds would be St. John's in the West, Oklahoma in the Midwest, and Michigan in the Southeast.

As a CBS camera focused on Villanova's gathering, the uncertainty was transparent. Massimino paced. Plansky, clutching a clipboard, scribbled notes so seriously it seemed he anticipated that there would be a test on the material. In the front row, Dawson shook his head emphatically from side to side often, expressing disagreement with one revealed entrant or another. After Bender launched into the Southeast bracket with the 1-16 matchup of Michigan–Fairleigh Dickinson, Villanova's players caught sight of their school's name, flanked by its seeding (8) and record (19-10). The visual confirmation of their fervent hopes simultaneously relieved and animated the room. Players jumped to their feet, roaring their approval, mugging for the camera, high-fiving teammates, team managers, and coaches.

Once the celebration abated, they looked to see who and where they would be playing. The coaches, if not the players, were slightly dismayed to learn that the answer to both questions was Dayton. The Wildcats would be meeting the Flyers, independents who had finished with the same 19-10 record, on their home court Friday night. If the fact that a No. 9 seed would have home-court advantage against a No. 8, or that they had home-court advantage at all, seemed inherently unfair—and the NCAA later would see it as such, preventing any team from again enjoying such an edge—it didn't seem to concern this committee. "We didn't worry about that," Schultz said. "Our main concern was to avoid replaying the conference championship games until the regional finals, and balancing the field. I think we did that." Later, the Wildcats would claim the Dayton-at-Dayton pairing hadn't concerned them, either. "Kids just want to play basketball. It's the adults who think it all out," said Pinone. "We were just happy to see our name go up on the board. The fact that we were going to play Dayton on their home court wasn't a big deal to us. It was like, 'We've got blue uniforms. They've got white. Let's go play.' We'd lost to Georgetown and St. John's by two points each, and I'm pretty sure we felt Dayton wasn't as good as those guys."

The longer Villanova's coaches studied the bracket, the more they came to realize their status probably hadn't been as precarious as they'd earlier feared. The Wildcats were one of six Big East teams in the field—the Big Ten also had six—and both Boston College (11) and Pitt (12) were seeded lower, indicating they'd been closer to the bubble.

Long before bracketologists would dissect NCAA fields in minute detail, the selection process seemed almost capricious. Sixteen twenty-win teams failed to gain entry. Kentucky made it at 16-12, but UCLA, which had the same record and a similar national reputation, did not. A committee source told the *Philadelphia Daily News* that Kentucky, Iowa State (21-12), and Old Dominion (19-11) were the last three at-large teams chosen, while West Virginia (20-8), Florida (18-11), and Weber State (20-9) were the last eliminated. Selecting the first twenty at-large teams, Bubas said, was relatively easy. "But the last six, seven, eight, we could've stayed in there for another week. . . . It was one of the most agonizing experiences I've ever undertaken."

Massimino, meanwhile, was just glad to have another meaningful game to coach. He and his staff immediately began making calls to learn what they could about Dayton. The coach wouldn't allow himself to look beyond that. "Once we got in the tournament, I had a feeling we could play pretty well," he said. "But a national championship? I don't know about that."

* * *

Privately, Massimino was upset about Dayton's home-court advantage. Though the Flyers technically would be the road team against Villanova, they had won fifteen of seventeen games at their arena that season. "Since we have their home bench, maybe it'll bring us luck," Massimino had cracked a day earlier. But the bracket contained some encouraging signs as well. There were no other Big East teams in the Southeast. So whatever team the Wildcats faced was going to be less familiar with their shifting defenses and quirky offensive sets. None of the players on top-seeded Michigan, Villanova's likely opponent if it got past Dayton, had ever been to an NCAA tournament. And despite the regular-season loss, Massimino felt his team was better than third-seeded Maryland. The only Southeast team that scared him, really scared him, was North Carolina.

As for Dayton, Villanova clearly had a talent edge. But with the advantages of a home court and a home crowd in the always chaotic opening round, who could predict anything? "They're a very deliberate and well-coached team," Massimino said of the Flyers. "They won't beat themselves." Translated, that meant Dayton wasn't the kind of team the Wildcats preferred to play. They were too similar. Massimino enjoyed going up against teams that wanted to run and gun and rack up points. Then he could slow it down, make them impatient, drive them crazy. Dayton wasn't like that. Instead, Donoher's team would be perfectly content to play at Villanova's pace.

Whatever concerns the Villanova coach had weren't allayed by the result of the opener of Friday night's doubleheader. Buoyed by the raucous support of most of the 13,260 fans—a group that would be supporting Dayton in the nightcap—underdog Fairleigh Dickinson nearly upset top-seed Michigan, losing by just four points, 59-55.

Just as the seeders had anticipated, Villanova-Dayton went back and forth. The Wildcats held the game's biggest lead, 43-37, but Dayton kept getting to the foul line and converting its free throws. The Flyers would take seventeen and make them all, a feat that almost was enough for them to overcome 32 percent shooting from the floor.

It was tied at 49-49 when Villanova went to its four-corners offense. Jensen, with the ball about twenty feet out and along the sideline, suddenly sensed an opening and decided it was time to make something happen. The handsome 6-foot-5 sophomore from Connecticut was a puzzle. Blessed with a textbook jumper, good size, and an almost obsessive work ethic, he could cancel out all those assets with grave self-doubts. Jensen would hit four or five in a row and look as though he was never going to miss again. Then he'd misfire at a crucial point in a game and his confidence would vanish, his mood darken. McClain nicknamed him "Norm," after the Norman Bates character from the movie *Psycho*. It was a reference not only to his resemblance to Tony Perkins, the actor who played the deranged killer, but also to the moody intensity that sometimes frightened his teammates. "He was scary," said McClain.

Jensen had made just 36 percent of his shots as a freshman and averaged only 2.7 points a game. Though he began his sophomore season with that 10-for-10 performance at Vermont, his seasonal statistics had improved only minimally (43 percent, 4.5). By the tournament, Jensen was such a psychological mess that he requested a meeting with Massimino. There he suggested to the coach that perhaps he didn't even deserve to be on the team. Who needed a shooter, after all, who couldn't shoot? "Harold was a guy that wanted to do so well that he'd get wound a little too tight, tried a little too hard," said Pinone. "He was trying to do so much and be so good he just couldn't relax himself." Massimino tried to reassure him. "Look," the coach said. "You're a great student, a great kid. It's basketball. Just relax. If you have a bad game, it happens. Just go get them the next game."

Now, just when it looked as if there might not be a next game this season, Jensen put a spin move on a Dayton defender who fell. A path cleared, the Villanova guard headed for the lane. Two Flyers, reacting slowly to the sudden break from the four corners, came at him from each side but arrived just a split second late. Jensen laid the ball off the backboard. It bounded against the thin cylinder of the rim, rolled dangerously close to its front edge, and fell in. The Wildcats were ahead, 51-49, with 1:11 left. Jensen relaxed as he raced down court. A burden had been lifted.

"That layup," Pinone said, "was the light that let him think, 'I'm a good player. I'm not going to stress over every missed shot. If I make a turnover, I'm not going to kill myself over it.' And he went on to have a great tournament. Just phenomenal."

Dayton held the ball until, with twenty-seven seconds remaining, Donoher signaled for a timeout. There would be ten seconds left when Dan Christie, on his first shot of the game, missed. The Flyers got the offensive rebound but Toney's off-balance shot at the buzzer spilled out. Villanova had survived.

"Dayton at Dayton was our toughest game," said Mc-
Clain. "When we won that one, we felt we might be able to do
some damage in the tournament." After all, Sunday's matchup
with Michigan would come on St. Patrick's Day. And they had
a leprechaun on their bench.

"There was something you couldn't miss about Jake," Bob
Powers, a former Villanova basketball star once said of Villanova's trainer. "It was something spiritual. He had this quality that
glowed and radiated." The leprechaun—who was well under
five feet tall but preferred to list his height as "4-foot-12"—
kept a neat garden behind the house where he spent his entire
life. It contained the statues of seven magical gnomes that,
Nevin liked to point out, looked a lot like him. Whenever a
child visited, he liked to show off the gnomes. "Those gnomes,"
Nevin would inform the mesmerized youngsters, "come alive
at night."

Few children doubted him. They were drawn to the man
because he was their size and because he really looked like
one of the supernatural little beings they'd read about in fairy
tales—a leprechaun, a gnome, an elf. They sensed this little
man with the twinkling blue eyes and impish smile possessed
some special powers. Massimino's youngest son, Andrew, used
to trail after the trainer like a puppy dog. When his father
asked the boy what he wanted to be when he grew up, Andrew didn't hesitate. "I want to be like Jake."

The magic garden was located behind Nevin's small but
foreboding Bryn Mawr home. The old house, whose Victorian-
age atmosphere brought to mind the Brooklyn residence in

Arsenic and Old Lace, only added to its occupant's mystique. Nevin was born there, lived all his seventy-five years there, and would die there. And there were ghosts. In an upstairs bedroom, Nevin had hung on the walls people-shaped, plywood cutouts that backed photographs of Villanova's greatest athletes. "Sometimes when I'm outside," Nevin once said. "I look up through the window and see their shadows on the wall."

Like his body, Nevin's world was compact. He never married, never drove, never developed many interests beyond Villanova sports and cigars. He lived just a few miles east of campus. Nevin rode the bus back and forth to work. When that wasn't possible, he walked. He got a job at the school in 1929 and became its full-time athletic trainer four years later. In the subsequent half-century, there were few days when he couldn't be found attending to the needs of the athletes on the basketball, baseball, football, and track teams. There were always ankles to tape, stories to tell, spirits to lift. After his parents died and his siblings moved away, Villanova's athletes and coaches became Nevin's family.

He could sense when athletes were down. And whether it was with a joke or an encouraging word, he could lift them up. "He is one of the people who never lost faith in me, even when I lost faith in myself," recalled Pressley. Talk to any Villanova athlete who knew him and each will have stories about Nevin. About the prank he played, the joke he told, the psyche he soothed, the powers he possessed. "Jake," said Jim Murray, a Villanova grad who went on to serve as general manager of the NFL's Eagles, "was just magical." It didn't take long for basketball players to realize that. If Nevin said something was going to happen, it happened. If you touched his head before entering a game, you played well. If he took care of an injury, it healed faster. "By the end, when we had another full-time trainer, Jake still did some taping. When he taped your ankle, the tape would be loose and practically disintegrating by the time you got in the game," said Everson. "But everyone wanted him to do it because no one he taped ever hurt an ankle. Ever."

Before he was a seer and a sorcerer, Nevin was a practical joker. Growing up unusually small in a wise-cracking Irish family, he quickly learned to give as good as he got. Few people ever departed from an encounter without having ashes from his omnipresent cigars surreptitiously dumped into one of their pockets. Pinckney once was reading a newspaper in the locker room when he looked down to find that Jake had set it aflame. Whenever he was asked how long he'd been at Villanova, Nevin invariably replied, "Since about 8:30 this morning."

In the 1930s, Nevin found a particularly easy target in Severance, the basketball coach who was also a hypochondriac. "During a train trip to an away game, Nevin kept telling Severance he looked flushed and maybe ought to see a doctor," Jack Devine, who played for Severance, recalled in 1986. "The coach didn't know it, but Nevin had stuffed several bricks into his suitcase. Finally, as Severance struggled onto the platform at the end of the trip, he told Jake, 'Maybe you're right. I'm so weak I can barely lift my suitcase.'"

Though records later would reveal that Nevin had been

born on February 9, 1910, while he was alive no one ever knew his actual birthday. "Jake had birthdays every season," Lou Ferry, a former Villanova football coach once said. "He'd have a birthday every football season, basketball season, track season, and baseball season."

By the 1984–85 basketball season, when he and his illness had become a popular topic during Villanova telecasts, Nevin was a nationally known figure. People would send him letters and postcards addressed simply, "Jake Nevin, Villanova," or "Jake Nevin, 19010."

If the upset of Georgetown were indeed a miracle that could be attributed to Nevin, it wouldn't be the last. They continued even after his death. In the final weeks of his life, Nevin's arms and legs were paralyzed. On the day he died, his nephew John Morris, his full-time caretaker, placed a blue-and-white Villanova pillow under one arm. When he returned a short while later, he found his uncle dead and the pillow now beneath his head. "Who could possibly have put it there?" Morris wondered. "There wasn't anyone else in the house but me."

Not long after Nevin's death, several Villanova players visited his unmarked grave in Ardmore. The players all lit cigars in his honor. One was moved to plant a lit cigar into the ground above his grave. "Now you know that unless someone is sucking on a cigar no smoke comes out," said Everson. "Well, all of a sudden these two big puffs of smoke rise up from that cigar. We all said, 'Whoa, let's get out of here.'"

On at least two occasions following his death, campus security guards reported seeing a stranger roaming at night near the darkened field house, by then renamed in Nevin's honor. When shown photos of the late trainer, they identified him as the prowler. "Then, on his first birthday after he died, the power went out in the Pavilion during one of our practices," recalled Everson. "Someone said let's try the field house even though it had no power, either. As we walked in, and I'm not making this up, the sunlight started streaming through these little windows up high in the building. Jake made sure we were able to practice on his birthday."

When Nevin stuck the plastic leprechaun's hat on his head, the buzzer might as well have sounded. There were still several minutes left in Villanova's Southeast Regional matchup with Michigan when the little trainer flashed the victory signal he'd promised Massimino. Someone had given him the cheap, party-store hat that week. Nevin immediately saw its significance. He told Massimino that if, in that St. Patrick's Day game with Michigan, the Wildcats had a late lead—and he fully expected they would—he intended to put it on. That, he said, would seal the deal. Though the Wolverines were the region's top seed, they hadn't impressed the Wildcats or anyone else with their narrow first-round victory over Fairleigh Dickinson. Massimino planned to slow the pace, constantly change defensive looks, and thoroughly confuse his more athletic, higher-ranked opponents.

While being the No. 1 seed would prove to mean little in this matchup, it did have its advantages. Michigan was housed in one of Dayton's finer hotels, while Villanova lodged at a roadside Ramada. There, one fellow guest, a weary trucker, had parked his pig-loaded rig in the parking lot outside their rooms. "I can still recall that smell," said Pinone. "It was brutal."

The results of the first two games in Dayton had created a happy scenario for Villanova. Michigan, primarily because of its heated football rivalry with Ohio State, was despised in every corner of the Buckeye state. So most of the 13,200 fans at Sunday's final were vociferously in the Wildcats corner. With three outstanding players—Roy Tarpley, Gary Grant, and Antoine Joubert—the Wolverines were 26-3 and had won eighteen straight. Coach Bill Frieder told reporters he hoped for a game in the 70s or 80s, a point total that against Villanova they'd have needed three halves to achieve.

The Wildcats packed in their zones, switched them often, and made Michigan beat them from the outside. Guards Grant and Joubert looked as listless as their surprisingly flat teammates. Both fouled out, Grant after going 6 for 13 from the field, Joubert 0 for 4. Offensively, Villanova wasn't much better. They went nearly eight minutes at the start of the second half without a basket. But thanks to its befuddled ineptitude, Michigan could build only a five-point lead, 35-30. "Without the clock," said Joubert, "we were inexperienced in controlling the tempo and being patient."

Once the Wildcats got a lead, they went into their stalling offense. Frustrated, Michigan fouled often and Villanova hit 13 of 16 free throws down the stretch to forge a 59-55 victory and extend their season into at least one more March weekend. McClain finished with a game-high 20 points. Pinckney held Tarpley in check and contributed 14 points. "It helps," Pinckney explained to those who sought his secret against Tarpley, "playing against Patrick Ewing twice a year." More significantly for what was to come, McLain turned the ball over just once in thirty-seven minutes. "Thank God the forty-five-second clock was turned off for this tournament," Massimino said. "Down the stretch our kids did what we do best. We've been through this before. We've held the ball quite a bit."

Sitting at the postgame news conference, Frieder stared intently at the stat sheet, as if hoping it would reveal some secret that Villanova's record had not. "Villanova certainly didn't play like a ten-loss team," the Michigan coach said upon looking up. "They played a perfect game." He would not be the last that season to utter those words.

Half the teams in the Sweet Sixteen came from either the Big East (Villanova, Georgetown, Boston College, and St. John's) or the ACC (Maryland, North Carolina, Georgia Tech, and North Carolina State). In Birmingham that Friday, the Wildcats would play Maryland, while North Carolina and Auburn would meet in the other game.

"Beating Michigan was nice," McLain said that week. "But all it did was get us to the Sweet Sixteen. We've been there before. We want more. We want to be remembered." McLain apparently was so convinced that Villanova would be moving on that, like Nevin, he purchased some good-luck headgear, a Final Four hat he bought for $8 in Birmingham that week. Tempting fate and risking a reaction from Villanova's opponents, the point guard wore it to a pregame news conference.

Maryland's Driesell didn't need any more motivation. He'd had several great teams in the last decade and a half but had gotten none to a Final Four. Now here he was on the doorstep again, with a twenty-seven-win team whose schedule was rated the nation's toughest, and all anybody wanted to talk about was Villanova and the Big East. Worse, his Terrapins, despite having defeated the Wildcats earlier, were two-point underdogs.

Meanwhile, Villanova's players were delighted with the matchup. "They'd beaten us in regular season at Cole Field House," Pinone said, "but we had just played a bad game. We knew we were better than them. We were very confident that on a neutral court we'd beat them." In their minds, they had played their next-to-worst game of the season in the loss to Maryland and still come within three points. Pinckney's career day (29 points and 16 rebounds) had canceled out Bias's 30 and 13. But in that nationally televised defeat, the rest of the Wildcats played the way McLain described his own performance, "discombobulated."

This time Massimino was going to make sure that the score didn't reach the 70s. The result that March 22 was an ugly defensive struggle, a style Villanova liked. Neither team shot well, and Villanova led, 43-36, when Massimino popped up off the bench and shouted, "We've got enough!" his signal for the team to run the four-corners. This time it almost backfired on him. Pressley missed a foul shot with just under three minutes to play. The Wildcats got the ball back but soon turned it over. Bias's dunk made it 43-38. Another turnover, an Adrian Branch jumper, and it was 43-40. Three Wildcats free throws around another Branch basket left the score at 46-42 with forty-four seconds remaining. The lead was three when a Branch air ball that Pinckney corralled ended another unsightly Villanova victory.

The Wildcats shot a woeful 39 percent, Maryland 36 percent. During the regular season, Villanova went 6-7 when it failed to make at least half its shots. Yet in the NCAA the 'Cats had shot under 50 percent in each of their first three games—and would do so in the next two as well—and won them all. "I wouldn't want to play against us," Pinckney said when asked about the matchup trouble the 'Cat's defense gave Michigan. "It's so frustrating. You can see it in their faces. They're hesitant to get into their offense, and when they finally do, they're shuffling around and by then we've changed it again." Jensen, after making the game-winning shot versus Dayton, had gone 0 for 5. Up to that point, he was shooting 37.5 percent for his career.

North Carolina defeated Auburn in the other semifinal, setting up the Southeast Region final matchup that Massimino both anticipated and feared. Back in 1982, the three current seniors' freshman season, Villanova and North Carolina had met in another regional final. Carolina, led by Michael Jordan, earned the Final Four trip with a 70-60 victory. The following February, the Tar Heels were ranked No. 1 again when Villanova traveled to Chapel Hill for a nationally televised Sunday afternoon game. Two days earlier, Philadelphia and much of the East had been blanketed by more than twenty inches of snow. Anticipating that the Wildcats might not be able to get to North Carolina, Digger Phelps, whose Notre Dame team had played in the state that weekend, volunteered to hang around and take Villanova's place in the spotlight game.

Phelps was a protégé of Dick Harter, the former Penn coach who, at Oregon then, had gleefully run up the score in a rout of rookie coach Massimino's Wildcats. Massimino, according to Pinckney, "hit the roof" when he heard about Phelps's offer. He gathered his team and, after making his feelings known about "Notre Dame's arrogance," asked them to vote on whether they wanted to try to make the trip to North Carolina and play the game. Not surprisingly, they all voted to go.

Philadelphia's airport had been closed by the fierce storm, but Villanova found a bus company willing to take the team seventy miles east to Atlantic City, which had been spared the worst of the snow. There the Wildcats chartered a forty-eight-seat aircraft and flew to Raleigh, where they got on another bus, finally arriving in Chapel Hill at 12:45 A.M. Sunday.

Their travel trouble was worth it—the motivated Wildcats upset the top-ranked Tar Heels, 56-53. The ACC was by then playing with a thirty-second clock and a three-point shot in league games, and the mid-schedule shift to a non-conference game without either, Jordan said afterward, proved a difficult adjustment. It was also another game when, the Villanova point guard would later admit, McLain was high.

After upsetting Michigan and Maryland, underdog Villanova had become a popular topic before the regional final. For one of the few times in memory, Dean Smith complained that one of his teams was being overlooked. "I'm getting up-set," the affable coach said, only half-jokingly. "We've won twenty-seven games, but people keep saying we're beatable."

The Tar Heels' shooting (at 54.3 percent, second best in the nation) and size worried Massimino. North Carolina had 6-foot-11 Brad Daugherty, 6-foot-11 Joe Wolf, and 6-foot-10 Dave Popson across the starting front line and had the talented 6-foot-11 Warren Martin in reserve. "What can we do?" Massimino said when asked about the height disadvantage. "We can't recruit anybody new at this point. But our three inside guys have played against big people all year, be it Georgetown or St. John's." It was a subtle reminder to the ACC-centric media that the Wildcats were from the nation's best conference and were, thank you very much, quite used to playing against big and talented teams.

Before this latest game on the brink, Pinckney, McClain, and McLain reminded each other of the pact they'd made as freshmen. This was the Expansion Crew's opportunity to make its mark, to fulfill the promise to get to a Final Four. Their hearts were thumping like rock-band drums when the game began. And then they went out and played horribly off-key in the first half, exiting at intermission with Villanova trailing, 22-17.

The 'Cats shot a miserable 23 percent from the floor and missed nearly half their foul shots (4 of 9) in the opening twenty minutes. "We were too high or too low or something," recalled Pinckney. "But whatever it was we weren't very good." "As bad as they shot," Smith would say, "we should have been up 14, 16, 18 at halftime." A key moment occurred with time running out in the half. The Tar Heels, with an eight-point lead, had been holding the ball for a last shot when they turned it over in the final seconds. McClain scored on an offensive rebound, was fouled, and hit the free throw. What could easily have been a ten-point Carolina halftime advantage was a much more manageable five.

Villanova fans couldn't help but wonder whether this was going to be a third regional final stumble for the Wildcats in four years. An irritated Massimino was determined that wasn't going to happen. When the locker room door shut he went ballistic, jumping, spewing, twisting, yelling. And then came the totally unexpected but tension-disintegrating reference to linguini and clams—with lots of cheese, of course. "It might have sounded crazy, talking about spaghetti at that time," Pressley said, "but that was his way of telling us to relax, to go out there and have some fun in the second half." The Wildcats, once they stopped laughing, did just that.

Massimino made one change at intermission. He inserted Jensen for Wilbur. "I took it as a sign that the coach had confidence in me," Jensen said. "I stopped worrying and just went out there and played. I felt like something huge had been lifted from my shoulders." Having watched films of Jensen's misfires throughout the season, Smith directed his defense to focus elsewhere, particularly down low on Pinckney. It worked on Pinckney, who was limited to just six shots and ended up with 9 points. But freed up on the edges, Jensen, after missing his first attempt, connected on five straight jumpers.

On offense, the Wildcats rediscovered their patented patience. "If you noticed, we were making at least four passes before every shot in the second half," said Massimino. Perhaps as a result, they got the ball inside consistently. McClain and Pressley took more than half of the team's 47 shots and scored 11 and 13 points, respectively. Villanova outscored its opponents, 14-4, in the opening eight minutes to leapfrog ahead, 31-26. A hook shot by Brad Daugherty got North Carolina back to within a point, 31-30, with fourteen minutes remaining. But Villanova responded with a 12-3 run and with just over eight minutes to play, in a game without a shot clock, led 43-33. North Carolina, a tall and plodding team not built to come back from big deficits, never recovered.

Even a coach as savvy as Smith was having difficulty recognizing and reacting to Villanova's ever-changing defensive sets. And the Wildcats extended their pressure so far that the Heels often were trying to get the ball to their big men from thirty-five feet out. Point guard Kenny Smith seemed particularly baffled, finishing with just four points and three turnovers. "They pretty much ran a clinic on us," Smith said afterward.

It was, for all intents and purposes, over when, with 3:30 to play, Jensen caught up with an errant North Carolina pass and converted it into an easy layup that put Villanova ahead by 11, 47-36. The lead was at 12 and Villanova was holding the ball with under a minute to play, when the Wildcats saw Smith signal his team to back off. Surrender. They were going to the Final Four.

In retrospect, it was a preview of what was to come. Villanova shot 76 percent in the second half. Only Daugherty, with 17 points, managed to score more than 6 points for the Tar Heels. North Carolina managed only 44 shots, making 20, and got to the foul line just seven times. Pressley paced

Villanova with 15 points, while McClain and McLain had 11 apiece.

Even before the horn sounded, Pinckney and McLain embraced. The entire Villanova bench got to its feet and applauded. When it was over, Pinckney, as he had promised to his teammates that morning, leaped onto the scorer's table, screamed with delight, then jumped down into McClain's arms. "I did a lot of things today I never did before," Pinckney said when asked about his uncharacteristically emotional reaction. The Final Four dream had been realized. Another one, even grander, had already replaced it.

Villanova's players react wildly on March 10 after learning they'd made it into the NCAA tournament. Had not the '85 event been expanded to include for a first time sixty-four teams, the 19–10 Wildcats might not have made it. (Photo courtesy of Chuck Everson.)

Despite their physical differences and competitive spirits, the two coaches, John Thompson (left in this 1991 photo) and Rollie Massimino, were good friends and possessed a mutual respect. Thompson would say the championship-game loss was a little easier to bear since it had come against a Massimino-coached team. (Photo courtesy of *The Philadelphia Inquirer.*)

During their Final Four stay in Lexington, Massimino (center) and players gather in front of the breeding shed at one of the area's famous thoroughbred stables, Spendthrift Farms. (Photo courtesy of Chuck Everson.)

Villanova's traveling party, with ailing trainer Jake Nevin flanked by a pair of Kentucky motorcycle policemen, poses outside its Final Four hotel. On the day of the game, Massimino would take his team into that same parking lot to work on a new defense. (Photo courtesy of Chuck Everson.)

Villanova's players, with McLain front right, come together before a meal during Final Four week in Lexington. Meanwhile, Thompson, who jealously shielded his team from distractions, housed the Hoyas that week in Louisville, eighty miles from Rupp Arena. (Photo courtesy of Chuck Everson.)

Villanova's Harold Pressley is defended by Georgetown's Horace Broadnax early in the championship game. (Photo courtesy of Georgetown Sports Information.)

One of the keys to the Wildcats' tournament success was the shooting of sixth-man Harold Jensen, seen here in a later game against Big 5 rival Temple. After an erratic sophomore season in 1984-85, Jensen became an integral part of Villanova's run to the title. (Photo courtesy of *The Philadelphia Inquirer*)

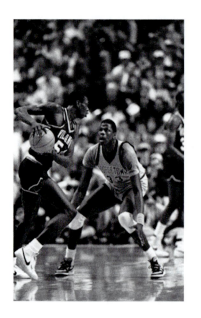

As he did so often in the upset, Pinckney challenges Ewing. Villanova's title-game scouting report urged players to take the game directly to Georgetown's center, widely considered the college game's best defender. (Photo courtesy of Georgetown Sports Information.)

Villanova's Ed Pinckney goes up for a shot between the Hoyas' David Wingate (left) and Patrick Ewing. (Photo courtesy of Georgetown Sports Information.)

During a timeout, Thompson talks strategy with (from left) Perry McDonald (No. 10), David Wingate, Michael Jackson, and Reggie Williams. (Photo courtesy of Georgetown Sports Information.)

John Thompson instructs backup center Ralph Dalton, who replaced Ewing when the Hoyas star picked up three quick fouls in the second half against the Wildcats. (Photo courtesy of Georgetown Sports Information.)

Nearing the end of what is still considered one of the great upsets in sports history, Villanova's bench celebrates. (Photo courtesy of Chuck Everson.)

Pinckney (left) and Gary McLain celebrate in the aftermath of Villanova's upset. The two, who along with Dwayne McClain comprised the self-styled Expansion Crew, had fulfilled a vow they'd made as Villanova freshmen. (Photo courtesy of Chuck Everson.)

A crowd estimated at 75,000 jams a Center City Philadelphia plaza to greet the returning national champions. (Photo courtesy of *The Philadelphia Inquirer.*)

Massimino, surrounded by (from left), Pinckney, Dwight Wilbur, Veltra Dawson, and Mark Plansky, displays the NCAA championship plaque at the April 2 parade in downtown Philadelphia. (Photo courtesy of the *The Philadelphia Inquirer.*)

Massimino and players peer out from one of the flatbed trucks utilized in the victory parade through Center City Philadelphia. (Photo courtesy of *The Philadelphia Inquirer.*)

The morning after their team's historic upset, thousands of students gather on Villanova University's Main Line campus to await the players' return. (Photo courtesy of Chuck Everson.)

President Ronald Reagan holds up the Villanova jacket —complete with its "Mr. President" designation—during an April 4 ceremony honoring college basketball's champions. Gary McLain, who later wrote that he was high on cocaine at the event, can be seen just above coach Rollie Massimino's head. (Photo courtesy of *The Philadelphia Inquirer*.)

The 1985 national champions' official team photo, with the autographs of all the players. (Photo courtesy of Chuck Everson.)

CHAPTER ELEVEN

We didn't try to get people to hate us.

—Craig Esherick, Georgetown assistant coach

Before it even began, the 1984–85 college basketball season looked as if, much like any of the *Rocky* sequels, it was going to be spectacularly uninteresting. It was hard to envision the plot as being anything but predictable. The promise of drama was virtually nonexistent. And if any legitimate challengers surfaced, Georgetown figured to knock them out quickly.

For nearly four months, Thompson's Hoyas did nothing to alter those expectations. The defending NCAA champions kicked off Ewing's senior season with eighteen consecutive victories, extending their two-season win streak to twenty-nine. As they did, the nation's mythmakers were busy securing them a spot on the college sport's Mount Olympus. In those eighteen victories, Georgetown revealed itself as an equal-opportunity destroyer. During that span, the Hoyas routed a traditional early season rival (80-46 over St. Leo's), a crosstown rival (82-46 over American), and a Big East rival (85-44 over Providence). On the road, they won in pits, both literal (New Mexico's Pit) and figurative (Pittsburgh's Fitzgerald Field House). They were victorious in their tiny campus gym (McDonough) and in their spacious home away from home (the Capital Centre). They beat small black schools (North Carolina A&T) and large state schools (Tennessee). They won laughers (the margin in four of the wins topped 33 points) and squeakers (two Big East victories came in overtime). They beat the unranked (Hawaii-Loa) and the highly ranked (No. 2 DePaul). "They are," said Indiana coach Bobby Knight, not an easy man to please or impress, "as good a team as I have ever seen."

NBA scouts predicted that perhaps four of Georgetown's starters could be first-round NBA picks. (Two—Ewing and Reggie Williams—eventually would be; the other three— Billy Martin, David Wingate, and Michael Jackson—all would go in the second round.) Ewing, ever more savvy and dangerous as a senior, was a gigantic force at both ends of the floor. Williams and Wingate, the two Baltimore schoolboys, provided points, toughness, and attitude. Point guard Jackson was smart and lightning quick. Martin did almost everything well. On the bench, Horace Broadnax was a defensive stopper who could shoot. Ewing had more than adequate backups in 6-foot-11 Ralph Dalton and 6-foot-10 freshman Grady Mateen. Thompson also could rely on his other two freshmen, Perry McDonald and Ronnie Highsmith, the latter an Army veteran brought in to replace the departed muscle of Michael Graham.

Defensively, with Ewing's shot blocking as their backstop, the Hoyas were able to gamble, trap, press, and create abundant turnovers. Offensively, they had the big man with the jump hook that coach Rick Pitino had helped him perfect down low, two or three slashers, and some legitimate outside threats. Somehow, largely because of Ewing, they had pulled off the unthinkable. They had lost three key contributors from a national championship team and emerged even stronger. "That was the best team of Patrick's four years, no question," Esherick said of the 1984–85 Hoyas. "They could play any way you wanted to play—slow, fast, zone, half-court defense. They were a tough team. And they had guys that could shoot. The team that won the national championship might have been a little better defensively, with Freddie Brown, Gene Smith, and Michael Graham, but that was probably its only edge."

Graham, who would be seen as a case study in all things Georgetown, should have been on the 1984–85 Hoyas as well. Despite the fact that he wasn't used extensively until the Big East tournament, played only one season there, and averaged fewer than 5 points a game, Graham would become the epitome of Georgetown basketball—or at least what a sizable chunk of the public perceived to be Georgetown basketball. It would be Graham, not Ewing, who appeared on a *Sports Illustrated* cover with Thompson following the Hoyas' 1983–84 national title. The shiny-headed enforcer was a tireless rebounder and defender and someone who liked the rough-and-tumble of hard-nosed basketball in the paint—in other words, the ideal man for Thompson's style. More importantly, in doing all that, he relieved some of the enormous pressure on Ewing.

In the NBA, the concept of a basketball enforcer was

hardly a new one. Auerbach's Celtics had used "Jungle" Jim Loscutoff, who retired just before Thompson got to Boston, to great effect. Sculpted Maurice Lucas had Bill Walton's back when Jack Ramsay's Trail Blazers were NBA champions in 1977. And by the late '80s, a whole new breed of tough guys had entered the league—Rick Mahorn, Bill Laimbeer, Charles Oakley, Anthony Mason. In the college game, which the NCAA would have the public believe was populated by angelic student-athletes, there wasn't supposed to be a need for enforcers. But after watching opponents surround, push, grab, elbow, batter, and generally mistreat Ewing for two seasons, Thompson became convinced that a big, physical power forward could help his star center in two important ways: He could clear space for him, and he could run interference.

Things had gotten so nasty for Ewing that at one point Thompson vowed that if his star continued to "be held, pushed, and mauled," he'd urge him to leave school early and declare for the NBA's Hardship Draft. That threat was obviously a little of Thompson's gamesmanship directed at Big East officials. But the gripe wasn't without justification. Ewing, who could dish it out as well as he absorbed it, clearly was being targeted by rough play. "Patrick is definitely being beat up out there," Fred Brown said in Ewing's sophomore season. His opponents' rough tactics always pushed Ewing to play even harder and, occasionally, to push back. "Patrick doesn't complain," said Thompson, "he retaliates." Typically, the coach counseled Ewing to stay silent on the subject of the physical play and the response it sometimes dictated. But during one of the player's rare interviews, a reporter struck a nerve by characterizing him as "overaggressive." "I'm overaggressive?" Ewing said. "I'm usually the one that had the concussion or got hit in the eye. I'm all scarred up, and I'm the one who's overaggressive?"

Georgetown found an answer to the problem, as it turned out, just a few miles from its campus.

In the 1982–83 season, the 6-foot-9, 210-pound Graham was a sensational rebounder and defender for Spingarn High, a perennial Washington powerhouse. But as impressive as his basketball attributes were, there was plenty about Graham that scared off many college recruiters. Newspapers reported that he'd fathered a child out of wedlock, that he had battled publicly with his high school coach, that he'd struggled academically and hadn't earned enough credits to graduate. Yet Maryland and Georgetown still wanted him. Thompson spoke with the player and subsequently told reporters he'd been assured by the youngster that he intended to work as hard academically as athletically. Soon after, Graham signed a letter of intent with Georgetown, though without informing his high school coach. With the backing of Thompson and other university administrators, he was admitted through the Community Scholars program. (After signing with Georgetown, Graham enrolled in a summer program and graduated from high school.)

That next year Ewing had the wingman he'd lacked, and the 1983–84 Hoyas responded by winning thirteen of their first fourteen games. Observers saw it as no coincidence that when academic problems kept Graham out of a game against Boston College, Ewing was pushed around and got into a scrape with BC guard Michael Adams.

The freshman power forward, who had a full head of hair in high school, shaved his head that year. The bald head, the well-muscled physique, the often-menacing glare, and his penchant for utilizing elbows all enhanced Graham's image as college basketball's bad boy—and Georgetown's as the game's most disliked team. "Part of that was because we won," said Esherick. "Some of it was because of Patrick's personality on the floor. It certainly wasn't anything we intended. There's no one who wants people to dislike them. Other than maybe someone who works for the Oakland Raiders. We didn't try to get people to hate us."

Technical fouls, wild elbows, confrontations, and the occasional fight became regular features of Georgetown games. And Graham usually could be found in the midst of it all. With him as its poster child, the "Hoya Paranoia" concept went viral. A team that always had an aggressive, physical style suddenly was seen as a collection of outlaws. No discussion of Ewing, or Georgetown basketball in general, was possible without a soon-to-be familiar verbal litany: "us-against-them," "thuggish," and, the most popular of all, "intimidating."

But while the negative imagery got under Thompson's thin skin, it continued to play well in the black community. "Ewing and his team were like that classic Ice Cube distinction," wrote author Todd Boyd in his book *Young, Black, Rich, and Famous,* "[they were] the wrong niggers to fuck with." After a Graham–Andre Hawkins bout marred a Big East tournament battle with Syracuse, *Sports Illustrated* writer Curry Kirkpatrick, who would develop an antagonistic relationship with Georgetown and its coach, added to the mystique and inflamed the racially charged atmosphere. In a critical piece on the Hoyas' tactics, Kirkpatrick wrote of "Georgetown's plundering legions," calling Thompson and his players "Grandmaster Flash and the Furious Twelve." As the belief that the all-black team was a collection of thugs widened, questions from a befuddled and now often hostile press increased. "People base their perception of you as a human being on the look you have on your face, the demeanor, your attitude," said Esherick. "But there's much more to everybody than what you see in competition. We had a lot of guys that were very competitive. Patrick was extremely competitive. David Wingate. So some of it was they saw a guy that got up for big games, was competitive, didn't apologize, and was aggressive and people took that a little too far."

Thompson, at the heart of this new media narrative, was beset by reporters who, unable to detect any basketball challengers to the Hoyas, smelled a new angle. Sometimes Thompson ignored the questions. Other times he angrily countered their implications. And on still other occasions he could be biting and sarcastic in response. "Keep it coming," Thompson at one point said of the ongoing criticism he and his program provoked. "I love it." By sheltering his team from public view and media scrutiny, the coach likely exacerbated those negative perceptions. Was he doing it to spite his critics? Was it just another layer of mystery for opponents to ponder? Was it a legitimate response to what he felt was the hurtful way his team was being portrayed? Was it his answer to the banana tossing, the racial stereotyping, the death threats?

Jackson has since said the thug act was contrived, a means to a competitive end. Others continue to insist it was as real as the championship trophy the Hoyas brought home from Seattle. The truth appeared to exist somewhere in between. The Hoyas knew their physical style, unsmiling faces, and remoteness were going to generate criticism. And they didn't care. The more the media and white fans complained about it, the more that style became a badge for the players. They scared the hell out of white America and it was kind of cool. They wouldn't back down. "Georgetown, like hip-hop, never attempted to minimize those fears by softening its image," wrote Boyd.

While the jackals barked, the caravan rolled on. The 1983–84 Hoyas won the Big East regular-season and tournament titles. And except for a slowed-down, two-point win over SMU, they never really were challenged throughout the NCAA tournament. In one of those postseason victories, over Dayton, Graham confirmed the Hoyas' image, flagrantly shoving Flyers star Sedric Toney to the court. The outrage grew louder. Curiously, at that season's Final Four, Graham emerged as something more than an enforcer. Never much of an offensive threat, he collected 22 points in the final two victories, including a 7-for-9 shooting performance in the championship-game win over Houston. No one knew it would be his basketball swan song. The 1983–84 Hoyas finished with the school's first NCAA title and a 32-3 record. Everyone but Fred Brown and Gene Smith would be back. Or so it seemed.

Graham's classroom troubles worsened that spring, when

he reportedly skipped several final exams. In late August, Thompson announced that the bruising power forward would be sitting out the next season to catch up academically, though he would retain his scholarship. Meanwhile, the coach tried to convince a skeptical media that Graham was not basketball's Jack the Ripper. "The kid has never been a hoodlum or any of that stuff," Thompson said. "Michael's biggest problem is motivating himself to do his schoolwork." Four months later, Graham surprised everyone, including Thompson, by announcing that he was transferring to the University of the District of Columbia, a nearby Division II school. He would never play there. Or at any other college.

To help make up for Graham's absence, Thompson recruited Highsmith, a 6-foot-8 power forward who had been a sergeant in the U.S. Army. Early speculation suggested Highsmith might also have been as old as twenty-five. Asked for the player's age, Bill Shapland, the school's sports information director, said, "We don't do ages."

Midway through the 1984–85 season, it appeared this Georgetown team would be one for the ages. The only unresolved questions were whether the Hoyas would finish the season unbeaten and where they would rank among the college game's all-time dynasties. With little on-court drama to record, sportswriters began comparing them to other repeat champions—Russell's San Francisco in the 1950s and the Alcindor and Walton UCLA teams of the 1960s and early 1970s. Wherever the Hoyas stood historically, virtually everyone expected them to become the first team since Walton's 1971–72 and 1972–73 UCLA teams to capture back-to-back national titles. Maybe, if everything broke right for them, they could even become the first unbeaten team since Knight's 1975–76 Indiana. "Who on earth is supposed to keep Georgetown from winning its second straight NCAA championship?" asked *Washington Post* columnist Tony Kornheiser. "The line forms on the right. When the Celtics show up, call me."

Their road to the coronation took a slight detour in late January when the Hoyas lost consecutive Big East games to St. John's and Syracuse. But the two close losses—by one and two points, respectively, to what probably was the nation's second-best team and a legitimate top-ten conference foe on the road—didn't dissuade many Georgetown believers. That January 26 home loss to St. John's, 66-65, not only ended the undefeated talk but allowed the Redmen to briefly supplant Georgetown atop the national rankings. But the Hoyas would regain it by winning their final nine regular-season games, including a much-ballyhooed, schedule-ending rematch with St. John's at Madison Square Garden.

The Hoyas averaged 74 points a game for the season and permitted just 58. Four starters, led by Ewing's 14.6 per game, averaged double figures. Most impressively, their opponents combined to shoot a woeful 39 percent against them. "They were one of the best defensive teams I've ever seen," said Villanova's Harold Pressley. "I still look back and think, 'Wow, those guys were truly amazing.' We'd sit and watch film and watch them on TV and were in awe of how quick they were and how they could trap you. They always seemed to have everybody covered." What made the Hoyas even more formidable, of course, were the intangibles. They began to believe they were the team most people thought them to be. They could stare down and intimidate opponents, win games during warm-ups. They got into teams' faces and heads and never, ever relented.

On February 27, No. 2 Georgetown, which had won seven in a row, traveled to New York for a rematch with No. 1 St. John's, winner of nineteen straight. The dream pairing generated a level of hype that hadn't accompanied a Madison Square Garden sporting event since Ali-Frazier in 1971. "This is the biggest game of all time that's not a championship," said St. John's coach Lou Carnesecca. "You could play this game at Yankee Stadium and fill it." That was true even though there was little at stake but the ultimately meaningless No. 1 ranking and perhaps a slightly better seeding in the Big East and NCAA tournaments. The Hoyas, with two league losses, weren't going to catch unbeaten St. John's for the regular-season league title. And, besides, the two were probably going to meet again a week later in the conference event. "We're both playing for pride and that's about it," said Thompson.

But, as was almost always the case when Georgetown was involved, the game's appeal reflected something deeper than its statistical surface revealed. The possibility that St. John's, with its white superstar, Mullin, might again defeat Ewing and the nasty Hoyas excited many white fans who were tired of Georgetown's act—as well as the all-black team's dominance. As the two best college players in America, Ewing and Mullin were constantly being compared, occasionally to the Georgetown star's detriment. The apples-to-oranges comparisons irritated no one more than Thompson. An adoring, mostly white press, perhaps without any ill intent, liked to portray the Brooklyn-born St. John's star as a hustling, hardworking gym rat who had transformed himself into a great talent. Ewing, meanwhile, was seen as a naturally talented seven-footer, implying, for Thompson at least, that hard work and dedication had less to do with his success than the physical abilities with which he was born. The same attributes that won praise for Mullin often brought scorn to Georgetown players. "If Chris Mullin hustles, he's tough," Thompson had said the previous season. "If Gene Smith hustles, he's dirty."

Into this highly charged atmosphere, Thompson tossed a little fuel by rebuffing an interview request that week from New York sportswriters. In advance of the big game on Wednesday, the Metropolitan Basketball Writers Association wanted to do a Tuesday teleconference with the coach. But Shapland informed them that would be impossible since the Hoyas were traveling to New York that day. The group then offered to move the call to Monday but again was rebuffed. When a writer asked Shapland what time Thompson would be getting to New York, he was told, "None of your business." An association official reported that it was the first time in fifty-two years that anyone had declined its invitation. The snub looked worse when Carnesecca, despite suffering from a bad cold, showed up, sat through several speeches, and then answered the reporters' questions for an hour. "And you wonder why St. John's is everyone's sentimental favorite,"a *Chicago Tribune* sportswriter noted in a story on this latest Georgetown controversy.

A day later Thompson defused some of his critics with a whimsical wardrobe choice. The superstitious Carnesecca had been wearing the same multicolored sweater for good luck throughout his team's winning streak. When Thompson learned that T-shirt versions of the sweater were available, he ordered one. He was wearing it beneath his sports jacket when, after the Hoyas were met by boos as they walked onto the Garden floor, he flashed the familiar pattern to a greatly amused sold-out crowd of 19,591.

The game that followed wouldn't be nearly so entertaining. Ewing dominated the Redmen in an 85-69 victory that returned the Hoyas to the top of the polls and reaffirmed the inevitability of the season. He had 20 points, 9 rebounds, and 6 blocks. Best of all for those Georgetown fans who were always looking for racial messages, Ewing emphatically swatted away two Mullin shots when a St. John's comeback still seemed possible.

A week later in the same arena, Georgetown and St. John's, as expected, met again in the Big East tourney final. The Hoyas, now playing their best and most physical ball of the season, seemed to use the occasion as a public sparring session in advance of the NCAA tournament. After St. John's had defeated Villanova in one semifinal, Syracuse star Pearl Washington and Ewing exchanged punches in the other, a game won easily by Georgetown. "He shoved me, and I hit him in the ribs," explained Washington. "It was just a reaction." Ewing, whose public image had softened a bit following his successful stint with Knight's gold-medal-winning U.S. Olympic team the previous summer, refused to discuss this latest altercation. "I don't wish to get into that," he said.

This time, it had been Carnesecca who provided a little pregame levity, entering the court with a dozen white towels knotted over his left shoulder, an exaggerated version of Thompson's famous quirk. Then the tone quickly turned serious. After the two had shoved each other, Williams punched St. John's Ron Rowan, triggering an altercation that concluded with both players being ejected. Earlier, a technical foul had been assessed on the Georgetown bench for some unrevealed but apparently inappropriate comment. And the Hoyas' Perry McDonald was whistled for a flagrant foul after a particularly hard collision with Mullin. No matter, the Hoyas won going away, 92-80. What was even more impressive was that Ewing, in foul trouble, had played just nineteen minutes. "The only team that can beat Georgetown is maybe Georgetown," Redmen assistant Brian Mahoney said afterward.

During the postgame celebration, Ewing presented Thompson with the net he and his teammates had just cut down. "I told him," Thompson said, "those weren't the strings I wanted." For those, he'd have to wait three more weeks.

And so, having twice in ten days defeated by a combined 28 points the team generally conceded to be the nation's second-best, having shown all the other contenders its literal and figurative muscle, having assured itself the NCAA tournament's top seed, Georgetown returned to its campus feeling invincible. "I think," said Thompson, "that this team is as good as last year's."

* * *

The only Selection Sunday drama for the Hoyas was the identity of their first NCAA victim. Georgetown was assured the No. 1 overall ranking, which meant they'd stay in the East Region. So it was hardly a great surprise that the Hoyas drew Lehigh, the only team in the tournament with a losing record. The Engineers from Bethlehem, Pennsylvania, had lost twice as many games as they'd won until three surprise victories in their East Coast Conference tournament left them with the unlikely combination of a 12-18 record and a tournament bid. That quirk infuriated a lot of coaches whose teams had showier records, tougher schedules, but no NCAA berth. "Whether or not we deserve to be in is arguable," admitted Lehigh coach Tom Schneider. "But we belong in there. We won our conference tournament and that's the way the system works." Even though he knew his team was almost certainly going to play the Georgetown–St. John's winner, Schneider said he hadn't watched Saturday night's Big East final. Instead, he'd gone to see his daughter in a high school play.

Since Lehigh had a 6-foot-7 center and one starting guard who weighed 150 pounds, the game figured to be a physical as well as competitive mismatch. Forget about any delusions of victory, Lehigh just hoped it could get the ball over half-court consistently against the Hoyas' press. "We're working against seven defenders in practice to get a feel for how tough it is," assistant coach Gordon Austin said of Lehigh's practice tactic, which was something Massimino often did to prepare Villanova for the Hoyas.

All the dismissive talk about Lehigh made Thompson uncomfortable, as did the Las Vegas point spread for the game—Georgetown was a thirty-five-point favorite. "I'm a little tired of everybody harping on Lehigh and whether they should be here," he said. "I don't feel sorry for them. They didn't win a vote to get here. They earned a spot by beating some people. We've got a great team. That's probably an understatement. [But] we're beatable. We never come into a game—no matter who the opponent is—thinking someone is terrible. If we perceive it that way, we'll be in trouble."

When the game began at noon that Thursday in the Hartford Civic Center, it was as lopsided as everyone had imagined. The Hoyas led 39-11 at the half. At one point, when Lehigh center Don Henderson tried to challenge Ewing, the Georgetown center, without ever leaving his feet, caught the shot in his hands and initiated a fast break. With the starters on the bench for most of the second half, Georgetown prevailed, 68-43.

Next came another Pennsylvania opponent, Temple, in what would be a matchup of two of the college game's most prominent black coaches. A longtime coach at Division II colleges, winning a national title in 1978 at Cheyney State, Temple's John Chaney, fifty-three years old, had landed his first Division I job just three years earlier. At the coaches news conference the day before their teams met, Chaney, who had called Thompson the best "teacher/coach" in the country, presented his counterpart with two gifts—a luggage tag and an apple. One was a desperate hope that Thompson might soon be packing for home, the other an acknowledgment of the Georgetown coach's teaching ability. "John Chaney is a competitor," Thompson said, when asked about the gifts.

"This is indicative of that. I'll take the name tag. But you all know how paranoid I am. I don't know what's in that apple."

A day later his Hoyas took a bite out of Temple in a relatively painless 63-46 triumph. Thompson again showed that he, too, could use the absence of a shot clock to his advantage. Twice in the second half when Temple closed to within eight points, he ordered a four-corners set. Twice it led to easy baskets for Jackson. Having test-driven its stall offense and handled Temple's zone, Georgetown confidently returned to its campus, where it would prepare for the following weekend's East Regional in Providence.

"Sixteen teams are still alive as regional play begins Thursday," John Feinstein wrote in the *Washington Post* on March 18. "Actually there are fifteen teams and Georgetown. If the first week of play confirmed anything, it is that only a monumental upset will prevent the Hoyas from winning a second straight national title."

Historically and culturally, if not competitively, Georgetown's next opponent, Loyola of Illinois, was a fascinating one. In 1963, the little Catholic school in Chicago not only won a national championship but helped push the college game a little closer to racial equality. Loyola had opened the '63 NCAA tournament by destroying Tennessee Tech, 111-42, its sixty-nine-point margin establishing an NCAA record. The Ramblers' next opponent was supposed to be Mississippi State. "Supposed to be" because three times in the previous four years, the Bulldogs had earned a tournament bid but not played.

At the red-hot apex of the civil rights struggle, Mississippi's segregationist leaders were concerned that the school would have to face integrated squads in the tournament, something that actually violated that state's reactionary Jim Crow laws. So after each of those previous NCAA bids, Mississippi officials had decreed that coach Babe McCarthy's Bulldogs could not compete. When in 1963 Mississippi State captured its third SEC title in five seasons, school president Dean Colvard vowed that this time, "unless vetoed by a competent authority," the team would play its scheduled NCAA tournament game in East Lansing, Michigan.

Colvard's statement touched off a firestorm in the state, the atmosphere souring further when Mississippians learned that the Bulldogs' scheduled foe, Loyola, started four blacks. Typical of the overheated response was an editorial in the race-baiting *Jackson Daily News*: "Harping over a crack at a mythical national championship isn't worth subjecting young Mississippians to the switch-blade society that integration spawns," it warned hysterically.

On March 13, two Mississippi legislators got an injunction preventing Mississippi State from participating. But this time McCarthy outsmarted them. Anticipating the move, the coach, his assistant, and the athletic director had flown to Nashville earlier that same day. His players, having surreptitiously boarded a separate flight before anyone from Jackson, a two-and-a-half-hour car ride from their Starkville campus, could prevent them from doing so, joined him there. Out of the reach of Mississippi authorities, all made it safely to Michigan.

In the game itself, Mississippi State was successful in

slowing down Loyola, which had averaged an astounding 91.8 points a game that season. But the Bulldogs still lost, 61-51.

Loyola, with its four black starters, went on to win the national title, laying the groundwork for Texas Western's memorable victory three years later. The fact, however, that Loyola's lone white starter, John Egan, was the point guard only confirmed racial stereotypes. Many whites didn't believe blacks had the intelligence to play certain positions—quarterback in football, catcher or shortstop in baseball, point guard in basketball. "A lot of people felt that way," said Jerry Harkness, a Loyola starter that year. "They'd say, 'Well, they [blacks] can play well at center but nowhere else.' Then there would be a great black forward and they'd say, 'Well, they can play well at forward and center but nowhere else.' Then they'd say the same thing about other positions when blacks proved they could play them, too. The last one was point guard. A lot of whites had to have something to hold on to."

Much had changed since 1963. The shunned black players that Loyola recruited so easily then were now in greater, broader demand. The number of blacks in college basketball had more than doubled in the interim. The typical Division I team now had six. Georgetown, which so famously had twelve, had little trouble with Loyola, defeating the stubborn Ramblers, 65-53. With a record of 33-2, the Hoyas had only to top Georgia Tech in Sunday's regional final to get back to the Final Four for a third time in Ewing's four seasons. To that point, Thompson and his team appeared remarkably relaxed.

There hadn't been any ugly on-court incidents in the tournament, no hiding out, no angry exchanges with reporters, no "Hoya Paranoia." "I'm probably just not as anxious as I used to be," Thompson said when asked about the apparent change. "I still get nervous about the same things. But you deal with the things you can control." And there wasn't a soul in America who didn't believe he and his Hoyas were going to control Georgia Tech.

Few teams, however, get to a Final Four without at least one scare, and Georgetown's came in the 60-54 victory that sent it to Lexington. Ewing spent much of the game on the bench with four fouls. His backup, Dalton, collected four as well. In the second half of the close game, Thompson had to insert 6-foot-10 freshman Grady Mateen. Had Tech star Mark Price shot a little better than 3 for 16, it all might have ended right there for the Hoyas. Up by just a point at halftime, Thompson tore into his players for what he saw as their lackadaisical performance. "But after I bawled them out," he said, "I reminded them that they had been in this situation before." With fourteen seconds remaining and Georgetown up by a basket, 56-54, Dalton hit two crucial free throws and the Hoyas held on. "I knew I had to make those," Dalton said, "or not go back to the bench."

Afterward, there was a great release of joy among the Hoyas, greater even than after their NCAA championship a year earlier. Ewing, grinning widely, collapsed to the floor, his large body spread-eagled in delight. Teammates dove atop him, the indistinct ball of humanity rolling around the court in Providence for several seconds. "I've always said," Thompson told a postgame news conference, "that it's much harder to get to a Final Four than win a national championship." None of those who at that moment already were conceding the 1984–85 title to his team knew how right he was.

CHAPTER TWELVE

I've waited for this all my life, dreamed about it, thought about it, talked about it.

—Rollie Massimino, at the Final Four

Though Lexington was the racehorse capital of the world— the calcium content in its native bluegrass being ideal for equine bone growth—the planet's most famous horse race took place elsewhere in the state. Likewise, while the city's University of Kentucky was home to one of the nation's legendary basketball programs, Lexington had never been the site for the NCAA tournament's Final Four. Meanwhile, much to the chagrin of proper Lexingtonians, Louisville—damn, low-class Louisville, eighty miles to the west and, to their minds, much farther away on the civility scale—not only was home to the Kentucky Derby but had hosted college basketball's foremost event six times. Nothing could be done, of course, about moving the Derby from Churchill Downs. But the other great civic slight finally was corrected in July of 1980, when the NCAA's Division I Basketball Committee awarded 1985's Final Four to Lexington.

For a city without a professional sports team, with barely 200,000 residents, landing the Final Four was a major coup. The NCAA tournament had blossomed into a national sporting institution, one that, in terms of the broad-based interest it generated, rivaled the Super Bowl and World Series. And the culmination of it all was the Final Four. All over America, it seemed, tens of millions of fans who couldn't distinguish a double-team from a double dribble were filling out NCAA brackets. The event, like golf's Masters, had developed into one of television's springtime sports rituals. Thirty-five million viewers had watched the Magic Johnson–Larry Bird showdown in 1979's championship game. Five years later, CBS paid the NCAA $96 million for a three-year rights deal. The '85 tourney would generate gross revenues of $33 million and attract 422,519 fans to thirty-four sessions. Final Four schools that year would earn $708,000 apiece.

"The allure of the Final Four," said the *Boston Globe*, "aside from a slick marketing effort between the NCAA and CBS television, is that upsets do happen—all the time. Single elimination remains the most pressure-packed and scintillating format in sports." Amid all this hoops hoopla, it was difficult to recall that March Madness had begun with barely a nervous tic almost a half-century earlier.

Until the 1930s, college basketball, all basketball really, was a little-noted diversion between football and baseball seasons. The game itself was an aesthetic nightmare—plodding, floorbound, brutishly physical, governed by rules that impeded fluidity. The best teams regularly missed three of every four shots and rarely reached the fifty-point mark. But thanks in large part to a series of rules changes enacted in the '30s, the ugly duckling would be transformed, slowly, into a swan. The three-second violation and ten-second rule were added. The center jump after every basket was eliminated. Stanford All-American Hank Luisetti would launch an offensive revolution with his one-handed set shot.

Almost overnight, college basketball doubleheaders in big-city arenas became hot-ticket events. In 1934, for example, New Yorkers packed Madison Square Garden to watch NYU face attractive intersectional foes like Kentucky and Notre Dame. Riding the wave and looking for a way to extend the basketball schedule, the Garden's operators and New York sportswriters teamed up in 1938 to organize a National Invitation Tournament, a postseason gathering of what were purported to be the country's top collegiate teams. The inaugural NIT would feature three schools from the East (Temple, NYU, and LIU) and three from the West, which then was anything beyond Pennsylvania (Colorado, Oklahoma A&M, and Bradley). Well-attended and, not surprisingly, given the identity of its co-promoters, well-covered, that first NIT proved a great success.

At Ohio State, where the Buckeyes basketball team had captured the Big Ten title that year but had not been invited to New York, coach Harold Olsen noticed. He wrote to the NCAA, suggesting that the organization stage a postseason competition of its own. Agreeable for once, the regulatory body decided that beginning in 1939, it would sponsor a tournament. Its eight participants would be selected by regional panels of coaches and sportswriters.

The event's evolution would be a slow one. Decades would pass before the NCAA surpassed the NIT in prestige and popularity. Initially, most teams, particularly those in the East, preferred the NIT and New York's bright, urban spotlight to the more countrified NCAA. But with no rules prohibiting a school from competing in both, some did. In 1950, for example, CCNY not only played in both the NIT and NCAA but swept their championships.

The first NCAA tournament began on St. Patrick's Day 1939 with a doubleheader in Philadelphia. Three days later a second two-game set took place all the way across the country, in San Francisco. Though there's no indication Nevin, the Wildcats trainer then, too, was wearing any leprechaun's garb, Villanova opened that inaugural tournament by defeating Brown before a disappointing crowd of 3,500 at the University of Pennsylvania's Palestra. Ten days later, the four opening-game victors—it would be decades before the term "Final Four" was coined—met in Evanston, Illinois. Villanova lost there to Oregon in one semifinal. Then, in the first NCAA championship game, played in front of 5,500 fans in Northwestern's gym, Oregon topped Harold Olsen's Ohio State.

For a time, the championship of both the NIT and NCAA would be played at Madison Square Garden. But in 1951, a Garden-based point-shaving scandal shook the sport and the NCAA looked elsewhere. That same year, the NCAA expanded to sixteen teams and reserved ten of those spots for conference champions, a move that eventually would separate it from the NIT, which was bound by that acronym's middle word, "Invitation." "That was the cornerstone of the success of the NCAA tournament," Wayne Duke, the future Big Ten commissioner, told the New York Times in 1988. "It provided a solid basis for the tournament. It wasn't designed to knock the NIT out of the blocks, as people in the East were inclined to believe in those days. [Then NCAA head Walyer Byers] wanted the major conferences to support the tournament."

If the NIT, which maintained its home in America's best-known arena, was oriented toward the East, the early NCAA had a distinct Midwestern flavor. No eastern school would be NCAA champion until Holy Cross, in 1947. And between 1953 and 1964, nine championship games took place in either Kansas City or Louisville. Those sites made sense. Kansas City was where the NCAA was headquartered, and Louisville was in the heart of perhaps the most basketball-conscious state in the nation. But New York was the world's media capital, and its NIT received a level of ballyhoo the NCAA could only dream about. "If the Final Four were played on the West Coast," the Chicago Tribune's Phil Hersh noted in a 1985 piece looking at the event's origins, "news would drift into East Coast papers two days after the fact."

Billy Packer, who would be the color analyst on CBS's Villanova-Georgetown telecast, was a basketball fanatic growing up in Pennsylvania in the 1950s. Yet the NCAA tournament was so foreign to him that until Russell led the Celtics to NBA glory, he'd never known the center's San Francisco teams had won consecutive NCAA titles in 1955 and 1956.

The spectacular growth of the NCAA began in the late 1960s, with the dominance of John Wooden's UCLA teams, especially those that included 7-foot-2 Lew Alcindor. "There was always the curiosity of seeing who might beat UCLA with Alcindor," said Packer. "And that helped move the tournament from the second page to the front page." By 1971, the NCAA tournament was being televised nationally by NBC, and its field had ballooned to twenty-five teams. Indicative of its growing stature, that year's Final Four took place in the 60,000-seat Houston Astrodome.

Beginning in 1975, it was difficult for the NCAA to keep up with its burgeoning appeal. The tournament's field underwent a series of regular expansions. It swelled to thirty-two teams, then forty in 1979, forty-eight in 1980, fifty-two in 1982, and fifty-three in the 1984 event, which Georgetown won at Seattle's Kingdome.

The demand for growth continued from the 275 Division I basketball schools, all of whom, it seemed, believed they deserved a spot in the sport's spotlight and a crack at the pot of gold TV had provided. The National Association of Basketball Coaches lobbied hard for bigger tournament fields. And at its 1984 convention, the NCAA acceded again to its members' wishes. Beginning in 1985, the group decided, the tournament would include sixty-four teams, nearly 25 percent of the eligible total. Eleven schools that would have been shut out a year earlier could now dream of miracles.

Though Lexington would be the smallest city ever to host one, it was an inspired choice for a Final Four. Like the thoroughbreds reared on the four hundred farms that then ringed the Kentucky city, it had an impressive pedigree. Adolph Rupp, a hard-bitten martinet from the Kansas plains, had built the nation's top college basketball program there, at the University of Kentucky. For decades, no other school could compete with his Wildcats. "Kentucky [basketball]," the *Washington Post* would note in that era, "always seems a bounce pass or so ahead of the pack."

In a state without major pro sports, devotion to Kentucky basketball became a civic religion. Its players were minor deities, their mere affiliation with UK opening wide for them the doors of business, power, even politics. It was hardly a coincidence that when the Final Four teams arrived in Lexington that last week of March 1985, the mayor who greeted them, Scotty Baesler, had played for Rupp in the 1960s. "Outside our borders, our identity is racehorses," Baesler said then of his city. "But inside, it's basketball."

While other colleges struggled to attract a few thousand fans to games, Kentucky regularly sold out its 13,000-seat Memorial Coliseum. Later, the Wildcats would move to 23,000-seat Rupp Arena, where every game between its 1976 opening and the '85 Final Four had been a sellout. On nights when Rupp's teams played, there were few radios in the state not tuned in to Cawood Ledford's broadcasts. "The kids in Kentucky start listening to games when they are still being burped on their father's shoulder," Marquette coach Al McGuire once said. And when television became the medium of choice, they made the switch. At its peak, Rupp's Sunday night TV show—little more than a stiff rehash of the week's games—was watched by 83 percent of Kentucky's television viewers.

Lexington also had an interesting civic history. One of the oldest cities west of the Allegheny Mountains, it was founded in 1782 and named for the site of the Revolutionary War's opening battle. Briefly the state capital, it soon developed a prosperous merchant and political class. With an opera, a lively theater scene, and the West's first college— Transylvania—residents liked to call their city the "Athens of the West."

Henry Clay, the U.S. Senate's "Great Compromiser," was a Lexingtonian. So were James Buchanan's vice president, John Breckenridge; Confederate general John Hunt Morgan; and Abraham Lincoln's future wife, Mary Todd.

Horsemen, drawn there by the rolling hills and the benefits of the purple-blooming bluegrass, found the area ideal. They built handsome farms and enclosed them with white-oak fences, four planks high. Virtually all the great racing thoroughbreds were bred at Lexington-area farms like Calumet, the birthplace of Triple Crown winners Citation and Whirlaway. Another equine native, Man o' War, perhaps the best racehorse ever, was so beloved locally that in death he was honored with a life-size statue at the Kentucky Horse Park. (Curiously, Man o' War's pedigree provides two connections to Villanova's historic victory thirty-eight years after the great horse's death. Born at Lexington's Nursery Stud, Man o' War was sold as a yearling to Samuel Riddle. The wealthy son of a Pennsylvanian who had earned a fortune providing uniforms to the Union army, Riddle lived in Delaware County, Pennsylvania, which is where Villanova is located. Man o' War lost just one of his twenty-one races. The horse that beat him was named Upset, a term and a concept to which Villanova's triumph would lend deeper meaning.)

Kentucky did not make it to Lexington's Final Four, but another group of Wildcats would. And so would Georgetown. The presence of a team whose blackness was its signature in a city that was once a hub of the slave trade provided the event with a touch of historic irony. For most of Lexington's existence, an Old South gentility had coexisted with the cruelties of slavery and later Jim Crow segregation. Though residents there liked to think they were more enlightened than their Deep South brethren, slaves had been sold at its Cheapside Auction Block, not far from the future site of Rupp Arena, for more than a century.

Given that legacy, very few post–World War II Lexingtonians thought it wrong or even unusual that Rupp's teams, like almost all in the South, remained segregated. Beginning in the mid-1960s, however, spurred by federal mandates and changing attitudes, a new Lexington was emerging. Led by the university, the city's institutions were broadening, changing, even integrating. It wasn't something that came easily to a region the historian Ronald Oakley described as "a land of Bible Belt religious fundamentalism, with a strong belief in an orderly and hierarchical society, with everything and everybody in its place."

That description certainly would have applied to the manner in which the meticulously detailed Rupp ran his program. With both feet in the past, he operated Kentucky basketball with a harsh, dictatorial precision. "He didn't have many friends," said former Kentucky governor Happy Chandler, "and he didn't care." He also didn't care about integrating. Though university administrators increasingly prodded him to find at least one black player, Rupp's success and popularity rendered those pleas powerless. "I'm not sure that the president of the university could ever have told Adolph Rupp what to do," said Perry Wallace, who was recruited by Kentucky (but not by Rupp) and eventually integrated the SEC at Vanderbilt in 1966. "He was 'the Baron,' a figure of power and legend."

Despite his Midwestern roots, Rupp became the epitome of a Kentucky colonel. The "Baron" developed a drawl, a love of Kentucky bourbon, and even owned a farm where tobacco was grown and cattle bred. He was an unyielding and demanding leader, pushing himself and his teams to perfection. And he was successful. During his forty-two years as coach, Kentucky would win 876 games, four NCAA titles, and a national reputation as the top college team in the country.

In 1966, Rupp inadvertently became the villain in the morality play that was that year's NCAA title game. In a matchup nearly as memorable for its contrasts as its outcome, his all-white Wildcats lost to Texas Western, which started an unprecedented five black players. As a result, while Texas Western coach Don Haskins would later be hailed as a civil rights pioneer, Rupp would forever be viewed as an unpleasant reactionary. Late in his career, Rupp reluctantly added a token black player or two. But when he retired in 1972, his final team was lily-white, a racial distinction that by then even Deep South members of the SEC like Mississippi State, Mississippi, and Alabama could no longer claim. Even so, the Baron remained beloved in Lexington and when the city opened its new $45 million downtown arena in 1976, a year before the coach's death, it would be named in his honor.

Final Fours had been held before in Kentucky. Louisville's Freedom Hall, which could seat 16,000 spectators, had been the site of six between 1958 and 1969. But as the event and the media interest surrounding it blossomed so did the ambitions of its organizers. The bigger the city and the bigger and newer its arena, the better its chances of hosting. As successful as Lexington's Final Four turned out to be, it would very quickly be viewed as a basketball anachronism, like set shots and satin shorts.

When a record 31,765 fans poured into the Astrodome for that '71 championship game between Villanova and UCLA, NCAA officials got a tantalizing taste of the future. More dome Final Fours were periodically scheduled. In 1984, when Georgetown beat Houston, 38,420 fans watched in Seattle's Kingdome. Three years later, the Louisiana Superdome crowd for Indiana's third championship under Knight was 56,707. By 1997, the linkage was complete. The NCAA ruled that Final Fours could take place only in cities that possessed a domed stadium with a capacity of at least 40,000. That seating minimum would be upped to 70,000 in 2009.

Just as important as arena size were TV ratings. Until 1973, championship games were played on Saturday afternoons. Having witnessed the NFL's groundbreaking foray into prime time, the NCAA decided that its title games also would take place on Monday nights. The change paid immediate dividends. For that first prime-time final, a then record audience of 13.8 million viewers saw UCLA defeat Memphis State.

With a small-town enthusiasm, and a devotion to basketball that could be matched in few other places, Lexington was determined to stage a memorable Final Four. Once the four teams had been determined, civic leaders moved into high gear. Water trucks bathed the city's streets daily. Curbs were painted, signs replaced, landscaping freshened. Final Four banners fluttered everywhere. Empty storefronts were decorated and filled with the goods of nearby merchants to lend the downtown a more lively and prosperous air. A bourbon-flavored tournament party, hosted by the aristocratic horse breeders Preston and Anita Madden, who annually staged a splashy Kentucky Derby bash, was scheduled for a local polo grounds the night before the championship game.

Increasingly, the Final Four, like the Super Bowl, was being defined by all the events that surrounded it—coaches' meetings, athletic directors' conferences, basketball writers' gatherings, awards banquets, team dinners, and, maybe most notably, lavish parties. Of those corporations who had latched onto the event, none gripped so tightly as Nike. The Oregon-based athletic-gear giant then paid many of the top basketball coaches between $100,000 and $250,000 annually for the rights to dress up their teams and their programs. Nike had an especially close relationship with Thompson and Georgetown, especially after a sneaker the firm designed for the Hoyas turned into a national sensation.

The fight for Final Four tickets was, as expected, furious. Only 6,600 tickets a game were available—at $21.50 apiece—to the general public, and 140,000 people had entered a lottery for them. Even Rupp's widow had to enter, though eventually someone at Kentucky, which got 2,000 tickets as the host school, found seats for her and the rest of the arena namesake's family. Each of the four competing schools got 2,125 tickets, the NABC 2,600.

Since Georgetown had been to two Final Fours in the previous three seasons, and since Thompson preferred it that way, the team departed Washington that week with very little fanfare. The Hoyas had staged a brief, thirty-minute session with the local media that week, then retreated into their customary shell. Late Thursday afternoon, they flew to Kentucky.

Things were much different at Villanova, which had just one previous Final Four appearance on its résumé. Students poured out of their dormitories after the North Carolina win and turned rainy Lancaster Avenue into a riot zone. Drinking, climbing telephone poles, draping trees with toilet paper, blocking traffic, a dozen students suffered minor injuries and nearly that many were arrested. Eventually, the party shifted to the old field house where a raucous crowd of 6,000 students greeted the Wildcats at 1 A.M. on their return from Birmingham. They chanted, sang, held hastily composed signs aloft. One hand-lettered banner draped over the second-level's façade contained a particularly bold forecast: THE WILDCATS WILL BE NOBODY'S FOOL ON APRIL 1.

"It was like the whole student body was there," said Pinone. "They were just going crazy. Chanting. Throwing streamers. Waving banners. We'd been removed from it, playing the games, but the whole campus had been going nuts."

Perhaps more so than even the students, Massimino seemed in an emotional frenzy. At a Final Four send-off rally on Wednesday, spitting out his words like machine-gun fire, the coach told another spirited crowd how surprised he'd been to learn that some in the media had knocked the way he dressed. Swirling like a model, he displayed his outfit—a charcoal-gray sports coat punctuated by a maroon silk handkerchief in its breast pocket, houndstooth-checked gray slacks, blue shirt, matching tie, and tasseled black Italian loafers. "Are you kidding?" Massimino bellowed, prancing around the podium with a microphone in his hand and half a chip on his shoulder. "I am the best-dressed coach in the country. The best. You bring in any five guys and I guarantee you it'll be like Mickey Mouse against Mickey Mantle. I've bought twenty pairs of shoes in the last month. Look at this shirt. I bought this in Hong Kong for $104. I throw away more clothes than most of the coaches in the country buy."

It was an odd reference for a pep rally. As with his "linguini and clams" halftime speech a few days earlier, Massimino seemed to have a gift for using extraneous topics to get people excited about basketball. He himself needed no urging. Massimino hadn't been able to sleep since the North Carolina victory. "I've waited for this all my life, dreamed about it, thought about it, talked about it," he said. "It should happen to every coach at least once, just that feeling of looking at the clock in the final seconds of a regional and knowing you have it won." But he wasn't satisfied yet. At 6 A.M. on

Monday, the day after the North Carolina victory, he and the sleepy Wildcats assembled for practice.

Villanova, Georgetown, St. John's, and Memphis State arrived in Kentucky on Thursday. The teams' official airport greeters dripped Kentucky charm. Young women clutching parasols were costumed like Southern belles in crinoline and lace. They took players by the arms and walked them past a brass band to an official greeting station. There each visitor received a package of welcoming gifts that included various Kentucky products and mementos and, of course, Nike sweatshirts and jackets.

Villanova's traveling party checked into its Ramada Inn headquarters, about three miles from Rupp Arena, then gathered for a sightseeing tour of the area. Massimino wanted his players to relax, to forget for a moment about the significance of their journey south. The Wildcats visited a mall where they noticed Villanova was missing from the few dozen schools whose names appeared on the official Final Four pennants. "They were printed up a long time ago," one gift shop proprietor explained to a Philadelphia reporter. After that, the players went to Spendthrift Farm, one of the bluegrass region's best-known horse factories. "Coach Mass let us do things," recalled Everson. "He let us experience all that, which I thank him for. We got to visit a horse farm. We got to see Seattle Slew and Affirmed and Alydar."

Meanwhile, Georgetown's players were staying in Louisville, eighty miles away, so far removed from the Final Four festivities that they may as well have remained in Washington.

The choice of distant lodging was an irritant to reporters whose editors were demanding stories on Thompson, Ewing, and the powerful and enigmatic Hoyas. When one asked the school's often unhelpful sports information director why Georgetown had decided to stay so far away from the site of the games, he was told, as usual, it was "none of your business."

Once again, Thompson's Hoyas, who had barracked in Biloxi, Mississippi, during the Final Four in New Orleans three years earlier, were thumbing their noses at the media and the basketball establishment. The Hoyas' hotel choice became the week's overriding theme, so much so that even Villanova's players were asked about Georgetown's bunker mentality. "We believe in the exposure for the student-athlete," said McLain. "The interviews are part of it. We are capable of speaking for ourselves. Maybe Georgetown does it a little differently. Coach Thompson has his set of beliefs and it's always best to stick with your own set of beliefs."

Thompson didn't care about the hubbub he'd created. No matter what was said or written, Georgetown's coach was going to keep the crowds and the media away from his team. He demanded physical as well as psychological isolation. He wanted no distractions. No interactions. Sportswriters characterized it all in terms of Christians and lions. Thompson locked up the lions, kept them so hungry and agitated that when their cages sprung open, the poor Christians had no chance. The psychoanalysis began. What was Thompson hoping to gain by hiding his team? Was he paranoid? Was he justified? Was he foxy? Was he churlish?

"People were so accustomed to kissing the ass of the media," he explained. "I didn't do it."

If, as so often accused, Thompson was trying to foster an "us-against-them" attitude as a way to coax a better performance from his team, it was hardly a novel approach. What better motivation was there, coaches knew, than a belief that you were being unfairly scorned, targeted, excluded, over-looked? Thompson simply had honed the tactic to a fine point. Basketball was war. And if he wanted to build fortresses and a fearsome army, then outsiders were just going to have to deal with it. No one was going to tell him how to run his pro-gram. If you didn't like it, you could express your displeasure on the court. Whatever his intent, the result was that George-town basketball games turned into miniature crusades. The Hoyas played with a religious fervor, as if they understood it was their duty to slay the infidels.

Pinckney told the story of a pregame hallway encounter with Fred Brown before a Villanova-Georgetown game a year earlier. The two had been close friends, teammates in fact at Adlai Stevenson High School in the Bronx. But when Pinckney greeted Brown that night, he was met by total silence. "This Georgetown thing," the stunned Villanova center thought, "is intense."

In the decades since, some Georgetown alums, like Jack-son and Dalton, claim they were all just playacting, delighting in the fear and befuddlement they created in opponents. But as young men in or just barely out of their teens, it's doubtful they seriously questioned their coach's philosophy. And the deeper they were immersed in it, the more faithful followers they became. "Coach Thompson kept them away from everybody," said Everson. "When we played in the Big East tournament in New York City one year, they stayed in Rye [nineteen miles away in Westchester County]. The Big East used to have a brunch before the first set of games, and Mike Graham told me that when Georgetown guys went they weren't allowed to talk to anybody from another team. They couldn't even look at you. If you said hello, they'd turn their heads. They'd sit by themselves. Mike told me that was Coach Thompson. Either you played by his rules or you didn't play. He told me, 'You think I liked being a jerk to my friends at the Big East tournament?'"

But Dalton, Ewing's backup, insists that Georgetown's players were perfectly content and happy with the isolation. They were the nation's most visible college team. Reporters wanted interviews, fans wanted autographs. And a lot of nuts and racists despised them. They had no choice but to build walls. Still, they got to have some fun. Though few were aware of it that week or in the years that followed, Dalton said, the Hoyas even got to do some sightseeing in Lexington. "We went to the horse farm in Kentucky," Dalton said later. "John Thompson didn't lock us up. He provides an opportunity to do the things you have to do. You all call it 'hiding.' You have to draw the line someplace. The best thing that happened to me is that Coach Thompson provided that line for us."

Yet to many on the other side of the line, it all looked either sinister or contrived. Only Thompson knew for sure, and he kept insisting the hysterical reaction to the way he operated was just one more misrepresentation by a mostly white media that still viewed black players and coaches suspiciously. Thompson said it was perfectly logical to house his team in Louisville. He wasn't depriving his kids of fun, he was merely making sure they could have some. "It's just my style," he explained. "It's John Thompson's way. I think it [the isolation] brings my team together and allows them to laugh and talk and just be themselves."

Assistant coach Craig Esherick agreed. "Our staying in Louisville was done for privacy and trying to keep the players focused," he said. "We had a lot of people that took a huge amount of interest in us, in terms of reporters wanting to interview everybody. That could have played into John's thinking. And I think he also wanted to separate us from our fans. When you think about it, it's the same reason that NFL football teams take their players, and those guys are adults, to a hotel the night before a game." Esherick said he was certain Thompson later wished he'd housed the team a little closer to the Final Four site. The long rides to and from Lexington wore them all down as the week went on, and on championship-game day, heavier-than-anticipated traffic delayed their arrival at Rupp Arena.

The NCAA, though, didn't like it at all. They wanted to create a happy carnival atmosphere at the Final Four. Instead, Thompson had crawled out from under the big tent and fled. In response, not long afterward, the organization mandated that competing teams had to stay near the arena. Sportswriters who made the long trek to Louisville that week were frustrated to learn that even there they had little access to the Hoyas. Georgetown officials chased visitors from the gym where the team practiced and guarded the locker room doors. The *New York Times* George Vecsey complained of Georgetown's "confrontational tactics."

If it were all a case of Thompson looking for an edge, he had found another motivational tool earlier that week. Louisville *Courier-Journal* columnist Billy Reed had written a mocking column about Kentucky's search for a new basketball coach and all the self-imposed limits the school placed on itself. Reed listed several people who, as a result, would never be considered. One was Thompson. A Martian, Reed wrote, had a better chance of being elected president than a black man had of becoming a successor to Rupp. A lot of coaches, white and black, likely would have laughed off the tongue-in-cheek comment. Not Thompson. "I fail to see the humor in racism and I never have," the coach told reporters after citing the column during Wednesday's teleconference. "I read that column to my players because I want them to understand that very clearly."

The Final Four's Saturday semifinals are a curious beast. Teams struggle so long and hard to reach them that sometimes just getting there is a sufficient reward in itself. As a result, emotional letdowns are commonplace. The NCAA tournament pressures can either dissipate or intensify. Teams can play as if they're merely happy to be there or as if they are still desperate to advance. They can be relaxed or white-knuckle tense. They can frolic in the national glare or melt beneath it. It's impossible to predict, which is why Saturdays traditionally produce more surprises than Mondays.

For anyone psychologically handicapping the 1985 field, Georgetown clearly carried the heaviest load, the burden of having to validate itself as the dynasty everyone believed it to be. St. John's felt it could beat anybody, with the possible and notable exception of the Hoyas. Memphis State's bluster belied its self-doubts. And Villanova? Well, the Wildcats seemed strangely serene. "For some reason that week we all had that feeling, like we were going to win," recalled Pinckney. "We were just so loose. Even Coach Mass."

There certainly was no pressure on them. If the Final Four teams had been ranked by the attending sportswriters and coaches, Villanova almost certainly would have been No. 4. Virtually everyone in Lexington thought the national champion was going to emerge from Saturday's second semifinal, Georgetown versus St. John's for the fourth time that season, the third time in a month. "I think Georgetown and St. John's are the best teams in the country," said Pitt coach Roy Chipman, echoing the overwhelming sentiment, "and whoever wins will win the national championship." "That, right there," said Oklahoma's Billy Tubbs of the Saturday nightcap, "is for your championship."

The intense focus on that other semifinal permitted Villanova to fly beneath the radar, an altitude at which the Wildcats were perfectly comfortable. Memphis State ought to have been content to do the same. Instead, the Tigers seemed more interested in providing Villanova, a slight two-point favorite, with bulletin-board material.

On Friday, all four teams ran through pseudo-practices before a crowd of 15,000 at Rupp Arena, a crowd that booed the Hoyas when they ran onto the floor. Afterward, each team sat through mass interview sessions, then retreated to local gyms—or, in Georgetown's case, to one in Louisville—for their real workouts.

During its public appearances that week, the Wildcats were so laid-back they were playful. At one Rupp practice, the players switched uniform tops. Five-foot-ten R. C. Massimino, for example, wore 6-foot-9 Pinckney's No. 54, creating considerable confusion among the program-clutching fans. At another, as if in response to this Final Four's racial undercurrent, the Wildcats' black players scrimmaged against the white.

Privately, the Villanova players couldn't comprehend what was coming out of the Memphis State camp. Before its Midwest Regional final the previous weekend, coach Dana Kirk predicted the winner of his team's game with Oklahoma would be in the national title game. Questioned in Lexington about the prediction and whether he thought it unfair to Villanova, Kirk tried to back away from his words. "I just agreed with [Oklahoma coach] Billy Tubbs," he said. "Billy said that, and I agreed with him. But, at that time, I had not seen Villanova. Villanova is the hot team in the country right now."

No sooner had that flare-up faded then Vincent Askew created another. The Memphis State guard said he was looking ahead to a championship-game matchup with Georgetown, apparently assuming the Wildcats would not be much of a hurdle. "That's the one I'm really looking forward to," said Askew. "You can't hold anything against Villanova because it's a good ball club. But everywhere I go, I hear Georgetown this and Georgetown that. They can't be beat and all of that. They've lost two games. That proves they can be beat. And I believe we can beat them."

All the talk added another element to Villanova's pre-game arsenal. Already confident and on a roll, they now had an added weapon—their desire to shut the Tigers up. Like North Carolina, Memphis State had a massive front line—seven-footer William Bedford, 6-foot-10 Keith Lee, and 6-foot-7 Baskerville Holmes. But the Wildcats, who had defeated the Tigers in a 1982 NCAA meeting, were convinced that, when it came to talent and coaching, they held the advantages. "That was one game I think we all knew we were going to win," Pinone said. "We had a better game plan. We were better prepared. We could do things to stop them. They were kind of freelance. They weren't really a good half-court team. We felt we could frustrate them. And I think that's what happened."

It didn't happen immediately, though. The Tigers pulled ahead 13-7 with eleven minutes to play in the first half. But by halftime the game was tied at 23-23 and Lee had two fouls. Lee was one of three consensus first-team All-Americans at the Final Four, joining Ewing and Mullin. Massimino's defensive game plan was to swarm him on defense and attack him on offense. It worked on both counts. Lee would have as many fouls (two) in the opening twenty minutes as baskets.

Perhaps thinking they were working the second game, which most expected would be another physical Big East war, the officials were calling it extremely close—at least when it came to Memphis State. The Wildcats would take 26 foul shots, their opponents 9. Then, with just over seventeen minutes to play, Lee picked up his third personal. Emboldened, the 'Cats went on a 9-0 run and emerged with a 39-33 lead. Lee's frustrations continued and he fouled out with ten minutes remaining in the half, the fifth foul a silly over-the-back on a boxing-out of Pinckney. Bedford had foul troubles, too, and the twin towers would share the floor together for of only sixteen of the forty minutes.

Their star's disqualification spurred one last charge by the Tigers, an 8-0 streak that tied it at 41-41. Now Villanova really started to milk each possession, irritating both Memphis State and its fans. The arena echoed with chants of "BOR . . . ING! BOR . . . ING! BOR . . . ING!"

A McClain dunk with 2:01 to play put Villanova up by four, and when McLain hit a pair of free throws with under a minute to go, the lead was six, 51-45. Andre Turner, who had bad shooting luck all game, saw his layup roll out. Pinckney grabbed the rebound, Villanova made one more free throw, and, defying all expectations if not belief, the Wildcats had made it to the championship game.

It was the fourth time in five NCAA tournament games that the Wildcats had held their opponents under fifty points. McClain led them with 19 points. Massimino employed eleven different defensive sets to stifle and frustrate the Tigers, limiting them to 38 percent shooting. McLain, after an early stumble, had handled defender Turner's pressuring tactics perfectly. It was another remarkable outing for a player who, according to what he wrote later, had snorted a half-gram of cocaine before the game. No one had seen him do it. And, if he really had, no one noticed any negative effect. "I would be amazed [if he really had consumed a half-gram of cocaine]," said

Everson. "The guy played almost a flawless game. I don't know how somebody could have played like that if he was wired on the stuff like he said he was."

One of the signs a Villanova fan had held up before the game asked, WHO INVITED MEMPHIS STATE TO THE BIG EAST TOURNAMENT? With that conference advancing an unprecedented three teams to the Final Four, the Tigers felt like uninvited guests. Bothered all week by the Big East focus, their discontent bubbled over following their loss to Villanova. Several Tigers blamed the defeat on the officiating. "They have a good team," Holmes said, "but give us three different refs and we'll beat Villanova right now. They say the Big East is so rough. It didn't seem rough to me. We couldn't touch them, but they could rough us up."

If anyone who missed the other semifinal happened to walk in on Lou Carnesecca's postgame news conference, he'd have had no trouble discerning the outcome. Following a third one-sided loss to the Hoyas in thirty-one days, this one by a score of 77-59, the sad-eyed St. John's coach wore an air of resignation that was nearly as noticeable as the garish ski sweater he'd donned.

When asked if he had any advice for Villanova in Monday night's title match, Carnesecca, his psyche as black and blue as his defeated players' bodies, said, "Yeah, wear helmets." While there were no fisticuffs in this Georgetown–St. John's matchup, the Hoyas' Williams, as would be the case two nights later, was at the center of a halftime-buzzer controversy. Georgetown led 32-28 when Williams missed a jumper just as the buzzer sounded. Thompson thought his player had been fouled and lambasted official Charles Vacca. Vacca walked away. One of his colleagues, Jim Burr, dropped the basketball as he tried to hand it to the official scorer. The Georgetown coach picked it up and, while giving Burr an earful, played keepaway with the ball. Eventually he angrily heaved it at the official. Seeing this, Carnesecca yelled to Burr, "Call a T! Call a T! If I did that, you would!" The official ignored the incident and immediately after halftime the Hoyas inflated their lead, scoring the second half's first seven points. The completely psyched-out Redmen never got close again.

Williams, who hurt an ankle in the victory, had 20 points, Ewing 16. The Hoyas had used a box-and-one to deny Mullin the ball, and the Redmen star finished his otherwise sensational college career with an 8-point stinker. In describing the Hoyas' victory formula, Broadnax inadvertently revealed a weakness. "We like to get people looking up at the scoreboard when they're five or ten points behind, saying, 'We've got to catch up.' We don't like anyone to dictate the tempo to us."

So impressed was Carnesecca by now that, in trying to come up with an apt comparison for these Hoyas, he ran off a litany of the greatest college teams ever—San Francisco with Russell and K. C. Jones, Kentucky with Alex Groza and Ralph Beard, UCLA with first Alcindor and then Walton, Knight's unbeaten 1976 Indiana team and its four NBA first-rounder picks. Had he also mentioned the Celtics, Yankees, and Canadiens, no one would have flinched.

When Georgetown–St. John's started, some of Villanova's

players were still doing interviews. The rest went out to watch the first half, though heaven knows they weren't going to discover anything new about either of these familiar teams. They knew both almost as well as themselves. And nearly alone among the vast crowd, they were pulling for Georgetown. "We always seemed to beat them once a year," said Everson. "And so far we hadn't done that yet. We wanted another chance."

One of the last questions McLain took that night came from a reporter who, like everyone else, correctly assumed Georgetown would beat St. John's again. "Gary," he said, "what will it take for someone to beat Georgetown?"

McLain, as always, was ready with an answer. "It will take a perfect game," he said, before adding an equally significant coda. "But when you're in the mood we're in, you're ready to play anybody."

That mood was enlivened Saturday night back at the Ramada, where McLain did another half-gram, exhausting the Final Four cocaine supply a friend had given him. He and the Wildcats ate pizza, watched the end of Georgetown–St. John's, listened to music, and imagined how wonderful it would be when, just as Jake had been predicting all along, they walked out of Rupp Arena Monday night with the championship trophy.

Few others thought that possible. Taking Kirk's comments one step further, newspaper columnists and headline writers had fun with Monday night's championship pairing. "Cinderella and the Ugly Stepsisters," one called it. "Cinderella vs. the Crusher," said another. "Cinderella vs. Midnight" might have more accurately summed up the feeling in the basketball world.

But one coach, virtually unnoticed amid the coronation chorus backing up Georgetown, made note of another element, one that was generating very little discussion that week. "Villanova," said Columbia's Jack Rohan, "is playing as if its brilliant coach, Rollie Massimino, were on the floor moving the Wildcats with a magic wand."

CHAPTER THIRTEEN

Guys just suddenly knew what other guys were going to do before
they did it. . . . I still don't know how or why it happened.

—Ed Pinckney

In the minutes before the championship game's start, Rupp
Arena quivered like the cheerleaders' pompoms. Voices. Move-
ment. Music. Color. Light. Anticipation. It all blended together
into a palpaple force.

Amid all this pregame energy, from his seat behind a
basket, a Villanova student held up one of those hand-lettered
signs that pander to the hopeless self-promotional instincts of
college-age males and TV networks, the latter, in this case,
CBS.

C-OULD GEORGETOWN

B-E

S-ORRY?

It was a remarkably cautious—and equally telling—question
from the young Wildcats fan. Even at this joyous pregame

moment, when optimism ought to have been surging though him like testosterone, his faith was not unquestioning. He could not bring himself to create a bolder forecast. Sure, he hoped his Wildcats would win. But he was not dumb enough to predict such an absurdity. Hadn't Massimino that week called the 35-2 Hoyas "one of the best teams ever assembled in the history of college basketball"? The fan's youthful spirit was no match for the belief that Georgetown was going to spay the underdogs.

It was April Fools' night. And the sign-carrying student was no fool.

"Those forty-eight hours," Jensen would say, "were the longest of my life." With no game to ease the rabid anticipation, idle Sunday was torture for Villanova's players. Now, as Monday dawned, they were a curious combination of weary and excited. Pinckney hadn't slept much. A lingering cough from an earlier bout with the flu had kept him—and, by extension his roommate Pressley—up most of the night.

At 9:30 A.M., they all made their way to a hotel conference room for breakfast. Massimino's words there were like caffeine. He told them about Severance's sudden death. Most of the players knew the old coach, recalled that he'd been with them in Vermont way back in November. For those who didn't understand what Severance had meant to Villanova, Massimino provided a brief summary of the man's life. "Now," he said in conclusion, "we've got to do our best to remember him in the right way."

For the youthful Wildcats, it was eerie to think that

someone whose life had so many of the same touchstones as theirs had, in an instant, ceased to exist. Severance had been a member of the tiny Villanova basketball community. He'd coached in the same field house where they'd played and practiced. He'd been to Saturday's game, seated amidst their parents and their friends. He'd had a ticket for the championship game. He'd been staying in the same hotel, riding the same elevators, eating the same food. Sure, his glory days were in the past. But soon enough theirs would be, too. He'd be forgotten. So would they.

Or would they? If anything, Severance's death leant more substance to the airy dreams that had propelled them toward this moment. They now had an opportunity to affix footnotes to their own biographies. They could win a national championship. They could assure their immortality.

One of Villanova's assistant coaches recalled for the players that eleven years earlier, before the game in which his team would clinch hockey's Stanley Cup, Philadelphia Flyers coach Fred Shero had told his players, "Win today and we walk together forever." Now they knew what Shero meant.

Following breakfast, Massimino led them out to the hotel parking lot where, surrounded by buses, pickup trucks, and wide-bodied American cars, he installed a fifty-sixth set to his defensive playbook, this one designed to stifle Ewing. Villanova might get beat, he understood, but no one was going to outprepare him. "I've never seen anybody approach other teams with such an understanding and such preparation," said Jensen. "We were so prepared for every game. He was always game-planning."

Each of the Wildcats had been given a mimeographed scouting report prepared by assistant coach Mitch Buonaguro. It contained some general comments ("Key to beating Georgetown is getting back on defense and stopping their running game."); the Hoyas' tendencies at both ends of the floor; diagrams of some of their favorite plays; and individual player breakdowns. Under Ewing's name came the report's most important advice, its significance emphasized by capital letters: "MUST KNOW WHERE HE IS AT ALL TIMES!" The report went on to reiterate the importance of "containing him," then ended with a suggestion that was both unusual and, as things turned out, crucial—"Let's take the ball to him."

Massimino arranged his players in the crowded parking lot as if he were readying a chessboard. "In that situation he ended up taking one of the defensive sets we were going to rely on and modifying it so that our guards would squeeze back and help front Ewing. That way Eddie could play behind him or on the side," said Jensen. "We wanted to force him to give it up and force them to beat us on the perimeter." With the last-minute addition incorporated, the players and coaches boarded a bus to return to Rupp Arena for the traditional game-day shootaround. After the session ended, they all gathered near the center-court logo for their official Final Four photograph. Then it was back to the Ramada.

The Final Four could be a lot more tedious than outsiders imagined. "You just want to play the game," said Jensen. "It's torture." Players on both teams were by then wearying of all the yo-yoing between the hotel and the arena. For Thompson and his Hoyas, it had been even worse. On those occasions when it was mandatory for the Georgetown coach and his players to travel to Lexington that week, it had required a 160-mile round-trip by bus. And for them in Louisville, so far removed from everything, the wait seemed even longer. "We'd been to Final Fours before, so we knew you spend a lot of time doing nothing but waiting," said Jackson. "Waiting to practice. Waiting for interviews. Waiting to play. But for some reason the time between games there felt like it was even longer."

The Hoyas' game-day routine was similar to Villanova's. Breakfast. Shootaround. Photos. Lunch. Rest. Meetings. They just had to wrap everything up a little quicker to take into account their far, far longer journey. "I think if John had to do it all over again," said Esherick, "he'd have stayed closer." The Hoyas departed their Louisville hotel around dinnertime. The driver underestimated the Final Four traffic and his route took them directly into it. The snafu delayed their arrival at Rupp, where a rigid pregame agenda awaited them, by a nerve-racking thirty minutes.

Earlier that afternoon, the 1984–85 Wildcats had gathered for one last pregame meal, Mass, and meeting. Massimino wasn't taking any chances. The superstitious and extremely Catholic coach asked Lazor and two other priests—Father John Stack and Father Ed Hastings, a member of the '71 Wildcats—to cocelebrate the Mass. "At least half of us, maybe even more, weren't Catholics," said Pinone. "But that was never an issue. It wasn't like anyone was trying to force religion on you. [The pregame Mass] was just an accepted part of what was done here. If guys were spiritual they used it as a chance to reflect. Some guys might have dozed. Church can be whatever you want it to be."

Lazor delivered the homily, focusing on Severance and Nevin and the task that lay ahead. "You should know," the priest told the players, "that you'll have a guardian angel watching over you tonight. Al Severance will be up on the baskets, swatting Georgetown shots away, guiding yours in."

Massimino then spoke again, urging the players to return to their rooms for rest and reflection. "Think about tonight's game," he said, as if the players had any choice. "Reflect on it. Play it in your head. Play to win. Don't play not to lose. And think about what it will feel like tonight at eleven o'clock when you're national champions." Jensen would call his normally emotional coach's thoughtful speech that day "pretty moving, pretty emotional."

They went back to their rooms and did as he'd suggested. If McLain had wanted to add his own illegal touch to the preparations, he was out of luck. He'd used the last of his cocaine on Saturday night. In what would be the biggest game his life, he'd be playing straight.

Then they all put on suits or sports coats and dress slacks and came together again. It was sometime around 6:30 P.M. when they boarded a bus and rode off into history.

"Good evening, ladies and gentlemen . . ."

At the sound of public-address announcer Frank Fallon's clear and unemotional voice, Rupp Arena pregame din softened. Casual conversations faded. The musicians in the two student pep bands lowered their instruments. Those fans not already on their feet slowly rose. All eyes, except those of the sportswriters busily composing pregame stories and columns in the white-draped rows at courtside, were fixed on the court.

Villanova students, some with their faces painted, others wearing white or blue GO WILDCATS! painters' caps, strained their necks for a final pregame glimpse of their team. At its bench, a circle of players engulfed Massimino. Whatever the coach told them, it produced a collective laugh. To their left, Georgetown's Thompson, the trademark white towel flung across his left shoulder, lectured his Hoyas. There was no laughter. Across the court, a block of Georgetown fans in tuxedos ceased its rhythmic chant of "We Are . . . George-Town!" And at their courtside table, CBS's Brent Musberger and Billy Packer stopped chattering.

". . . and welcome to Rupp Arena for tonight's NCAA national championship game between the Villanova Wildcats and the Georgetown Hoyas. Now let's meet the starting lineups. . . ."

It was shortly after 9 P.M. when the players—Villanova's in navy-blue uniforms, Georgetown's in that all-too-familiar gray—were introduced alternately, by position. "For Villanova at forward . . . Harold Pressley . . . for Georgetown at forward . . . Billy Martin . . . for Villanova at forward . . . Dwayne McClain . . . for Georgetown at forward . . . Reggie Williams . . . for Villanova at center . . . Ed Pinckney . . . for Georgetown at center . . ."

As Ewing ran toward center court to shake hands with his counterpart, something smacked down near a corner of the floor. An arena attendant quickly gathered up the spent projectile, a now flattened banana, and toweled off the spot where it had struck. If the Georgetown star saw the hurled insult, he gave no indication. Few, in fact, appeared to notice. According to the *Washington Post*'s Michael Wilbon, the Georgetown beat writer, it was at least the tenth time that season a banana or banana peel had been thrown at Ewing. So common had the racist ritual become that Wilbon would not even note it in his stories the next morning. Neither would most of his 300-plus colleagues.

The players returned to their benches for final instructions. The assistant coaches and reserves took their seats as the starters moved slowly but eagerly toward the mid-court circle, unadorned but for the arena's name. There the ten young men coiled themselves in readiness as an official tossed a Wilson basketball into the air. Encircled by their eight teammates, Ewing and Pinckney launched themselves into the air, into history.

"Play to win. Don't play not to lose."

The Wildcats remembered their coach's earlier admonition as that opening toss hung in the air. The powerful Hoyas might beat them, but they weren't going to intimidate them. Villanova's players knew that act too well. The Wildcats were going to be aggressive, not cautious.

The nerves any championship-game participants experienced were eased in this case by the two teams' familiarity. The five seniors at center court were now playing in their tenth Villanova-Georgetown game. "We knew all these guys," said

Pinone. "It was just a certain comfort level. We were like, 'Okay, this is the third time we're doing it this year.' It just so happened to be for the national championship. It might as well have been a Saturday night in Landover or a Tuesday night at the Spectrum. I don't want to make it sound blasé, like it was just another game, but it almost had that feel. No one made it more than it was. It was the next game on the schedule."

Like any team going against Georgetown, the Wildcats were forced to concentrate on Ewing. This time, as Buonaguro's scouting report had emphasized, they were determined to challenge him at both ends of the floor. It was a strategy that worked with Memphis State's Lee in Saturday's national semifinal. They acknowledged the Georgetown center was the best player in the nation, but they were willing to concede him nothing.

Villanova's coach knew Thompson well enough to surmise that he wouldn't change anything for the title game. Why would he? The Hoyas were far and away the best team in college basketball and had been since virtually the minute Ewing arrived. They'd won their last seventeen games, hardly an argument for change.

"Coach Thompson wasn't going to change much for us, we knew that," said Buonaguro. "We stuck with what we did, and added a couple of little wrinkles." Defensively, they'd employ the parking lot plan. Offensively, instead of trying to devise ways to evade Ewing, Villanova wanted to take the game directly to him. For Massimino, the strategy's potential positives outweighed the negatives. Sure, the seven-foot All-American might block a shot. But how many during the course of a game? Three, four, maybe five? On the other hand, if the Wildcats went right at him, he might pick up some early fouls. And, by drawing his attention to the driving ball handler, four other Wildcats would be removed from his considerable sphere of influence and possibly open to receive a pass.

As for the Hoyas' trapping, full-court pressure, the cocky McLain, who had faced it for four years and believed he could beat Jackson like a drum, would handle it solo. Massimino knew the spotlight, the pressure, and Georgetown's status as an overwhelming favorite would ignite his spotlight-loving little point guard. As a final twist, Villanova tweaked its inbounds play. Georgetown liked to press and trap after made baskets, so, on occasion, the Wildcats would send a second man out-of-bounds.

A game plan is one thing. The confidence to carry it out in the intense heat of a national championship game, when your opponent wants it as badly as you do, is something else. But ever since they got into the tournament, the Wildcats had possessed a strange serenity. Or maybe, as some would later believe, they simply were possessed. Villanova had become something greater than the sum of its parts. Maybe the coming together was inevitable for so experienced and harmonious a team. Maybe it was just a case of good timing. Maybe they'd all entered a zone simultaneously. Or maybe, as some of them had begun to suspect, it was magic.

"Guys just suddenly knew what other guys were going to do before they did it," Pinckney said. "The chemistry in those two weeks was incredible. I still don't know how or why it happened."

* * *

Despite all their preparation and cohesion, the Wildcats were bothered immediately by the Hoyas' 1-3-1 trap. The constant hounding and harassing was not just a hallmark of the Hoyas' success, it was one of the primary reasons for it. Opponents who couldn't deal with it had no chance. "One of the keys to the game is not turning over the ball," the scouting report had pointed out. "We must control the tempo."

After McLain breezed past Jackson in the backcourt on the game's opening possession, Dwight Wilbur nearly turned the ball over in the corner. Then, having taken a pass near the top of the key, Pinckney, too, nearly kicked it away. Collecting himself and the ball, the Wildcats senior drove the lane. As Ewing rushed toward him, he dished to Pressley, who maneuvered around the suckered center, ducked under the basket, and, contorting his body, somehow scooped in a reverse layup. "Believe it or not, that was a shot we practiced from time to time," said Pressley.

"Why that was so effective," Billy Packer told his audience, "is Eddie Pinckney took it right at Patrick Ewing. . . . Ewing has such great leaping ability that, unless you take the ball to him, he'll cover two men at one time." Though neither Packer nor Brent Musberger mentioned it at the time, that first basket was as lucky as it was quirky. As such, it instantly confirmed everything positive the Wildcats had been imagining.

Wingate hit a jumper for Georgetown, but on the 'Cats' next possession, it was Wilbur who drove the lane and lured Ewing to him before passing the ball to McClain. The flat-footed Georgetown center decided not to contest this shot, and the Wildcats forward slammed home a dunk that gave his team a 4-2 lead. "Now we're thinking, 'Whoa! Something might be going on here,'" Pinckney recalled.

Another Wingate basket, an off-balance jumper, tied the score, and Georgetown showed patience early against Villanova's befuddling matchup-zones, which wasn't easy. "Our defense is so confusing," Massimino said, "that sometimes we confuse ourselves with it [at practice]." Despite public perceptions, the Hoyas, when they weren't creating turnovers, employed a controlled offense. They were far from the run-and-gun outfit many imagined them to be, a style that didn't fit neatly into the black-and-white view of the game. "Once they got into half-court game," said Pinone, "they were very deliberate. Very deliberate."

In an early attempt to counter the Hoyas' ferocious zone press, Pressley ran out-of-bounds, accepted a lateral pass from Wilbur, and got the ball in safely to McLain. "We hadn't seen that from them before," Williams admitted. "It took us some time to adjust." McLain, with a defender in his face, awkwardly heaved up a shot that went in. The Wildcats made their first four shots, but they were far from perfect, having turned the ball over four times in that stretch as well. Georgetown went ahead, 10-8, on a layin off an offensive rebound by Martin before Villanova finally missed, that shot, too, coming on a play where Pinckney directly challenged Ewing.

By then Massimino, hoping to stretch his opponents' defense and continuing with a pattern he'd established early in the tournament, had pulled Wilbur 5:06 into the game and inserted Jensen. It was a move Georgetown had hoped Massimino would make. "We felt like Wilbur was a better ball handler," said Esherick. "With him [Jensen] in the game, we felt like we might have a better shot at creating some turnovers."

A minute later, the switch paid off for Villanova. Jensen hit his first shot—a long jumper that two years later would be worth three points—and Villanova trailed, 12-10. A fourth basket without a miss by Williams, who as a sophomore had become the kind of corner jump shooter the Hoyas had sometimes lacked, increased Georgetown's advantage to 20-14 before the Wildcats responded with two baskets.

Already the game appeared to be infused with an astounding level of intensity. There was no relaxing. Every possession was a passion play. The performers appeared to know they were creating something permanent.

The Wildcats, as was their habit, kept shifting their matchups from 2-3 zones to 1-1-3 to 2-1-2. "Anything to keep them a little off balance," Massimino said. But the pace of play was quicker than Massimino, who had written "64" on the pregame blackboard as a defensive point target, had anticipated or desired. "At this pace this will be an eighty-point game," Packer pointed out. "Villanova's going to need to find a way to slow the tempo a little."

If there were still any thoughts that Villanova eventually would wilt beneath Georgetown's constant psychological heat, they vanished on the play that tied the game at 20. McClain got the ball in the corner and drove the baseline. As he did, a defender closed on him. McClain stopped suddenly, twisted around the Hoya, jumped and lifted a shot that arced just over Ewing's outstretched fingertips. On its soft descent, the ball dropped through the hoop.

As if sensing the play's symbolic significance—the brave lion tamer placing his head into the maw of the beast and emerging unharmed—the crowd, almost all of which seemed to be pulling for underdog Villanova, rose up and roared. Running back up court, McClain turned and theatrically spit on the court. The gesture was an emphatic reminder to the Hoyas that the Wildcats were going to stand toe-to-toe with the defending champions. "That's exactly what I was doing," McClain recalled. "I was making a statement that we didn't come here to fear Georgetown."

For Villanova, which had been shooting 44 percent for the tournament, it was their ninth basket in ten attempts.

In family rooms and dens across America, TV viewers, most of whom had been expecting a Georgetown romp, were beginning to sense something special. Maybe this game wasn't going to be a rout. Maybe it was worth watching. The ratings reflected this growing interest. A lofty rating of 20.2 for the game's initial thirty-minute segment jumped to 22.3 for its second, 23.9 for a third. For most of its second half, the number would be an unprecedented 27.8.

When Ewing missed a fifteen-foot jumper with just under six minutes to go in the half, an obviously upset Thompson yanked his star from the game and lectured him sternly when he arrived at the bench. Meanwhile, Williams rebounded the second of his two missed free throws and his put-back gave Georgetown a two-point edge.

Georgetown continued to force turnovers, though not at

its customary pace. When Williams stole the subsequent in-bounds pass, it was the Wildcats' seventh.

Ewing reentered, but backup center Ralph Dalton re-mained, indicating again just how much Thompson wanted to get the ball inside against the Wildcats' zones. It worked. With just under four minutes left in the half and Georgetown up by a point, Ewing got the ball down low and slammed home a dunk over Pinckney to put the Hoyas ahead by three.

But Villanova couldn't miss. On its next possession, Pressley fired a long, arcing shot that bounded off the metal a few times before dropping through. "We were unconscious," Everson said.

Then came a second straight Ewing dunk, only to be followed by a McClain basket. In an offensive rhythm now, the Hoyas' Jackson found Ewing again and the All-American responded with a third dunk in succession. Georgetown led, 28-25. Williams was draped on Jensen but somehow the Wildcats guard hit another long jumper to make it 28-27 Georgetown.

Without a shot clock, Villanova remained characteristi-cally patient on offense. Even so, through the first eighteen minutes, none of its possessions had exceeded the forty-five seconds a shot clock would soon mandate. But with just un-der two minutes to play in the half, with a one-point lead and Pinckney on the bench with two fouls, the Wildcats ran the last successful stall in college basketball history.

After Everson, in for Pinckney, got a hand on a Martin jumper, the Wildcats took over with 1:54 to go. As George-town sat back impassively, Villanova went into its four corners.

On CBS's telecast, Musberger noted the significance. "Folks," he said of the stall, "you're watching a relic." Packer, meanwhile, wondered aloud why Thompson was not making his Hoyas—some of whom had assumed such a passive posture that they had their hands on their hips—go out and defend the unchallenged 'Cats ball handlers. "This is really playing into Rollie Massimino's hands," the analyst correctly noted.

Just under five seconds remained when Pressley took a shot over Ewing, grabbed his miss, and put in the basket that would give Villanova a 29-28 halftime lead. With the Hoyas scrambling for what would be a misfired last-second shot, Everson tried to box out Williams. As the buzzer sounded, the Hoyas' forward responded with an elbow to Everson's face. Then, as casually as if he'd just tied his shoe, Williams turned and ran off the court with his teammates.

Fortunately, the era when sideline reporters routinely interview coaches as they exit the floor at halftime had not yet arrived. Massimino, his face contorted with fury, pursued an official and screamed that Williams's cheap shot should have resulted in either a technical foul or an ejection, probably both. The referee, apparently glad to have been spared potential trouble by the horn, shook his head and fled the court. Villanova's coach, his jaw now clamped in anger, pivoted and, pumping a fist in the air, jogged toward the locker room with malice marking each short stride. "Georgetown's philosophy and game plan was to intimidate people," said Harry Booth, a Villanova assistant. "But Rollie refused to be intimidated."

Rupp Arena's two dressing rooms were adjacent, and

players from both teams encountered one another in a narrow hallway. The tightly contested first half apparently hadn't chastened Georgetown. Several Hoyas, Everson said, were snickering at their opponents.

Inside his tiny locker room, Massimino now had more emotional ammunition to add to the tactical. Still upset about the Hoyas' last-second antic, he launched a spittle-spewing rant. "They are not giving that intimidation shit to us," he screamed. "Who the fuck do they think they are? Do they think we're going to lie down for them? That is not happening. They're trying to chump us, and it's bullshit!"

Everson, who would not play in the second half, never got a chance to retaliate. In fact, he wouldn't see Williams again until, during 2002's NBA All-Star weekend, the two men bumped into each other—innocently this time—in a Philadelphia hotel hallway. "When I saw who it was, I spun around and put my hands on Reggie's neck and said, 'Okay, I'm ready for you now,'" Everson recalled. The two men laughed and posed for a photograph that now hangs above the desk in Everson's home office. The image of the two smiling middle-aged men is surrounded by a series of four sequential shots that show the Georgetown star delivering the infamous blow.

"The first half," said Musberger, "was as good a half of college basketball as I've ever seen." And neither the quality nor the intensity would diminish in the twenty minutes of basketball that followed.

For Villanova, its one-point halftime edge could hardly

have been comforting. The Wildcats had led the Hoyas at the half in their previous meetings that season and lost both. Pinckney had two fouls. And despite their constant runs at him, Ewing had yet to pick up one.

In the Hoyas' locker room, Thompson told his center to roam a bit more freely on offense and urged Ewing's teammates to get him the ball, as they had done successfully late in the first half. Sure enough, on their first possession, Ewing got it in the high post, spun, and sank a jump shot. Georgetown was back in front, though Jensen's third basket on his third long jumper would soon switch the lead again.

Thompson's halftime plan would be short-circuited when, in the span of less than sixty seconds just five minutes into the half, Ewing collected three fouls. Williams was already nursing a sore ankle, and now Thompson had to replace his star with Dalton. With the Hoyas' two top offensive threats on the bench, Villanova's confidence inched even higher. Ewing's initial foul had come on a Pinckney shot that somehow rolled in. When Villanova's center hit the subsequent free throw, the 'Cats were ahead by four, 34-30.

In the second half, Villanova seemed even more determined to exploit the lack of a clock. After one minute-long possession, McLain, pushing the ball awkwardly from his chest in a motion that appeared to combine elements of a jump shot and a one-handed set, hit an ugly eighteen-footer. The Wildcats led by six, 38-32, with nearly sixteen minutes to go. Now they weren't the only ones who believed an upset was possible.

McLain clearly was enjoying his night in the spotlight. He would later claim that early in the game his counterpart,

Jackson, had called him a "scared punk." Now, every time he beat the Hoyas' defender off the dribble, scored, or set up a basket, he got in Jackson's face. "The battle lines were drawn," McLain said. "Michael Jackson couldn't guard me. I was taking it to him. When we were going up-court I'd be talking to him. 'I got you, boy. You're mine tonight.'"

When Ewing returned to the game, so did Villanova's obsession with him. At one point, when he caught a pass in the low post, four Wildcats converged, a defensive tactic that would be unthinkable in the three-point age that would dawn in the 1986–87 season. Despite all the attention they showed him, Ewing never got to the line that night. The Hoyas, in fact, shot just eight free throws the entire game, one fewer than the total Memphis State had griped about two days earlier. Since both teams played in the conference, this disparity couldn't be blamed on a Big East bias. Had Georgetown's reputation for rough, physical play influenced the officials? "I don't really think so," Pinckney would say. "I think it was just the result of the two different styles of defense we played."

After McClain banked in another improbable shot and followed it up with a free throw, Villanova was in front, 41-36. McLain and his teammates were handling the Georgetown pressure as well as they ever had.

The Wildcats' calm was in marked contrast to Massimino's agitated appearance. His power tie was askew, his shirttail untucked, the summer suit he wore on April 1 wrinkled as he prowled the sideline instructing and imploring. Patience now became an even greater priority for Villanova. Each possession was thoughtfully and slowly executed.

A Ewing jump hook closed the gap to 41-38 before Broad-nax collided hard with McLain and play was stopped. With his point guard apparently hurt, Massimino sent in Mark Plansky, a 57 percent free throw shooter, to take the one-and-one. Visibly nervous, the freshman missed badly.

Midway through the half, incredibly, the Wildcats had taken just five shots, made four, and led by a point, 41-40. Three minutes later, Villanova still led and Georgetown, for the first time, appeared concerned. "John Thompson," Packer said, "is starting to take this game seriously." When a Pinck-ney jumper stretched the Wildcats' lead to five, 53-48, Thompson signaled for a timeout. The big crowd yelled louder than it had all night. And as Villanova's players sprinted off the court, several held their arms above their heads, their confidence expanding. Georgetown, meanwhile, was beginning to understand how tough it was to beat a team that didn't miss. "We were all thinking that it was just a matter of time until they missed a shot," said Broadnax. "But it never came."

Apparently, the only way to keep their opponents from making every shot was to keep them from taking any at all. Georgetown ratcheted up the defensive pressure and a flurry of Villanova turnovers produced baskets that put the Hoyas up by one with 4:35 to play.

In all the pregame talk about tempo, the attention had been on Villanova. Few imagined that Georgetown might try to exploit the lack of a shot clock. But with just under four minutes left, in a plot twist worthy of O Henry, that's precisely what happened. Holding on to a one-point lead, Georgetown tried to ice the game with a stall. But early into the possession, Martin's unchallenged pass bounded off Broadnax's shin. It was a crucial moment of inattention, just whose, neither time nor the two players have ever been able to sort out. "I didn't expect it," said Broadnax.

The Wildcats recovered the errant pass and, with 2:35 to go, another Jensen jumper put them ahead, 55-54—ahead to stay, as it turned out.

The unforced Georgetown error and the lack of a clock permitted Villanova to turn the remainder of the game into a foul-shooting contest. With no clock or three-point shot, trailing teams then had little choice but to create end-of-game foul fests. And in that regard the Wildcats had a clear advantage. Two of the players Villanova had on the court at the time had free throw percentages that topped 80 percent, four were better than 72 percent. Four of Georgetown's five, meanwhile, made under 70 percent.

Four subsequent free throws by Jensen pushed the Wildcats lead to five. Before one of those one-and-ones, during a timeout, Nevin had signaled for Jensen. "Kid," the trainer whispered, "knock them both down." His team ahead, 61-56, with only fifty-two seconds remaining, McLain couldn't contain his exuberance any longer. "We got it!" he said aloud while running down-court. "We got it!" But Jensen and Mc-Clain, who had made twenty straight tournament foul shots to that point, each missed the front end of a one-and-one. An emphatic Ewing put-back following one of the misses kept Georgetown's hopes alive.

Massimino called a timeout. And in the huddle, with the finish of this fairy tale at last in sight, he tried to reassure his players. "Whatever happens," he said, "I love you." Jensen walked over to Nevin's wheelchair. He kissed the head of the old man who had foreseen this moment, stayed alive for it, helped make it possible. "This one's for you," Jensen told him.

Pressley made one free throw and it was 66-62 when, with six seconds left, Jackson scored to make it a two-point game. Again, a basketball quirk that would soon be corrected by the Rules Committee benefitted the Wildcats. Georgetown had no timeouts remaining. The clock did not then stop after made baskets. But following Jackson's score, Wingate had punched the ball into a clot of photographers. At this critical stage, a technical foul would have been unthinkable. The officials had little choice but to stop the clock with two seconds remaining and retrieve it.

An official handed the ball to Jensen. All the Villanova sophomore had to do was get it safely in-bounds. When McClain tried to spin free of his defender, Broadnax, the two collided. The Hoya tumbled backward in a desperate try to draw a foul. McClain, too, lost his balance. As the Wildcat forward was dropping to his knees, Jensen bounced the ball toward him. He caught it, hugging it to his body as he collapsed to the floor. Broadnax, like a football player making sure a ballcarrier was down, made one half-hearted slap at him then retracted his arm in resignation. McClain, the ball safely encircled by his arms and chest, slowly rose, one arm in the air.

The buzzer, the beautiful buzzer, sounded like cathedral bells. "That's it," Musberger said. "Villanova has done it."

Wildcats players bounded around the floor in an out-of-control delirium. The normally staid Pinckney and McClain, bouncing off well-wishers like pinballs, repeatedly screamed "April Fools'! April Fools'!"

Pinckney reprised his act from Birmingham, leaping onto a courtside table. His eyes searched for the Expansion Crew's two other members. Spotting them both, but unable to make himself heard amid the din, he jumped down from his perch and sought them out. He found McLain first and the two friends who had shared a small Sullivan Hall room as freshmen hugged tightly. Then they both remounted the table until they picked out McClain in the chaos. Reunited for one last time in Villanova uniforms, the three players retreated to the relative calm of their bench. "We did it!" they told one another over and over again, remembering their long-ago vow. "We did it!"

Their euphoria was duplicated at dozens of points throughout the arena. Villanova fans who never really believed they'd live to see their school win a national title were crying, screaming, hugging. Priests were embracing cheerleaders. Pep-band members left their instruments unattended as they joined in the celebration. Assistant coaches hugged team managers. Nevin's nephew, John Morris, wheeled his uncle around the court, stopping often. Everyone it seemed wanted to embrace, kiss, or shake hands with the lucky charmer.

Eventually things quieted down for the awards presentation. Pinckney had been named the Final Four's MVP, joined by Ewing and three other Villanovans—Jensen, McClain, and McLain—on the all-tourney team.

Villanova's players didn't want to depart the court. McLain held the rectangular NCAA championship plaque over his head and prayed that this moment would last forever. Players and coaches cut down the nets. One was draped around Nevin's neck. Some recall seeing a tear form in the corner of the old man's eye. "It was not possible to look into that face at that moment," the *Philadelphia Inquirer*'s Bill Lyon wrote of the scene around Nevin, "and not believe that special forces had been at work."

Thompson took his disappointed players aside and told them they'd shown themselves to be gracious victors a year ago. Now they could show the world—the skeptical world—that they knew how to lose with class. Standing on the court, their unhappiness in clear view, the Hoyas gamely applauded for their conquerors. Ewing stood with his coach. He looked remarkably relaxed, as if a great weight had been lifted from him. "It wouldn't surprise me if part of the reason Patrick Ewing applauded so enthusiastically was that he admired the way the game was won," the *Washington Post*'s Kornheiser observed, "and part was that he was relieved that these four years were over."

When Ewing, who had 14 points and 5 rebounds, was called to receive an award for having made the all-tourney team, he thrust an index finger into the air, his last on-court act as a collegian. "We might not have won the game," said Ewing, after what was just his twenty-third loss in 144 games at Georgetown, "but I still think we're No. 1."

Thompson held his postgame news conference, said the bitterness of defeat was eased somewhat by his respect for Massimino, then walked directly to the team bus.

Although the NCAA mandated that players had to make

themselves available to the media for an hour after games, several Hoyas also retreated quickly to the bus. The few who remained were besieged by swarms of sportswriters. "If you're looking for someone who's sad, you won't find him here," Dalton bravely told them. The intensely serious Mary Fenlon tried to break up the interview scrums, yelling at reporters, "Please, gentlemen, we've got to get home!"

Instantly, discussion about the game focused on how well Villanova had played, how brilliantly they'd shot the ball. The box score itself was even more astounding than everyone's recollections. Villanova took only 28 shots and made 22. In the second half they took 10, and made 9. Jensen was 5 for 5, McLain 3 for 3, McClain and Pinckney each 5 for 7, Pressley the slackard at 4 for 6. The Wildcats shot 78.6 percent against the best defensive team in the country, maybe the best defensive team ever. The previous best in a title game had come in 1960, when Ohio State, with Jerry Lucas and Thompson's old Celtics teammate John Havlicek, made 67.4 percent. "Any time you shoot that kind of percentage in the national championship game," Thompson said, "you deserve all the praise." Perhaps even more astonishingly, when you remembered how the Hoyas' pressure had never relented, McLain had just two turnovers.

CHAPTER FOURTEEN

The new Nat. Champs—Villanova's Basketball Team came to the
Rose Garden. I wound up with a jacket.

—Ronald Reagan, diary entry, April 4, 1985

Ronald Reagan was back in the picture. His face on the
cover of *Sports Illustrated*'s preview issue had kicked off this college basketball season. Now, posing alongside the long season's champions in another area of the White House, he would
end it.

The president had been an actor for so long that few
people, in or out of politics, knew their way around a script
as well. The Gipper could be so convincing with even the
most unfamiliar material that those he addressed usually forgot that the words he delivered with such smiling sincerity
were rarely his own. On April 4, 1985, just minutes before a
10:45 A.M. White House ceremony to honor Villanova, he re-
viewed the 658 words his speechwriters had prepared for the
Rose Garden gathering. "With the eyes of the nation on you . . .
you didn't buckle under the pressure. . . . Your personal courage has inspired greatness . . ."

Perhaps because of Reagan's fondness for sports these White House championship ceremonies had become accepted national rituals. From Super Bowl winners to Olympic gold medalists, athletes had come to regard them as perhaps their grandest perk. The president knew the routine well. He would acknowledge the coach and players. He would walk to the mike; deliver a few humorous comments; turn serious as he praised their performance; shake hands; graciously accept a hat, T-shirt, or team jacket; and then be off to the next engagement on his busy calendar.

Outside Reagan's office that morning, the victorious Wildcats were lining up awkwardly on the executive mansion's steps. Meanwhile, the rest of their party gawked at the ubiquitous Secret Service detail or proudly snapped photographs of the assembling champions. Some of the honorees were obviously nervous. A few players tried to appear cool, mumbling wisecracks to equally tense teammates. Others stood frozen.

And one, the short, caramel-complexioned young man whose spot in the middle row would put him directly behind the president, was high. Gary McLain had not abided by the dictum of Nancy Reagan's now infamous antidrug campaign and just said no. He had instead snorted a half-gram of cocaine in the lavatory of the bus that carried him and his teammates to the White House that lovely spring morning.

"I was standing in the Rose Garden, wired on cocaine."

Those ten words on the cover of Sports Illustrated's March 16, 1987, issue can still make Villanovans cringe. Like FDR's

"a date which will live in infamy," they conjure a past trag-
edy, a painful and damaging attack they never saw coming,
an end of innocence. The words comprised the opening sentence to a startling seventeen-page, tell-all story that forever
altered the way Villanova and its monumental upset of Georgetown would be remembered.

For the brief, shining moment that followed its 1985
title, Villanova had resembled Brigadoon, a paradise that only
recently had emerged from the mists. Life after "The Upset"
had a certain glow. The people there were happy and proud.
It was always sunny in Philadelphia's favorite suburb. Until
then, the school's name was one of those vaguely familiar
capitalized words you encountered only in the sports pages,
like Valparaiso, Vardon, or Van Arsdale. Suddenly everyone
knew Villanova. Now Villanova was replete with a new significance. It was seen as an exemplar of college athletics, a
place that could be pointed to with pride as a counterpunch
to scandals like those that subsequently befell Tulane basketball and SMU football.

A year after the championship game, as a series of *Philadelphia Daily News* stories made clear, life at the university was
rosy on all fronts. Student applications had jumped by 15 percent. Alumni donations were at record levels. Phi Beta Kappa
had opened a chapter there. U.S. News and World Report
now ranked Villanova one of the East's top universities. Varsity football had been reinstated. A new campus arena had
opened. And a Philadelphia TV station had paid $800,000 for
the rights to televise a few games from the basketball team's
1985–86 schedule.

"Some schools win on the field but lose in the real world," Bob Capone, the alumni director, proudly told the newspaper. "We won on both fronts and people noticed. They had heard the name [Villanova] but they really didn't know what we were about until last year. Then they saw the way our players handled themselves in Lexington, the way they came across on TV. People said, 'Gee, what a nice bunch of kids. And they can play basketball, too. They must be doing something right at that school.' "

Massimino had turned down a $2 million offer from the New Jersey Nets to stay there. Ed Pinckney and Dwayne McClain were playing in the NBA. And that other departed senior, Gary McLain, he was . . . just what was he doing anyway? It was just before St. Patrick's Day 1987, with Villanova's happy campus virtually deserted for spring break, when that question was answered. Brigadoon vanished back into the mist.

Exactly two years after Villanova had begun its memorable NCAA run with a weekend in Dayton, the new issue of *Sports Illustrated* dropped out of the blue and hit the campus with a nuclear force. On its cover was an ethereal painting of McLain, his back to the public as if he were unable or unworthy to face the world. He is wearing his blue Villanova uniform, the one he wore that night in Lexington. His name and number are clearly visible. He is gazing at a basketball that, like him, is half-submerged in what appears to be cocaine.

For the first time in the splendid history of America's favorite sports publication, the article's title ("A Bad Trip"), author ("By Gary McLain"), and opening lines all appeared on the cover. McLain reportedly was paid $40,000, though the magazine has never confirmed that. His story, cowritten by Jeffrey Marx, was as sordid as the tale of the 1985 championship had been uplifting. In it, the former Wildcat point guard said he'd been an addict, that he'd smoked marijuana in high school, even on a recruiting visit to Villanova. It was at college where he discovered cocaine. He'd used it throughout the time he was a student, before the NCAA semifinal in Lexington, before visiting the White House. He said he sometimes sold the stuff, and when he needed money to get some he sometime sold the sneakers Villanova gave its players. He implied that his teammates had used drugs, too, though he never provided any names. He said fellow students, teachers, even Massimino knew, a claim the coach has continually and vehemently denied.

It took time to digest it all, to measure McLain's depressing story against the rosy recollections of 1985. The immediate reactions were, like the tale itself, all over the map. Villanova track coach Marty Stern called McLain "gutless" for smearing his teammates but not identifying them. A former classmate called him a "whore." Some alumni and fans around the country agreed with those assessments. Others saw it differently. "Exposing himself to public ridicule to help others is a Christian act indeed," Larry Goanos of Brighton, Massachusetts, wrote in a letter to the magazine.

McLain's public chronicling of the shocking details would puncture the pleasant mythology that had surrounded the Wildcats' remarkable upset of Georgetown. It would destroy the cheerful narrative about Villanova and Massimino.

Perhaps even worse for its cherubic-faced protagonist, it would tarnish the crucial role he played in the victory. For some, Massimino's lovable image evaporated in an instant. "Shame on Massimino," opined another SI letter writer. Others, like Villanova women's basketball coach Harry Perretta, defended him. "I know Rollie," said Perretta, "and I know he wouldn't tolerate that."

Almost immediately after the story appeared, reporters descended on the campus. "Even in our dorms, they were coming in and out, looking for scoops," said Jensen. Their investigative fervor was driven in part by the knowledge that, even though they should have been chastened by countless previous examples of hypocrisy, they had been duped again.

"It always happens, sooner or later, to the haughty," wrote columnist Mark Whicker in the *Orange County Register*. While he wasn't given any money directly at Villanova, Whicker noted, McLain wrote that he always knew he could get some from certain alums. "So Massimino is just another opportunist," the columnist concluded. "Even though he insisted he was so much more, that shouldn't shock anybody."

The public had the same curiosity as the journalists— What was true? What wasn't? Who knew? Who didn't? Was Villanova slandered or exposed? Those questions, to a surprising extent, still remain unanswered.

The basketball family closed ranks. Players were hurt. They formed a protective circle around Massimino, one they've maintained for the subsequent quarter-century. "You could see how hurt he [Massimino] was," said Jensen. "That didn't sit well with any of us. That pissed us off. We thought, 'Come on, this is just BS, just made up, just a guy trying to get back in the limelight who couldn't deal with not being on center stage.'"

McLain, who battled drug and personal problems in the coming years, long ago stopped discussing the article or the sins he alleged in it. "That," he said when declining an interview request, "was a long time ago." But he has never denied the accuracy of what he wrote.

Later, his Villanova teammates would say they had had suspicions about McLain, but apparently none ever saw the level of abuse he detailed. Most of them believe, then and now, that the attention-craving point guard, who had been fired from a job on Wall Street not long before the article appeared, enhanced his story to make it more sellable, more valuable.

"College kids are going to make mistakes and [Massimino] understood that," said Pinone. "But he felt hurt by the way it got portrayed, that maybe he'd turned the other way. And that accusation was out there." Everson said none of McLain's teammates believed "half the stuff that was written." "I've watched all the games and rewatched them. If he was on the stuff, he did an amazing job hiding it."

Partially as a result of the clamor created by the SI story, the NCAA in 1987 instituted drug testing for tournament participants. McLain drifted away from Villanova and his friends. He fell in and out of addiction, jobs, and rehab facilities. Eventually, at about the time he turned forty-five, he seemed to right himself for good, cleaning himself up, becoming a drug counselor, speaking to children about his story. "It was a life lesson," he said, "a hard life lesson."

Twenty-five years after his signature coaching victory, Massimino was hurrying home from a Northwood University practice for a plate or two of his wife's pasta. Neither diabetes nor the stroke he'd suffered in 2003 had tamed his taste for Mary Jane's cooking. She had, after all, been trained in the art by Massimino's beloved mother.

At seventy-six, Massimino looked tan and healthy in the Florida sun, although his hair and frame were both thinner than on that long-ago night when he'd so famously prowled, pirouetted, and prayed along the Rupp Arena sideline. He had relocated permanently to Florida after leaving Cleveland State in 2003. He'd tried retirement, playing thirty-six, sometimes fifty-four holes of golf a day with basketball buddies like Chuck Daly, Mike Fratello, and Billy Cunningham. But without coaching there was a void that nothing else—not golf or TV commentating or even pasta—could fill. "He was trying to make himself happy," Mary Jane said, "but he wasn't."

Then in 2006, Rick Smoliak, the athletic director at Northwood, a 620-student school in West Palm Beach, Florida, asked Massimino, with whom he'd worked at SUNY Stony Brook more than three decades earlier, to start a basketball program. Though Northwood would be playing at the small-school NAIA level, a long way down from the pinnacle Massimino had reached with Villanova, the coach eagerly bit. "To start from scratch," he said, "that really intrigued me."

Massimino dove into the program-building venture, micromanaging every detail. He designed the team's stationery, its uniforms, even the logo on the Northwood arena's floor. He recruited, schmoozed, hired, and, best of all, coached. "He missed it," said Everson, a reserve on Massimino's championship team at Villanova. "I think that for a while there he forgot how much he loved being around the guys, the practices, the game situations."

On that winter's day in 2010 when Massimino was hurrying home for pasta, Everson and a few other ex-Villanovans were with him. The old coach had kept his basketball family close. Several of the guys from the '85 team had been visiting him once a year, staying at Massimino's place in Jupiter, accompanying him to practices and games, speaking to Northwood's players. Leaving a West Palm Beach restaurant where they'd stopped for postpractice snacks and beer, Massimino and a former '85 player, Brian Harrington, were crossing a street. Suddenly, a car driven by an elderly Floridian came rolling around the corner. The vehicle, moving at about twenty miles an hour, clipped both men and sent them sprawling.

"Coach says, 'I'm okay,' gets up, starts wiping his pants off," recalled Everson. "But the old guy is scared. Coach goes up to him and says, 'Listen, pal, you really ought to consider not driving. It's not like we just stepped off a curb. We were in the middle of the street!' Anyway, everybody's worried about Coach. We're all telling him that he can't go home, that we need to call an ambulance and get him checked out. But he goes, 'Listen, my wife's making pasta. I like my pasta al dente.

And it's going to be mush if I start messing around with police and that stuff. We're going to eat. Get in the car.' "

For Massimino, the unkind hit was just one of the many he'd endured since 1985.

Almost exactly seven years to the day after Villanova upset Georgetown, Ed Pinckney was dressing for a game between his Boston Celtics and the Philadelphia 76ers. A local TV station's camera crew, dispatched to Boston Garden to get Pinckney's reaction to the news, had just informed him that Massimino had announced he was leaving Villanova for UNLV.

April Fools' Day 1992 was still a couple of hours off, but Pinckney was convinced he was being pranked. "No way," he told the TV crew. "I'm not falling for that." He remained steadfast in his disbelief even after a Boston sportswriter confirmed the news for him. So did a Celtics broadcaster. When still Pinckney scoffed, the sportswriter asked him to walk with him to a courtside phone. There he called his desk, asked an editor to tell Pinckney the news about Massimino, and put the player on the phone. And still Pinckney didn't believe.

Finally, one of the 76ers beat writers, a Philadelphia reporter Pinckney had known at Villanova, tracked him down and told him it was so. Massimino had indeed left for a four-year, $2.8 million deal at scandal-ridden UNLV, the University of Nevada at Las Vegas. "That's outrageous," Pinckney said when he collected himself. "UNLV is just so hard to believe. It's like the exact opposite of Villanova."

The remarkable fall of Roland V. Massimino was picking

up speed. In subsequent years, Massimino would keep descending the ladder of prestige in college basketball. The job at image-challenged UNLV was followed by one at another scandal-tainted school, Cleveland State. Then it was a period of exile before he arrived at Northwood, a rung so low few even knew it existed.

Massimino's surprising 1992 departure from Villanova had taken place beneath a black cloud. He later claimed he'd grown to feel unloved there. If that were so, by 1992 the feeling was mutual. Believing the coach had turned his back on Philadelphia and its beloved Big 5, the city's fans and media had turned on him. Even students at Villanova, where he'd so recently been embraced as a god after the national championship, cheered the news of his departure. Shortly before his unexpected exit, Massimino had decried his fall from grace. "I think at this point of my career, there should be respect," he said. "Wherever I go around the country, it's unbelievable. Then I come to Philadelphia."

Three weeks after those comments, when it was clear the respect was gone, he left Philadelphia for Las Vegas. He would bomb at UNLV and at Cleveland State, the brief stays at each as notable for controversy as for a lack of success.

After Cleveland State, he'd suffered a stroke, been diagnosed with diabetes, and, in September of 2011, undergone surgery for lung cancer, perhaps a byproduct of the Macanudo cigars he cherished almost as much as pasta and Italian shoes.

He'd plummeted so far and fast that it all would have

been unimaginable that night in Lexington. After upsetting Georgetown, he had careened around Rupp Arena like a pinball, bear-hugging players, assistants, friends, fans, students, his lucky tan suit growing more wrinkled with each embrace. The expression on his face that night was an odd mixture of joy and "I told you so" smugness, the latter a response to all those who had doubted him and his team. "No one thought we could do it," he'd crowed to CBS analyst Billy Packer immediately afterward. "But I did."

Anyone watching him closely after that game would have gotten a glimpse at a Massimino few knew. Despite his warm and fuzzy image, he could be vain, swaggering, and vindictive. As the years passed, he alienated as many people as he charmed. Author Bill Reynolds, in his 1990 book on the Big East, *Big Hoops*, would characterize Massimino as the "worst loser in the league." But on that night in 1985 he was a winner, one who could be excused for gloating.

Before the news conference that followed the upset of Georgetown, where he enjoyed watching the doubting Thomases of the press eat crow, he fired up a fat Royal Jamaican. "I usually smoke Macanudos," Massimino felt the need to explain, "but this was all I could find." Later, back at the Ramada Inn, there were lots of "We did it!" phone calls and, as always, plenty of good food and drink. Sometime around 4 A.M., his oldest son, Tom, uncorked a bottle of Dom Perignon champagne and toasted his father. This was no time for humility.

The next day, less than twenty-four hours after what already was being termed one of the greatest upsets in sports history, there was a victory parade in downtown Philadelphia, then a hero's return to Villanova's deliriously joyful campus. More accolades would follow in the coming weeks and months, as would a lucrative offer from the NBA's New Jersey Nets, one he turned down at the last minute. Villanova would write him a new contract, build him a new campus arena. It was the best time of his life. The worst was about to begin.

The good-guy reputation he had taken years to construct disintegrated rapidly. When Villanova stumbled, so did Massimino. His world had always been sharply divided. On one side was Daddy Mass's enormous extended family—relatives, friends, players, other coaches, and all those he'd helped and nurtured throughout his career. But beyond those walls enemy armies lurked. "With the inner circle there's a fierceness of loyalty," Bill Bradshaw, who has been the AD at LaSalle, DePaul, and Temple, once said of Massimino. "But anyone outside the circle better beware."

The love and loyalty Massimino inspired in those close to him was legendary. He wouldn't miss funerals or weddings. His house and office were always open. Every Christmas he telephoned all his ex-players. He was there when they needed a shoulder to cry on or a check to live on. He promised them good educations and he made sure they got them. He could be charming, caring, and considerate. "He'll scream and yell at the kids on the court but then take them into his office and talk to them about anything but basketball afterward," said his top assistant at Villanova, Mitch Buonaguro. "There's not a kid [he's coached] who docsn't love him."

Others knew a darker side. Never cross him, they said, or mess with a recruit he wanted, or beat his team in a game it needed, or question his strategy, or, God forbid, criticize him. He didn't forget. "He doesn't let anything go," said Jim O'Brien, who was Boston College's coach when he butted heads with Massimino.

Sportswriters in particular, including many who once had been great admirers, came to dislike him intensely. The often resentful Rollie they saw wasn't the roly-poly Rollie their readers loved. The one they knew had as much grizzly bear in him as teddy bear. That gap in perceptions between those inside and outside the walls Massimino built was enormous. "[He could be] such a magnanimous winner," wrote Jere Longman in the *Philadelphia Inquirer*, "and such a churlish loser."

While Massimino maintained a close relationship with many in the media, those he turned off couldn't be switched back on. In the midst of Final Four week in 1985, when Massimino was at the height of his career and popularity, the *Inquirer* ran a surprisingly critical and curiously timed profile. While pointing out how deeply his players admired him, the story also noted that several of his colleagues found him overbearing. "He believes you're either with him or against him," Pete Gillen, a onetime assistant, told reporter Chuck Newman. "You're either in the family or you're not."

That was all fine as long as Villanova kept advancing deep into NCAA tournaments. But when the winning stopped, so did much of his support. Some coaches, like DePaul's Ray Meyer, were lovable enough to survive the tough times. Massimino wasn't built that way. He kicked and screamed and fought back and in doing so made even more enemies.

When Massimino was an assistant at Cranford High in North Jersey, the head coach, Bill Martin, had advised him that critics were inevitable and that the best way to deal with them was either to confront or ignore them. "If you don't like what someone says," Martin told Massimino when the younger man left to take his first head-coaching job, "either tell them or walk away from them. Don't be a phony." Massimino clearly preferred to tell them. He once quarreled publicly with a male Villanova cheerleader because he had a ponytail. During a game at the Spectrum, he once pointed out a persistent heckler to security guards and insisted they expel him. He feuded ceaselessly with his most persistent critics, Philadelphia's sportswriters, many of whom were just as confrontational as he was.

"I still have many dear friends in the [Philadelphia] media," Massimino said after leaving Villanova. "But, yes, quite frankly the younger media, as we know them, I think somewhat made me very leery of the whole picture. I'm the type of guy who says what I feel, and I really, really don't want anybody to say what's not true. I'm a very loyal person. When you attack my players, when you attack my university, when you attack someone with whom I feel has done a tremendous job . . . now, I react."

The constant warfare wouldn't win him any friends. Consequently, when Villanova became the prime mover in the perceived dissolution of Philadelphia's cherished Big 5,

Massimino and his ambitions were blamed. The coach became an outcast in the city's close-knit basketball community. Even fellow Big 5 coaches, like LaSalle's Speedy Morris, criticized him openly.

"The big thing was the Big 5," Massimino would say about the ill will he generated. "It wasn't Villanova['s fault], it was Rollie. Rollie is Villanova. Well, Rollie's not Villanova. The decision was made by the institution."

Philadelphians didn't want to hear it. They couldn't tell you who Villanova's president was. For them Massimino was the face of the university. They blamed him. And as had happened with many of his coaching colleagues, winning a national title, they sensed, had gone to Massimino's head. "I think Rollie's a good coach," Pitt's Paul Evans, who had participated in a few public fights with him over recruiting issues, said in 1987. "I think he worked his ass off from the bottom steps up and he wins a national championship. Then, I thought, he fell in love with himself and turned off a lot of good friends."

Turned them off so thoroughly that eventually he felt he had to leave Philadelphia. So on the day before April Fools' Day 1992, almost exactly seven years after the city and school had paraded and praised him, Massimino said "enough" and departed.

The boos began that day with Villanova's students, who on hearing the news at an assembly gleefully chanted, "NA-NA-NA-NA . . . GOOD-BYE!" At the start of the 1994–95 season, Villanova commemorated the tenth anniversary of the school's lone championship. Massimino did not attend the ceremony. When emcee Bill Raftery mentioned his name, many in the Pavilion crowd booed. The hard feelings would persist for decades. "Every time Rollie comes back to Philly, he gets killed," Villanova coach Jay Wright said in 2007.

His friends, his ex-players, his golfing buddies couldn't understand it. "Twenty years of that man's life went into that city," said John Olive, who had played for and coached with Massimino. "I don't want to speak for Coach, but I think he was very disappointed with how Villanova University treated him. It was always a struggle. It was a continual struggle day after day with everyone around him. With the administration. With the media. I think he said, 'Hey, I don't need this anymore.'"

In his final seven seasons at Villanova, his teams never lost fewer than thirteen games, twice lost sixteen, and twice lost more than they won. He had hoped his son Tom, by then an assistant, would succeed him when he left for UNLV, but Lappas was given the job instead. Bitter, he wouldn't speak again to his old colleague for years.

Like McLain, he, too, found peace several years into the new millennium, when Northwood College called.

After Massimino was diagnosed with lung cancer in 2011, surgeons removed a portion of his lung in mid-September and he underwent rigorous chemotherapy treatment. But on November 2 he was back coaching at the tiny Florida school. "He's a pretty amazing guy," said Everson. "I got a phone call from him and he said, 'I've got cancer.' And I said, 'What are you worried about? You had a stroke and diabetes and you're still eating pasta all the time. You got hit by a car. You think this is going to be a problem?' Six weeks after his operation he was back on the bench, screaming, yelling like nothing happened. When the light comes on for a game or practice, he's just like he was twenty-seven years ago."

By the end of the 2011–12 season, he had cajoled his team to another national championship game appearance. But this time Massimino's Northwood squad had no magic, falling to Oregon Tech in the NAIA title matchup.

Jake Nevin's condition slipped rapidly after that night in Lexington. On November 22, 1985, Villanova renamed its old arena—the trainer's second home—the Jake Nevin Field House. Unable to move at all by then, he attended the ceremony in his wheelchair. Less than three weeks later, the field house was filled again for his funeral.

It was a sentimental Irish wake. Each speaker had stories about Nevin that topped his predecessor's. The next day's Philadelphia newspapers were filled with touching reminders of the man and the crucial role he'd played in the sporting miracle eight months earlier. His passing helped infuse Villanova's triumph with an almost supernatural aura. Somehow, with each opponent getting progressively better, the Wildcats had managed to do the impossible, to win six consecutive games and in doing so defying even the most generous expectations.

"It made no sense," wrote the *Inquirer's* Lyon. "At least it didn't if you only looked at it from the traditional sports perspective. But then you remembered that the players had dedicated every game of that season to Jake Nevin and, finally, it was enough to make you believe that this was all meant, somehow, to be."

Massimino, barely able to control his emotions at the ceremony, read a letter Nevin had composed before his death: "Thank you, Lord, for my nephew Johnny, my family, my friends, and those special people who were a part of it. You know the love we shared. Thank you for the many gifts you gave me, the wonderful people who touched me. You all were very wonderful. Thank you for the family spirit that was central to my life. You know how I valued that. Thank you for the beautiful, the simple, the great people that I knew who shared so many great moments with me. You know I gave them my very best. Thank you for all the kids at Villanova. I can truly call them my kids. You know how much I loved you and thanks, Lord, for December 9, 1985, when you rewarded my faith with eternal life.—Jake."

More than a year after Villanova's historic upset, in November 1986, Hollywood released a film that would eventually occupy a lofty spot in what might be the rarest of all movie genres—the intelligently rendered sports film. *Hoosiers*, a simple, sepia-toned story about the American heartland and the unlikely victory of a small-town basketball team over a daunting urban foe, was, certainly for all those whose memories of Villanova's historic upset were still fresh, an allegorical homage to the Wildcats. In particular, the inspiring pregame speech delivered by Gene Hackman, as coach Norman Dale, struck many as reminiscent of the "play to win, not to lose" talk Massimino had given his team on that April day in 1985.

In it, the fictional Coach Dale cautions the wide-eyed farmboys on his Hickory High team not to look past the game at hand. "I'm sure going to the State Finals is beyond your wildest dreams," he says, "so let's just keep it right there. Forget about the crowds, the size of the school, their fancy uniforms and remember what got you here. . . . And most important, don't get caught up thinking about winning or losing this game. If you put your effort and concentration into playing to your potential, to be the best that you can be . . . we're going to be winners."

As time passed and the impact of McLain's revelations eased, the '85 title game reacquired a positive and quaint luster. For a new generation of sports fans in the twenty-first century, Villanova's win was no longer so much about the issues that had made it so intriguing a quarter-century earlier, race and drugs. Instead, it came to be seen as a moment that spoke perfectly about sport's potential for the unexpected, for miracles, for magic.

When well into the new century, ESPN created a list of the greatest upsets in sports history, Villanova's was ranked third, topped only by the U.S. Olympic hockey team's "Miracle on Ice" at the 1980 Games and Joe Namath's called shot, his Jets upset of the Baltimore Colts in Super Bowl III. A 2012 *Sporting News* review of the greatest NCAA tournament games played since the expansion to sixty-four teams named it No. 2, behind only Duke's triple-overtime win over Kentucky in 1992.

"Because people can point to . . . Massimino, there is always some hope for even the most hopeless tournament," John Feinstein wrote in 1988. "Dreams do come true in the NCAA tournament, even impossible ones."

* * *

The horrifying photos that flashed around the world on August 18, 2011, provoked a familiar response: "Gee, a Georgetown basketball team involved in a brawl. What a surprise." But like so much of what people thought they knew about Georgetown basketball, then and twenty-five years earlier, those perceptions were mistaken.

On August 18, 2011, during the second game in a Hoyas' goodwill trip to China, basketball players from Georgetown and a Chinese professional club engaged in a wild brawl. Punches and kicks were exchanged. Chairs and water bottles were thrown. Fans rushed the court to participate. One branded a stanchion. John Thompson III, the son of the former Hoyas coach, now in his father's old job, eventually pulled his team off the floor.

The fight, by most accounts, was started by the Chinese team, which was comprised of military personnel and which had a reputation, according to at least one Chinese observer who had little idea of the irony, for "thuggery." No one was seriously injured in the frightening scene that, in America at least, resurrected long-dormant notions about Georgetown basketball. "If this game took place in 1985," wrote Sean Pendergast of the *Houston Chronicle*, "there would have been fifteen bloody, mangled Chinese basketball players scattered unconscious on the floor with Patrick Ewing, Reggie Williams, David Wingate, and Michael Graham all standing over them with their hands raised amidst a shower of jettisoned half full beers and sodas and debris."

Maybe. But in 2011 Georgetown wasn't Georgetown anymore. It really hadn't been since January 8, 1999, when

Thompson, in the midst of a messy divorce and a bad season, resigned. "No one, and I mean no one, could have made Georgetown a power better than John," Dean Smith said that day.

The fifty-seven-year-old coach, a longtime Nike board member, didn't need the money or the aggravation anymore. He was in the Hall of Fame and had compiled a record of 596-239 (.713) in twenty-six and a half seasons at a school he put on the sports map. He was, despite his distaste for talking about the milestone, the first black coach to win an NCAA tournament and the first to win one with an all-black team. His influence was such that he almost singlehandedly forced the NCAA to backtrack on academic reforms that he believed were ill-advised.

The real glory years ended with Ewing's departure, though Georgetown remained a formidable program for most of Thompson's last decade and a half there. Perhaps his most memorable post-1985 moment occurred four years after his most memorable loss, when news stories surfaced that an alleged Washington drug lord, Rayful Edmond, had befriended two of the Hoyas, including star center Alonzo Mourning. Thompson summoned Edmond to his office and told him he'd better stay away from his team or else. Edmond, now serving a life sentence on drug-related offenses, was never seen at another Hoyas game.

That title-game loss to Villanova stung Thompson and his players. As a legend sprang up and took root around that upset, it stung them even worse. More than twenty-five years later, Thompson and his players are seldom willing to discuss it. Ewing said he stopped watching ESPN Classic because the network occasionally replayed the game and he was afraid that some night he might inadvertently stumble across the painful memory.

Thompson's name would surface again in connection with several coaching openings, at both the pro and college levels, but he wouldn't go back. He did a popular D.C. talk-radio show for thirteen years before stepping aside in 2012. As a radio personality, he was, not surprisingly, outspoken and often controversial. In 2009, for example, he suggested on the air that Georgetown could use some "thugs" to help with rebounding, seemingly implying that that's what he would have done, that that's what he *had* done when he recruited Michael Graham. The comment briefly resurrected talk about Thompson's coaching style and "Hoya Paranoia," topics that had faded as the Hoyas' fortunes did the same.

In what must have come as a surprise to all those who thought him a racist, he handpicked his longtime white assistant, Esherick, to be his successor. Esherick would stumble and he would be followed in the job by Thompson's eldest son, John Thompson III, in 2004. By then, the swagger and the fear that had made Thompson's teams such a phenomenon had long since dissipated. So had many, though certainly not all, of America's racial hang-ups, stereotypes, and animosities—the elements that once had helped make the Hoyas gods in so many African-American communities and devils elsewhere.

In 2008, a black president moved into the same White House where Ewing had been stopped at the gate, where so many presidents had used race to divide and conquer.

Hip-hop was, by the turn of the century, mainstream music, and the staid Georgetown campus the site of an annual Global Hip-Hop Festival.

The hot racial issues that once inflamed the sports world had cooled some by 2004, when Thompson's Princeton-educated son was installed at Georgetown. There, in what was once the quintessential black program, he would employ that most stereotypical element of white basketball—Pete Carril's Princeton offense. It raised few eyebrows. One of the players who performed in that offense for Thompson's son was Ewing's son, Patrick Ewing, Jr., who, though few knew it at the time, had been born a month after Georgetown's 1983–84 title.

All those players on Thompson's 1984–85 team, so virulently derided as thugs, earned degrees. Most moved on to extremely successful careers beyond basketball. Jackson attended Harvard's Kennedy School of Government and would work as an executive with the NBA, Nike, Turner Sports, and the U.S. Olympic Committee. Dalton was a successful stockbroker, Broadnax an attorney and college coach. Wingate had a lengthy NBA career. Ewing became a superstar with the New York Knicks, though he would never win a championship, and later served as an assistant with the Orlando Magic.

"It's not what people used to think about Georgetown. A lot of them are very successful guys," said Everson. "We still have nothing but respect and admiration for those guys. Especially a guy like Patrick Ewing. He made you play at your best. You see them now, they say hello, how you doing. They're all nice guys. They just had that Hoya Paranoia thing going on."

By the time Barack Obama became the nation's forty-fourth president, the Georgetown mystique was so distant it was difficult to recall. The college that once sold more licensed merchandise than any other had by 2009 fallen to No. 70 on that list.

The morning after their championship, before they returned to campus for yet another rally there, Villanova's players and coaches were paraded through downtown Philadelphia. The blue-collar city warmly embraced the team of outsiders from the blue-blooded Main Line. The brief, ten-block event, in which the victors rode atop three flatbed trucks, ended at City Hall Plaza, where a crowd of 75,000 assembled to greet the basketball-obsessed city's first collegiate champions in thirty-one years. Beneath a MISSION COMPLETE banner, Massimino, tired but still giddy, wearing a finely tailored blue suit and a pink tie, memorably and inadvertently remarked, "It's really a pleasure to be the national champions of the nation." In the subsequent twenty-seven years, his players have never let him forget the verbal gaffe.

A photo-mural depicting the 'Cats at that celebration lines a long wall just inside the main entrance of the university's Pavilion. The great upset still hangs in the air throughout Villanova's campus, where time has helped ease—but never quite erased—the pain and the memories engendered by McLain's story.

Villanova's basketball program remains a prominent one, even as the lure of football money and constant conference shifting have threatened the future of the once indomitable Big

East. Jay Wright, who replaced Steve Lappas, got the Wildcats back to another Final Four in 2009, where they lost in a national semifinal to a familiar postseason opponent, North Carolina. Occasionally, during basketball games in the cold Pavilion, the band still strikes up "My Old Kentucky Home." The reference is clear to all, even if the memories of that Final Four week there have dimmed considerably since 1985.

Wright has also been a wonderfully successful peacemaker, helping to soothe the bad feelings generated by and directed at McLain and Massimino. He has brought both men back to campus, where they have been feted and warmly received during '85 anniversary celebrations and other basketball events.

The twelve players, too, bound together eternally by that one unforgettable game, remain close, all but Veltra Dawson, who transferred to Evansville that next season and disappeared from their exclusive little circle. Thanks primarily to Everson, they all talk frequently on the phone, gather for weddings, funerals, and Villanova functions. They tell stories about one another, about Coach Massimino and Nevin. Especially Nevin. Several of them tried to buy a headstone for the late trainer's unmarked grave in Ardmore, not far from campus, but Johnny Morris, Nevin's nephew, angered by a pension dispute with the university, would not allow it. Morris has since passed away and the players hope to resurrect the project.

Middle-aged men now, the players have moved past that game, though it is never far away for any of them. An FBI agent, a stockbroker, basketball coaches, a fund-raiser, an oil-company executive—all of them realize they will always be defined by those forty minutes of implausible basketball. No matter what life throws at them, they can retreat to April 1, 1985.

Jensen, who always walked a fine emotional line in life, subsequently suffered from depression and anxiety, conditions he attributes as much to the medications he was taking to combat the maladies as to his intense nature. For him, the upset and the role he played in it have always been buoys. "For me, that game has become even more remarkable as time goes on," he said. "That it really did happen, and that we were a part of it, makes me feel that much more lucky. Seeing what happens in the tournament every year, when teams that everyone thinks have the most talent or the best coaching don't always win—most of the time don't win—I appreciate what we did that much more."

The championship rings many still wear are inscribed with the words, UNITY, TRUTH, LOVE. When they were young, those virtues seemed so easily sustainable. Now they try, as best they can, to adhere to them, to keep them alive among themselves.

In 2005, the twentieth anniversary, HBO aired a documentary on the game, *The Perfect Upset*. For Everson, a regional executive with Sunoco who has become the team's social director, that felt like the right time for McLain and Massimino to come together. "I said, 'You know what? It's time to put this to bed.'" So on a day when McLain came to speak at a basketball camp Everson operated on Long Island, the seven-footer also arranged for Massimino to attend. When the coach arrived, Everson directed him to a back room and told him McLain was there and that his old point guard wanted to talk. They did that—and more. "It was the first time they'd really talked," said Everson. "There was yelling and there were tears but they came out arm in arm."

At the time, McLain tried to summarize what he told the coach who had called the appearance of McLain's SI story "the worst moment of my life." "I told him, 'I wasn't trying to tarnish your image. I didn't do it in a menacing way. I wanted to tell the truth. I do apologize for any ill that I've caused you and I love you.' Coach Mass is a very proud person. He's been everything to me—not only a great coach, but a great mentor and his intentions were always the best for me."

A few years later, the players and coaches all gathered at Wright's Villanova home to view, for the first time as a group, a videotape of the win over Georgetown. Massimino had always avoided watching it, worried, he claimed, that perhaps the outcome would change and his life's grand moment would disappear like a coin in a magician's hand.

They all laughed through much of the replay, as much at the cultural relics as the game moments and the background incidents they alone remembered. Ever the coach, Massimino noted their errors, though obviously they were few. As the championship game's joyful conclusion neared, the mood grew more profound, the lumps in the throats a little larger. The laughter stopped before the game did. By then the room was silent.

All of them have that long-ago moment tattooed on their brains. The men who wore Villanova's uniforms that night will always inhabit that tiny sliver of time just before the Rupp Arena buzzer sounded, when McClain gathered Jensen's in-bounds pass to his chest and fell to the floor. "Whenever I feel down, I close my eyes," McClain would say. "And Lexington is right there."

SELECTED BIBLIOGRAPHY

And the Walls Came Tumbling Down: Kentucky, Texas Western, and the Game That Changed American Sports, by Frank Fitzpatrick, Simon & Schuster, 1999.

Beyond the Shadow of the Senators, by Brad Snyder, Contemporary Books, 2003.

Big Hoops: A Season in the Big East Conference, by Bill Reynolds, New American Library Books, 1989.

Big Man on Campus: John Thompson and the Georgetown Hoyas, by Leonard Shapiro, Henry Holt, 1991.

Cages to Jump Shots: Pro Basketball's Early Years, by Robert W. Peterson, Oxford University Press, 1990.

Can't Stop, Won't Stop: A History of the Hip-Hop Generation, by Jeff Chang, St. Martin's Press, 2005.

Coach: The Life of Paul "Bear" Bryant, by Keith Dunnavant, Simon & Schuster, 1996.

Ed Pinckney's Tales from the Villanova Hardwood: The Story of the 1985 NCAA Champs, by Ed Pinckney and Bob Gordon, Sports Publishing, 2004.

Elevating the Game: Black Men and Basketball, by Nelson George, HarperCollins, 1992.

Encyclopedia of College Basketball, by Mike Douchant, Gale Research, 1995.

The Final Four, by Joe Gergen, Sporting News, 1987.

From Set Shot to Slam Dunk, by Charles Salzberg, E. P. Dutton, 1987.

God's Country: America in the Fifties, by J. Ronald Oakley, Dembner Books, 1986.

A History of Georgetown University, by Robert Emmett Curran, Georgetown University Press, 2010.

Illustrated Basketball Rules, by Edward Steitz, Dolphin Books, 1976.

The Negro in Sports, by E. B. Henderson, Associated Publishers, 1939, rpt. 1969.

Nova No. 1, by the staff of the *Philadelphia Inquirer*, News Books International, 1985.

The Other America, by Michael Harrington, Penguin Books, 1992.

The Perfect Game: Villanova vs. Georgetown for the National Championship, by Kyle Keiderling, Morning Star Books, 2012.

Philly Hoops: The Magic of Philadelphia Basketball, by the staff of the *Philadelphia Daily News*, Camino Books, 2002.

Pride of the Lions: The Biography of Joe Paterno, by Frank Fitzpatrick, Triumph Books, 2011.

The Punch, by John Feinstein, Little, Brown, and Co., 2002.

Racism in College Athletics, by Dana D. Brooks and Ronald C. Althouse, Fitness Information Technology, 1993.

The Reagan Diaries, edited by Douglas Brinkley, HarperCollins, 2009.

Sports & Freedom: The Rise of Big-Time College Athletics, by Ronald A. Smith, Oxford University Press, 1988.

Villanova University, 1842–1992: American, Catholic, Augustinian, by David R. Contosta, Pennsylvania State University Press, 1995.

The Year of the 'Cat: Villanova's Incredible NCAA Basketball Championship Story, by Craig H. Miller, Villanova University Athletics Department, 1985.

Young, Black, Rich, and Famous: The Rise of the NBA, the Hip Hop Invasion and the Transformation of American Culture, by Todd Boyd, Doubleday, 2003.

SCHOLARLY PAPERS AND JOURNALS

"The Black Athlete in Big-Time Intercollegiate Sports," by Donald Spivey, Phylon 44, 1983.

"Hoya Paranoia: How Georgetown Found Its Swagger During the Reagan Years," by Zach Tupper, Senior Honors Thesis, Georgetown University Department of History, 2009.

"Jim Crow in the Gymnasium: The Integration of College Basketball in the American South," by Charles H. Martin, *The International Journal of the History of Sports* 10, No. 1, 1993.

"Racial Participation and Integration in Intercollegiate Basketball, 1958–1980," by F.J. Beghorn, Norman Yetman, and F. R. Thomas, *Journal of Sports Behavior* 5, No. 1, 1988.

VIDEO

"Beyond the Bubble: John Thompson Jr. Interview," WJLA-TV, Washington, D.C., 2011.

"Patrick Ewing: Standing Tall," Fox Home Entertainment, 1993.

Perfect Upset: The 1985 Villanova vs. Georgetown NCAA Championship,
    produced by Jordan Kranis, HBO Sports Documentaries,
    2005.

"1985 NCAA Championship Telecast," CBS-TV, 1985.

"1985 Villanova Wildcats—A 'Cat's Tale," Comcast Sports
    Network Philadelphia, 2005.

ARCHIVES

Falvey Memorial Library Special Collections, Villanova Uni-
    versity.

Georgetown University Library Special Collections Research
    Center.

NEWSPAPERS

Allentown Call

The *Atlanta Journal-Constitution*

The *Boston Globe*

The *Charlotte Observer*

The *Courier-Journal* (Louisville, KY)

The *Hoya*

Las Vegas Sun

Lexington Herald-Leader

Los Angeles Times

The *Miami Herald*

New York Daily News

New York Post

The *New York Times*

Newsday

Palm Beach Post

Philadelphia Daily News

The Philadelphia Inquirer

The Plain Dealer (Cleveland)

Seattle Post-Intelligencer

Seattle Press

The Times Herald (Raleigh)

The Times-Picayune (New Orleans)

The Villanovan

The Wall Street Journal

The Washington Post

The Washington Times

MAGAZINES

The New Republic

Newsweek

Sports Illustrated

Time

The Washingtonian

The Washington Post Magazine

INDEX